More praise for
What Einstein Told His Cook

"I have enjoyed Bob Wolke's column in the *Post* for years, and his book is as good a read on the science of cooking as there is. Bob is not only well educated, he is a wit and a wonderful, gifted writer who can make anyone understand what's behind the 'magic' that happens in the kitchen. His sound, clever recipes are a welcome bonus."

hing

"The best book on food (not a cookbook) of 2002. Robert Wolke's book is so full of useful information that you'll find yourself referring to it again and again. . . . Not only does he have the penetrating mind of a chemistry professor, but Robert Wolke also has a tremendous sense of humor. Besides being packed with all kinds of interesting food science tidbits, this book is just plain funny."

—SauteWednesday.com

"Robert Wolke's terrific book will be invaluable and accessible to every cook. The style is clear, the text is honest, and perhaps best of all the book is fun to read, filled with the 'why's and 'how's of the kitchen."   —Paula Wolfert, author of *Mediterranean Cooking* and *Mediterranean Grains and Greens*

"The occasional recipe adds diversity but facts are the book's strong point. *What Einstein Told His Cook* is a scientifically accurate but witty and entertaining study of the chemistry of food and cooking."

—Elliot Ketley, *Restaurant* (UK)

"This book should be on the shelf of any serious cook's library. By demystifying the fundamentals of the kitchen, it empowers the cook to navigate recipes with confidence and control."

Lidia Matticchio Bastianich, author of
Lidia's Italian-American Kitchen and *Lidia's Italian Table*

"Wolke [is] a chemist with a preternatural ability to explain complex chemical reactions in simple terms. Whatever the magnitude of the topic, Wolke addresses it with the same understated intelligence and paternal humor." —Tim Carman, *Washington City Paper*

"If you read Bob Wolke's *What Einstein Told His Cook*, you may have to kick some old wives' tales right out of the kitchen. . . . One of the book's joys is that some quirks of the kitchen may never have occurred to us. That's what makes Bob Wolke the science teacher we wished we had when we were stuck with Big Bad Science Snob. He's not afraid to lunge at a joke to explain a concept when Big Bad would have bored us silly with irrelevant detail."
—Suzanne Martinson, *Pittsburgh Post-Gazette*

"Robert L. Wolke's recipes are lab experiments you can eat. That's what makes reading *What Einstein Told His Cook* so much fun for the avid home chef who derives as much pleasure from understanding food as eating it." —*New York City Record*

"For the kitchen nerd with a sense of humor. An absorbing read."
—*Food & Wine* (Ireland)

"Good science only adds to the enjoyment of the culinary arts. With a sauce of wit and panache, Wolke serves up commonsense answers to every question that a curious cook could ask."
—Roald Hoffman, 1981 Nobel Laureate in Chemistry

W. W. NORTON & COMPANY

New York London

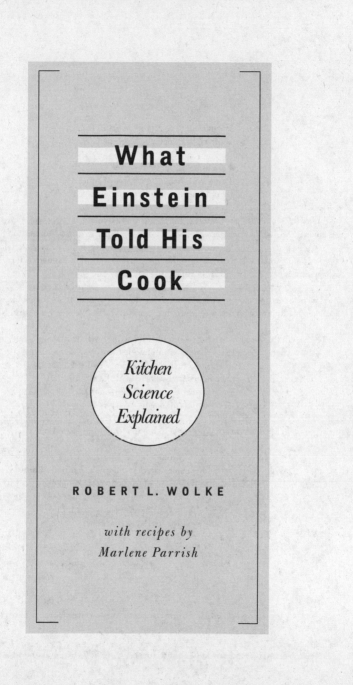

What
Einstein
Told His
Cook

*Kitchen
Science
Explained*

ROBERT L. WOLKE

*with recipes by
Marlene Parrish*

Recipe for Chocolate Velvet Mousse adapted from Chocolate Mousse with Olive Oil, published in *The Best American Recipes 2000*, Houghton Mifflin, 2000. Adaptation printed by permission of Teresa Barrenechea. Recipe for Champagne Jelly in *The Best American Recipes 1999*, Houghton Mifflin, 1999. Recipe copyright 1998 by Lindsey Shere. Reprinted by permission of Lindsey Shere.

For information about permission to reproduce selections from this book, write to Permissions, W. W. Norton & Company, Inc., 500 Fifth Avenue, New York, NY 10110

The text of this book is composed in Filosofia, with the display set in Grotesque Bold
Composition by Sue Carlson
Manufacturing by Courier Westford
Book design by Barbara M. Bachman
Illustrations by Alan Witschonke
Production manager: Andrew Marasia

Library of Congress Cataloging-in-Publication Data

Wolke, Robert L.
What Einstein told his cook : kitchen science explained / Robert L.
Wolke ; with recipes by Marlene Parrish.— 1st ed.
p. cm.
Includes bibliographical references and index.
ISBN 0-393-01183-6 (hardcover)
1. Cookery. 2. Science—Miscellanea. I. Parrish, Marlene. II. Title.
TX652 .W643 2002
641.5—dc21   2002001708

ISBN 978-0-393-32942-1 pbk.

W. W. Norton & Company, Inc., 500 Fifth Avenue, New York, N.Y. 10110
www.wwnorton.com

W. W. Norton & Company Ltd., Castle House, 75/76 Wells Street, London W1T 3QT

1 2 3 4 5 6 7 8 9 0

This book is dedicated to my wife, partner, colleague, and motivator, Marlene Parrish.

CONTENTS

What is raw sugar? · Is refined white sugar unhealthful? · How can you soften hardened brown sugar? · What are treacle, sorghum, and sulphured molasses? · What's the difference between cane sugar and beet sugar? · How do you dissolve two cups of sugar in one cup of water? · What does "caramelize" mean? · How are starches and sugars related? · How do they get corn syrup from corn? · What is Dutch process cocoa? · Why does chocolate melt in the mouth? · How do they make white chocolate? . . . and more.

What are all those special salts and tenderizers in the supermarket? · What are salt substitutes? · Why do we add salt to the water for boiling pasta? · What's so special about sea salt? · Kosher salt? · Freshly ground salt? · Can a potato remove the excess salt from over-salted soup? · Why do recipes tell you to use unsalted butter and then add salt? . . . and more.

Chapter Three • THE FAT OF THE LAND   65

What's the difference between a fat and a fatty acid? · Why are oils only partially hydrogenated? · Why do we clarify butter? · How do they make corn oil? · How do the various cooking oils compare? · What can you do with used cooking oil? · How do nonstick cooking sprays work? · What noodles contain fat? · Is heavy cream really lighter than light cream? . . . and more.

Chapter Four • CHEMICALS IN THE KITCHEN 93

What do home water filters do? · What's the difference between baking powder and baking soda? · Is aluminum dangerous? · What is baking ammonia? · Sour salt? · Cream of tartar? · Artificial vanilla? · MSG? · Why is there "no calcium" in cream cheese? · Why does lasagne dissolve metal? · How is vinegar made? · Are green potatoes poisonous? · How is lye used in our foods? . . . and more.

Chapter Five • TURF AND SURF   124

Is a rare steak bloody? · What makes ground beef brown? · Is prime rib prime beef? · Why is the meat near the bone "sweetest?" · What do bones contribute to a stock? · What's the best way to skim fat from a stock? · How do they make all those different hams? · How does brining work? · How long is "overnight"? · What makes gravy lumpy and greasy? · Why does fish cook so quickly? · Why does fish smell fishy? · What is surimi? · Are oysters on the half-shell alive? · Should lobsters be boiled or steamed? . . . and more.

microwave oven? · Can the microwaves leak out of the box and cook the cook? · What makes a container "microwave safe"? · Why do some "microwave safe" containers still get hot in the oven? · Is it dangerous to heat water in a microwave oven? · Do microwaves change the molecular structure of food? · Do microwaves destroy the nutrients in food? · Why does microwave-cooked food cool off faster than food cooked in a conventional oven? . . . and more.

Chapter NINE · TOOLS AND TECHNOLOGY   269

Why doesn't anything stick to nonstick cookware? · What's the "best" kind of frying pan? · Does a magnetic rack affect the sharpness of your knives? · What's the difference between a pastry brush and a basting brush? · How can you get the most juice out of a lemon or lime? · What's wrong with washing mushrooms? · Does tarnish affect the properties of a copper frying pan? · What's the easiest way to clean silverware? · Why are there separate measuring cups for liquids and solids? · How do "instant-read" thermometers work? · How do pressure cookers work? · How do induction-heated ranges and light ovens work? · Why do crackers have those little holes in them? · What are the pros and cons of food irradiation? · What are all those special compartments in your refrigerator? . . . and more.

INTRODUCTION

Along with the recent explosion of interest in food and cooking has come a growing desire to understand the chemical and physical principles that determine the properties and behavior of our foods.

This book explains the science behind both the foods themselves and the tools we use to prepare them. Its organization and index have been devised to make it easy to find a particular fact or explanation.

Home cooks and professional chefs not only cook but they must first buy ingredients. Today's technology produces such a baffling variety of food products that many cooking problems begin in the market. I have therefore included discussions of both natural and prepared foods, where they come from, what they are made of, and what the practical consequences may be for the cook and consumer.

Having taught at universities for more years than I care to count, and having spent ten of those years as the founding director of a Faculty Development Office helping faculty members to improve their teaching, I recognize two possible approaches to explaining kitchen science. I'll call them the college method and the experience method.

In the college method, I would write what amounts to a textbook on kitchen science and then bid my "students" to go out into the world and apply their acquired knowledge to solve practical problems that arise in the future. That approach presumes that all the "course content" will have been mastered and recalled whenever needed. But both my experience as a teacher and undoubtedly yours as a former student testify to the futility of that approach. (Quick: Who fought in the Battle of Hastings?)

In short, the college method attempts to supply answers before the questions arise, whereas in real life, questions crop up without warning and must be dealt with on the spot.

But what if you didn't have to plow through a lot of science, yet every time you were mystified by something you could ask a scientist to explain that specific problem, no more and no less? While you can't have a scientist (much less an Einstein) always at your elbow, the next best thing might be to have at your disposal a compilation of answers to questions that you yourself might be likely to come up with, along with plain, no-nonsense explanations of what's happening. That's the experience method. In this book, I have selected well over a hundred questions that have been asked of me by real-life cooks, readers of my Food 101 column in *The Washington Post* and other newspapers.

In addition to explanations of the underlying science, you will find a number of unusual and imaginative recipes developed by my wife, Marlene Parrish, a food professional. The recipes were specifically designed to illustrate the principles being explained. They may be thought of as a lab course that you can eat.

Each question-and-answer unit is designed to stand by itself. Whether prompted by the table of contents, the index, or a question that pops into your head, you can open the book and read the relevant unit without having had to master a series of earlier concepts.

To ensure that each unit is conceptually complete, and because many topics are interconnected, I have often had to repeat very briefly a concept that is explained more completely in another unit. But a bit of repetition now and then only enhances understanding.

While I have been careful never to use a technical word without defining it the first time it is used, you will find a brief glossary at the back of the book to refresh your memory when necessary.

There is of course no limit to the things that people may wonder about, and any book such as this can explain only a small fraction of what's going on in our kitchens and markets. I therefore invite your questions, along with your name and town, sent via e-mail to questions@professorscience.com. While I cannot reply individually, a Question of the Week will be answered on my web site, www.professorscience.com.

May you derive as much pleasure from understanding your food as from eating it.

ACKNOWLEDGMENTS

After many years spent in another career while doing freelance writing on the side, I owe my "big break" in food writing to Nancy McKeon, former food editor of *The Washington Post*, who gave me the opportunity to write a food science column in that distinguished newspaper. Food 101 has been running in *The Post* and other newspapers for some four years now, thanks to the continued confidence and support of the current food editor, Jeanne McManus, who allows me complete freedom to "do my thing."

The road that led to this book began when I met and married Marlene Parrish, a food writer, restaurant critic, and cooking teacher. As a food-loving scientist-writer and avocational cook, I began to write more about food and the science that lies behind it. Without her loving confidence in me, this book would not exist. Marlene developed and tested all the recipes in the book, each one specifically designed to illustrate and put to work a scientific principle being explained. Moreover, throughout my long, hard months of writing and rewriting, she made my lunches.

Once again, I must express my gratitude to my literary agent, Ethan Ellenberg, who has served my interests over the years with honor, sound advice, and good cheer, even when the road became unexpectedly rough.

I am remarkably fortunate to have had Maria Guarnaschelli as my editor at W. W. Norton. Focusing uncompromisingly on quality, Maria was always there to steer me gently back onto the right path whenever I strayed, all the while being a fountain of encouragement. Whatever this book may have turned out to be, it is infinitely better than it would have been without Maria's sharp instincts, knowledge, and judgment, and without the trust, respect, and friendship that have grown between us.

Authors don't write books; they write manuscripts—mere words on paper until converted into books by corps of patient, diligent professionals in a publishing house. I am grateful to all those at W. W. Norton who exercised their talents to transform my text into the handsome volume you now hold in your hand. My special thanks go to Norton's director of manufacturing Andrew Marasia, art director Debra Morton Hoyt, managing editor Nancy Palmquist, freelance artist Alan Witschonke, and designer Barbara Bachman.

In spite of the convictions held by my daughter and son-in-law, Leslie Wolke and Ziv Yoles, I don't know everything. Writing a book like this inevitably required consultations with food scientists and food industry representatives too numerous to mention. I thank them all for their willingness to share their expertise.

Probably every contemporary writer of nonfiction owes a huge debt to that omniscient but disembodied and ethereal entity called the Internet, which puts all the world's information (along with much misinformation) literally at our fingertips—the flick of a finger on a mouse. I trust that the Internet, wherever it is, will appreciate my heartfelt expression of gratitude.

Finally, if it were not for the fabulous readers of my newspaper column, this book could not have been written. Their e-mail and snail-mail questions and feedback have continually reassured me that I might indeed be providing a useful service. No author could desire a better audience.

What Einstein Told His Cook

Chapter One

Sweet Talk

....

O F OUR FIVE CLASSICALLY recognized senses—touch, hearing, vision, smell, and taste—only the last two are purely chemical in nature, that is, they can detect actual chemical molecules. Through our remarkable senses of smell and taste, we experience different olfactory and gustatory sensations from contact with the molecules of different chemical compounds.

(You'll be seeing the word molecule frequently throughout this book. Don't panic. All you need to know is that a molecule is, in the words of a first-grader of my acquaintance, "one of those eentsy-weentsy things that stuff is made of." That definition, plus the corollary that different stuff is different because it's made of different kinds of molecules, will stand you in good stead.)

The sense of smell can detect only gaseous molecules floating around in the air. The sense of taste can detect only molecules dissolved in water, whether in the food's own liquid or in saliva. (You can't smell or taste a rock.) As is the case with many other animal species, it is smell that attracts us to food and taste that helps us find edible—and appetizing—foods.

What we call flavor is a combination of odors that our nose detects and tastes that our taste buds detect, with additional contributions from temperature, pungency (the "sting" of spices), and texture (the structure and feel of the food in the mouth). The olfactory receptors in our noses can differentiate among thousands of different odors and contribute an estimated 80 percent of flavor. If this figure appears high, remember that the mouth and nose are connected, so that gaseous molecules released in the mouth by chewing can travel upward into the nasal cavity. Moreover, swallowing creates a partial vacuum in the nasal cavity and draws air up from the mouth into the nose.

Compared with our sense of smell, our sense of taste is relatively dull. Our taste buds are distributed mostly over the tongue, but are also found on the hard palate (the front, bony part of the roof of the mouth) and the soft palate, a flap of soft tissue ending in the uvula, "that little thing hanging down" just before the throat.

Traditionally, it has been thought that there are only four primary tastes: sweet, sour, salty, and bitter, and that we have specialized taste buds for each. Today, it is generally agreed that there is at least one other primary taste, known by its Japanese name, *umami*. It is associated with MSG (monosodium glutamate) and other compounds of glutamic acid, one of the common amino acids that are the building blocks of proteins. Umami is a savory kind of taste associated with protein-rich foods such as meat and cheese. Moreover, it is no longer believed that each taste bud responds exclusively to a single kind of stimulus, but that it may also respond in lesser degrees to others.

Thus, the standard "map of the tongue" in textbooks, illustrating sweet buds at the tip, salty buds on either side of the tip, sour buds along the sides, and bitter buds at the back, is an oversimplification; it shows only the areas where the tongue is most sensitive to the primary tastes. What we actually taste is the overall pattern of stimuli from all the taste receptors, the cells within the taste buds that actually detect the various tastes. The recent success in sequencing the human genome has enabled researchers to identify the probable genes that produce the receptors for bitterness and sweetness, but not yet for the others.

When the combined taste, smell, and textural stimuli reach the brain, they remain to be interpreted. Whether the overall sensation will be pleasant, repulsive, or somewhere in between will depend on individual physiological differences, on previous experience ("just like my mother used to make"), and on cultural habituation (haggis, anyone?).

One taste sensation is undeniably the favorite of our species and of many others in the animal kingdom from hummingbirds to horses: sweetness. To paraphrase a famously ungrammatical advertising slogan, nobody doesn't like sweetness. Nature undoubtedly set us up for that by making good foods such as ripe fruits taste sweet and poisonous ones, such as those that contain alkaloids, taste bitter. (The alkaloid family of plant chemicals includes such bad actors as morphine, strychnine, and nicotine, not to mention caffeine.)

In our menus, there is only one taste that has an entire course devoted to it: the sweetness of dessert. Appetizers may be savory, main courses may have any complex combination of flavors, but dessert is invariably and sometimes overwhelmingly sweet. We love sweetness so much that we use its concept in terms of endearment (sweetheart, honey) and to describe almost anything or anyone that is particularly pleasant, such as sweet music and a sweet disposition.

When we think of sweetness, we think immediately of sugar. But the word *sugar* does not denote a unique substance; it is a generic term for a whole family of natural chemical compounds that, along with starches, belong to the family of carbohydrates. So before we indulge our sweet tooth—before beginning our scientific repast with dessert—we must see where sugars fit into the scheme of carbohydrates.

FILL 'ER UP

*I know that starch and sugar are both carbohy-
drates, but they're such different substances. Why
are they lumped together in the same category
when we talk about nutrition?*

. . . .

In a word: fuel. When a runner loads up on "carbs" before a race, it's like a car filling up at the gas station.

Carbohydrates are a class of natural chemicals that play vital roles in all living things. Both plants and animals manufacture, store, and consume starches and sugars for energy. Cellulose, a complex carbohydrate, makes up the cell walls and structural frameworks of plants—their bones, if you will.

These compounds were named carbohydrates in the early eighteenth century when it was noticed that many of their chemical formulas could be written as if they were made up of carbon atoms (C) plus a number of water molecules (H_2O). Thus, the name carbohydrate or "hydrated carbon." We now know that such a simple formula isn't true for all carbohydrates, but we're stuck with the name.

The chemical similarity that unites all carbohydrates is that their molecules all contain glucose, also known as blood sugar. Because of the ubiquity of carbohydrates in plants and animals, glucose is probably the most abundant biological molecule on Earth. Our metabolism breaks all carbohydrates down into glucose, a "simple sugar" (Techspeak: a monosaccharide) that circulates in the blood and provides energy to every cell in the body. Another simple sugar is fructose, found in honey and many fruits.

When two molecules of simple sugars are bonded together, they make a "double sugar" or disaccharide. Sucrose, the sugar in your sugar bowl and in the nectar of your centerpiece's flowers, is a disaccharide made up of glucose and fructose. Other disaccharides are maltose or malt sugar and lactose or milk sugar, a sugar found only in mammals and never in plants.

Complex carbohydrates or polysaccharides are made up of many simple sugars, often as many as hundreds. That's where cellulose and the starches fit in. Foods such as peas, beans, grains, and potatoes contain both starch and cellulose. The cellulose isn't digestible by humans (termites can do it), but it's important in our diets as fiber. Starches are our chief source of energy, because they break down gradually into hundreds of molecules of glucose. That's why I said that loading up on carbohydrates is like filling a gas tank with fuel.

As different as all these carbohydrates may be in terms of their molecular structures, they all provide the same amount of energy in our metabolism: about 4 calories per gram. That's because when you come right down to it, they're all basically glucose.

Two pure starches that you probably have in your pantry are cornstarch and arrowroot. You don't need to be told where cornstarch comes from, but have you ever seen an arrowroot? It's a perennial plant grown in the West Indies, Southeast Asia, Australia, and South Africa for its fleshy underground tubers, which are almost pure starch. The tubers are grated, washed, dried, and ground. The resulting powder is used to thicken sauces, puddings, and desserts. But arrowroot does its thickening job at a lower temperature than cornstarch so it's best for custards and puddings that contain eggs, because they can easily curdle at higher temperatures.

A RAW DEAL

In a health-food store I saw several kinds of raw sugar. How do they differ from refined sugar?

. . . .

Not as much as you may be led to believe. What health-food stores call raw sugar isn't raw in the sense that it is completely unrefined. It's just refined to a lesser degree.

From the dawn of history, honey was virtually the only sweetener known to humans. Sugar cane was grown in India some three thousand years ago, but it didn't find its way to North Africa and southern Europe until around the eighth century A.D.

Luckily for us, Christopher Columbus's mother-in-law owned a sugar plantation (I'm not making this up) and, even before he married, he had a job ferrying sugar to Genoa from the cane fields in Madeira. All of which probably gave him the idea of taking some sugar cane to the Caribbean on his second voyage to the New World in 1493. The rest is sweet history. Today, an American eats about forty-five pounds of sugar a year, on the average. Think of it: Empty nine 5-pound bags of sugar onto the kitchen counter and behold your personal quota for the year. Of course, you didn't get it all from the sugar bowl; sugar is an ingredient in an astounding variety of prepared foods.

The claim is often made that brown sugars and so-called raw sugars are more healthful because they have a higher content of natural materials. It's true that those materials include a variety of minerals—so does the perfectly natural dirt in the cane field—but they're nothing you can't get from dozens of other foods. You'd have to eat a truly unhealthful amount of brown sugar to get your daily mineral requirements that way.

Here's a quick overview of what goes on at the sugar mill, usually located near the cane fields, and the sugar refinery, which may be located some distance away.

Sugar cane grows in tropical regions as tall, bamboo-like stalks about an inch thick and up to ten feet tall, just right for being chopped down with a machete. At the mill, the cut cane is shredded and pressed by machines. The pressed-out juice is clarified by adding lime and allowing the juice to settle, and then boiled down in a partial vacuum (which lowers its boiling temperature) until it thickens into a syrup, colored brown by concentrated impurities. As the water evaporates, the sugar becomes so concentrated that the liquid can't hold it anymore; the sugar turns into solid crystals. The wet crystals are then spun in a centrifuge, a perforated drum similar to the drum in your washing machine that flings water out of your laundry during the spin cycle. The syrupy liquid—the molasses—is flung out, leaving wet, brown sugar containing an assortment of yeasts, molds, bacteria, soil, fiber, and other miscellaneous plant and insect debris. That's the real "raw sugar." The U.S. Food and Drug Administration (FDA) declares it to be unfit for human consumption.

The raw sugar is then shipped to a refinery, where it is purified by washing, re-dissolving, boiling to re-crystallize it, and centrifuging twice more, making the sugar progressively purer and leaving behind progressively more concentrated molasses, whose dark color and intense flavor are due to all the non-sugar components—sometimes called the "ash"—in the cane juice.

Health-food stores that claim to be selling "raw" or "unrefined" sugar are usually selling turbinado sugar, which is a light brown sugar made by steam-washing, re-crystallizing, and centrifuging raw sugar for the second time. In my book, that's refining. A similar pale brown, large-grained sugar called demerara sugar is used in Europe as a table sugar. It is made on Mauritius, an island in the Indian Ocean off the coast of Madagascar, from sugar cane grown in rich, volcanic soil.

Jaggery sugar, made in rural India, is a dark brown, turbinado-like sugar made by boiling down the sap of certain palm trees in an open container, so that it boils at a higher temperature than in the partial vacuum of the usual cane sugar refining method. Because of the higher temperature, it develops a strong, fudge-like flavor. The boiling also breaks down some of the sucrose into glucose and fructose, making it sweeter than plain sucrose. Jaggery sugar is often sold pressed into blocks, as are other brown sugars in many parts of the world.

The unique flavor of molasses has been described as earthy, sweet, and almost smoky. The molasses from the first sugar crystallization is light-colored and mildly flavored; it is often used as a table syrup. Molasses from the second crystallization is darker and more robust, usually used in cooking. The last, darkest, and most concentrated molasses, called blackstrap, has a strong, bitter flavor that is an acquired taste.

A cleaned-up piece of raw sugar cane, by the way, can be a real treat. Many people in cane-growing areas, especially children, like to chew on sticks of sugar cane. They're very fibrous, but the juice is, of course, delicious.

MY SUGAR IS SO REFINED

Why do people say that refined,
white sugar is bad?

. . . .

This nonsensical claim is a mystery to me. It seems that some people take the word *refined* as an indication that we humans have somehow defied a law of Nature by having the audacity to remove some undesirable materials from a food before eating it. White sugar is just raw sugar with those other materials removed.

When sugar is refined by three successive crystallizations, everything but pure sucrose is left behind in the molasses. The less-refined, browner sugars from earlier stages in the process are more flavorful because of the traces of molasses that they contain. Whether you use light brown or the slightly stronger-flavored dark brown sugar in a recipe is purely a matter of taste.

Many brown sugars sold today in the supermarket are manufactured by spraying molasses onto refined white sugar, rather than by stopping the refining process in midstream. Domino and C&H brown sugars are still made in the traditional way, however.

My point is this: In raw cane juice you have a mixture of sucrose plus all the other components of cane that end up in the molasses. When the molasses components are removed, will someone please explain to me how the remaining pure sucrose suddenly becomes evil and unhealthful? When we eat the more "healthful," browner sugars, we're eating just as much sucrose along with the molasses residues. Why isn't the sucrose evil in that form?

Refined, Divine, and Superfine

> ### *Meringue Kisses*

These crunchy confections are almost pure refined, white sugar; its superfine granulation makes it dissolve quickly in the egg white. Meringues are notorious for picking up moisture from the air, so make these on a dry day only.

Why are they called kisses? They are shaped like Hershey's Kisses Chocolates, but Hershey admits that they aren't sure where the name came from.

This recipe is for three egg whites. But whenever you have a number of extra egg whites on hand, use this formula: For each 1 egg white, add a pinch of cream of tartar, beat in 3 tablespoons superfine sugar, and ½ teaspoon vanilla. After beating, fold in 1 tablespoon superfine sugar. Then continue with step 3.

---

   3 **large egg whites, at room temperature**
   ¼ **teaspoon cream of tartar**
  12 **tablespoons superfine sugar**
  1½ **teaspoons vanilla**

---

1. Preheat the oven to 250°F. Line two baking sheets with parchment paper.
2. In a small, deep bowl, beat the egg whites with the cream of tartar using a hand-held or electric mixer until they hold a shape. Gradually beat in 9 tablespoons of sugar and continue beating until the mixture is smooth and stiff peaks form when the beaters are lifted. Beat in the vanilla. Using a spatula, fold in the remaining 3 tablespoons sugar.
3. Put ½ teaspoon of the meringue mixture under each of the four corners of the parchment paper to keep it from skidding. Drop teaspoonfuls of the meringue mixture onto the paper-covered cookie sheets. If you want to be fancy, put the meringue into a pastry bag fitted with a star tip and pipe out the kisses.

4. Bake for 60 minutes. Turn off the oven and allow the meringues to remain in the cooling oven for 30 minutes. Remove from the oven, cool for 5 minutes, and store in airtight containers, where the meringues will stay crisp almost indefinitely.

MAKES ABOUT 40

A SUPERFINE GLASS OF TEA

To sweeten my iced tea quickly, I added
powdered sugar. But it turned into gummy lumps.
What happened?

. . . .

Good try, but you used the wrong sugar.

Ordinary table sugar is "granulated," meaning that it consists of individual granules or grains, each of which is a single crystal of pure sucrose. But when pulverized into a fine powder, sugar tends to pick up moisture from the air and cake. (Techspeak: sugar is hygroscopic.) To prevent this, the manufacturers of powdered sugar add about 3 percent of cornstarch. It's the starch that gummed up your tea, because it won't dissolve in cold water.

What you should have used is superfine or ultrafine sugar, which is not a powder in the strict sense. It consists of tinier crystals than those in ordinary granulated sugar, and it therefore dissolves more easily. It's used by bartenders because it dissolves quickly in cold mixed drinks and by bakers (it's sometimes called baker's sugar) because it blends and melts faster than ordinary granulated sugar.

ROCK SALT SÍ, ROCK SUGAR NO!

My brown sugar has turned into rock.
What can I do to soften it?

. . . .

That depends on whether you need to use it right away. There's a quick fix that gives temporary results—long enough for you to measure some out for a recipe—and there's a more time-consuming but longer-lasting fix that will restore your sugar to its original, manageable form.

But first, what makes brown sugar turn hard in the first place? Loss of moisture. You didn't reseal the package tightly enough after opening it, and it dried out to some extent. It's not your fault; it's almost impossible to reseal an opened box of brown sugar completely. So after you use some, always repackage the remainder in an airtight (more exactly, a vapor-tight) container such as a screw-top jar or a plastic food storage box with a tight lid.

The brown sugar sold in stores consists of white sugar crystals coated with a thin film of molasses, the thick, dark liquid left behind when sugar-cane juice is evaporated to allow crystals of pure sugar—sucrose—to separate out. Because the molasses coating has a tendency to absorb water vapor, fresh brown sugar is always very soft. But when exposed to dry air, the molasses loses some of its moisture and hardens, cementing the crystals together into lumps. You then have a choice: either restore the lost water or try somehow to soften the hardened molasses.

Restoring the water is easy, but it takes time. Just seal the sugar in a tight container overnight along with something that gives off water vapor. People have recommended everything from a slice of apple, potato, or fresh bread to a damp towel or, for no-nonsense types, a cup of water. The most effective setup is probably to put the sugar in a tight-lidded container, cover it with a sheet of plastic wrap, place a damp paper towel on top of the plastic wrap, and seal it all up. After a day or so when the sugar becomes soft enough, discard the towel and plastic wrap, and reseal the container tightly.

Many food books and magazines inform you that brown sugar hardens because it loses moisture, which is true, and then go on to tell you to heat it in the oven to soften it, as if the oven somehow restores moisture. It doesn't, of course. What happens is that the heat softens, or thins, the molasses "cement," which then re-hardens as it cools.

Some brown sugar packages recommend placing the hardened sugar in the microwave oven along with a cup of water. The water isn't there to hydrate the sugar, though, because in the couple of minutes it takes for the heat to do its job, water vapor from the cup doesn't have enough time to diffuse through the mass of sugar and hydrate it. The water is there only to absorb some of the microwaves, because microwave ovens shouldn't be operated in an empty or nearly empty condition (see p. 258). If you're zapping at least a cup or so of sugar, you probably don't need the water.

A chef of my acquaintance puts brown sugar out in his restaurant kitchen every day and it dries out rapidly. When it becomes very hard, he puts a few drops of hot water on it and massages it with his hands until it returns to its original texture. That's fine for the pros, but massaging sugar probably isn't the average home cook's idea of fun.

Speaking of molasses, a former Peace Corps volunteer once told me that many years ago in Mhlume, Swaziland, they used to pave dirt roads by spraying them with molasses from the local sugar refinery. It dried out and hardened very quickly, taking a few months to wear back down to the dirt. *(Note to my city's Public Works Department: Maybe if you used molasses instead of lowest-bidder asphalt, our roads would last longer.)*

Finally, if all else fails there is always Domino's Brownulated or free-flowing sugar, which pours like a dream and never turns into a brick. Domino's manufacturing trick is to break down some of the sucrose (Techspeak: hydrolyze it) into its two component sugars: glucose, aka dextrose, and fructose, aka levulose. (Some sugars have multiple names.) This mixture, called invert sugar, holds onto water tightly, so hydrolyzed brown sugar granules don't dry out and cake. Brownulated sugar, however, is intended for sprinkling on oatmeal and such, not for baking, because it doesn't measure out the same as the ordinary brown sugar that cookbooks specify.

> If you're in a hurry to soften hard brown sugar, your trusty microwave oven will come to the rescue with a quick, but temporary, fix. Just heat the sugar for a minute or two on high, probing it every half minute or so with a finger to see if it's soft yet. Because ovens differ so widely, no exact time can be stated. Then measure it out quickly because it'll harden again in a couple of minutes. You can also soften the sugar in a conventional oven at 250° for 10 to 20 minutes.

BEET ME WITH A CANE

What's the difference between cane sugar and beet sugar?

. . . .

More than half of the sugar produced in the U.S. comes from sugar beets, misshapen, whitish-brown roots that resemble short, fat carrots. Sugar beets grow in temperate climates, such as in Minnesota, North Dakota, and Idaho in the U.S., and in much of Europe, whereas sugar cane is a tropical plant, grown in the U.S. mainly in Louisiana and Florida.

Beet sugar refineries have the more difficult task because the beets contain many bad-tasting and foul-smelling impurities that must be removed. The impurities survive in the molasses, which is inedible and fit only for animal feed. For that reason there's no such thing as edible brown beet sugar.

Once refined, cane sugar and beet sugar are chemically identical: they're both pure sucrose and therefore should be indistinguishable from each other. Refineries don't have to label their sugar as cane or beet, so you may be using beet sugar without knowing it. If it doesn't say "Pure Cane Sugar" on the package, it's probably beet.

Nevertheless, some people who have long experience in making jams and marmalades insist that cane and beet sugars don't behave the same. Alan Davidson, in his encyclopedic *Oxford Companion to Food* (Oxford University Press, 1999), says that this fact "should cause the chemists to reflect, humbly, that they are not omniscient in these matters."

Touché.

A sugar beet.

Courtesy of the American Sugarbeet Growers Association.

THE CLASSES OF MOLASSES

My grandmother used to talk about sulphured molasses. What is it?

. . . .

The "sulphur" in sulphured molasses is a good starting point for understanding several interesting aspects of food chemistry.

Sulphur is the old-fashioned spelling for sulfur, a yellow chemical element whose common compounds include sulfur dioxide and sulfites. Sulfur dioxide gas is the choking, acrid odor of burning sulfur and is reputed to pollute the atmosphere in Hell, probably because volcanoes belch sulfurous fumes from the nether regions of our planet.

Sulfites release sulfur dioxide gas in the presence of acids, so their action is the same as that of sulfur dioxide itself. Namely, they are bleaching agents and are anti-microbials. Both properties have been used in sugar refining.

Sulfur dioxide has been used to lighten the color of molasses, the dark, sweet byproduct of sugar refining, and to kill its molds and bacteria. The molasses is then said to be sulphured. Virtually all molasses produced today is unsulphured, however. Sulphured molasses is not to be confused with Great-Grandma's sulphur and molasses, a spring tonic that supposedly "purified the blood" after a hard, cold winter. She mixed a couple of teaspoons of gritty, powdered sulfur into some molasses and fed it to as many children as she could catch. The sulfur is harmless because it isn't metabolized.

Sulfur dioxide gas is used to bleach cherries white, after which they are dyed a Disneyesque red or green, then flavored with oil of bitter almonds, packed in syrup, and christened *maraschino*, after the liqueur whose flavor these garish creations are striving to imitate.

Sulfites counteract oxidation. (Techspeak: sulfites are reducing agents.) "Oxidation" most commonly refers to the reaction of a substance with oxygen in the air, and it can be quite a destructive process. Witness the rusting of iron—a pure example of what oxidation can do, even to metals. In the kitchen, oxidation is one of the reactions that make fats turn rancid. Assisted by enzymes, oxidation is also what makes sliced potatoes, apples, and peaches turn brown. Dried fruits are therefore often treated with sulfur dioxide to keep that from happening.

But oxidation is a more general chemical process than the simple reaction of a substance with oxygen. To a chemist, oxidation is any reaction in which an electron is snatched away from an atom or molecule. The electron-deprived "snatchee" is said to have been oxidized. In our bodies, such vital molecules as fats, proteins, and even DNA can be oxidized, making them unable to fulfill their critical jobs of carrying on our normal life processes. Electrons are what holds molecules together, and when an electron is snatched away, these "good" molecules can break down into smaller, "bad" molecules.

Among the most voracious electron snatchers are the so-called free radicals, atoms or molecules that desperately need another electron and will snatch one from almost anything it encounters. (Electrons like to exist in pairs, and a free radical is an atom or molecule that has an unpaired electron desperately seeking a partner.) Thus, free radicals can oxidize vital life molecules, slowing down the body, causing premature aging, and possibly even heart disease and cancer. The problem is that a certain number of free radicals occur naturally in the body from a variety of causes.

Antioxidants to the rescue! An antioxidant is an atom or molecule that can neutralize a free radical by giving it the electron it wants before it steals one from something vital. Among the antioxidants we obtain from our foods are vitamins C and E, beta-carotene (which turns into vitamin A in the body), and those ten-syllable tongue-twisters you see on the labels of many fat-containing products to keep them from turning rancid by oxidation, butylated hydroxyanisole (BHA) and butylated hydroxytoluene (BHT).

Back for a moment to sulfites. We should note that some people, especially asthmatics, are very sensitive to sulfites, which can cause headache, hives, dizziness, and difficulty in breathing within minutes of eating them. The FDA requires specific labeling of products that contain sulfites—and there are many, from beer and wine to baked goods, dried fruits, processed seafoods, syrups, and vinegars. Search the labels for sulfur dioxide or any chemical whose name ends in -sulfite.

TREACLE, TREACLE, IN THE JAR, HOW I WONDER WHAT YOU ARE

What are those sweet syrups called treacle and sorghum, and how are they different from cane syrup?

. . . .

Cane syrup is simply clarified sugar-cane juice, boiled down to a syrup in much the same way maple syrup is made by boiling down the thin, sucrose-rich sap of the North American sugar maple and black maple trees. Black birch trees also have a sweet sap that can be boiled down into a syrup.

Treacle is a term used mainly in Great Britain. Dark treacle is similar to blackstrap molasses and has blackstrap's somewhat bitter taste. Light treacle, also known as golden syrup (a significant improvement in nomenclature), is essentially cane syrup. The most popular brand, Lyle's Golden Syrup, can be found in American specialty stores.

Sorghum is made neither from sugar cane nor sugar beets, but from a grass-like cereal grain plant with tall, strong stalks. It is grown around the world in hot, dry climates, mostly for use as hay and fodder. But some varieties have a sweet juice in the pith inside the stalks that can be boiled down into a syrup. The resulting product is called either sorghum molasses or sorghum syrup or sometimes just plain sorghum.

Molasses and Ginger: A Classic Combination

Molasses Gingerbread Cake

Ever since colonial times, Americans have paired the sweet/bitter flavor of molasses with ginger and other spices. This dark, dense, and moist cake is good plain or dressed up with whipped cream. Cooks who avoid dairy products can substitute ¼ cup plus 2 tablespoons light-flavored olive oil for the butter. The strong flavors of ginger and molasses will make the switch undetectable.

- 2½ cups all-purpose flour
- 1½ teaspoons baking soda
- 1 teaspoon ground cinnamon
- 1 teaspoon ground ginger
- ½ teaspoon ground cloves
- ½ teaspoon salt
- ½ cup (1 stick) butter, melted and slightly cooled
- ½ cup sugar
- 1 large egg
- 1 cup dark unsulphured molasses
- 1 cup hot (not boiling) water

---

1. Adjust the oven rack to the middle position. Spray an 8- by 8-inch pan with nonstick cooking spray. Preheat the oven to 350°F for a metal pan or 325° F if using an ovenproof glass pan.

2. In a medium bowl, stir together the flour, baking soda, cinnamon, ginger, cloves, and salt with a wooden spoon. In a large bowl, whisk together the melted butter, sugar, and egg. In a small bowl or glass measure, stir the molasses into the hot water until completely blended.

3. Add about one-third of the flour mixture to the butter-sugar-egg mixture and whisk together just to moisten the ingredients. Then whisk in about half of the molasses mixture. Continue by adding another third of the flour mixture, then the other half of the molasses mixture, then the final third of the flour mixture. Whisk just until all the patches of white disappear. Do not overmix.

4. Pour the batter into the prepared pan and bake for 50 to 55 minutes, or until a toothpick inserted into the cake comes out clean and the cake has pulled away somewhat from the sides of the pan. Cool in the pan for 5 minutes.

5. Serve warm from the pan, or turn the cake out onto a rack to cool. This is a good keeper and will stay fresh for several days, covered, at room temperature.

MAKES 9 TO 12 SERVINGS

A TIGHT SQUEEZE?

*My recipe for fondant tells me to dissolve
two cups of sugar in one cup of water.
It won't fit, will it?*

. . . .

Why didn't you try it?

Add two cups of sugar to one cup of water in a saucepan and stir while heating slightly. You'll see that all the sugar will dissolve.

One of the reasons is very simple: Sugar molecules can squeeze into empty spaces between the water molecules, so they are not really taking up much new space. When you get right down to the submicroscopic level, water isn't a densely packed pile of molecules. It's a somewhat open latticework, with the molecules connected to one another in tangled strings. The holes in this latticework can accommodate a surprising number of dissolved particles. This is especially true of sugar, because sugar molecules are built in such a way that

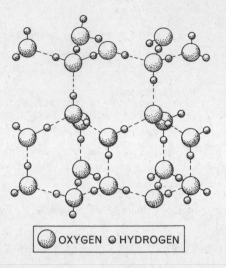

OXYGEN ⊙ HYDROGEN

A snapshot of the arrangement of H$_2$O molecules in water.
The dashed lines represent hydrogen bonds, which are continually
breaking and re-forming between molecules.

they just love to associate with (Techspeak: hydrogen-bond to) water molecules, and that makes sugar very mixable with water. As a matter of fact, with heating, you can coax more than two pounds (5 cups!) of sugar to dissolve in a single cup of water. Of course, by the time you get that far, it's not clear whether you're dealing with a boiling solution of sugar in water or with bubbling melted sugar containing a little water.

And that's how candy was born.

Yet another reason is that two cups of sugar is considerably less sugar than it seems. Sugar molecules are both heavier and bulkier than water molecules, so there won't be as many of them in a pound or in a cup. Also, the sugar is in granulated form, rather than in the form of a liquid, and the grains don't settle down into the cup as tightly as you might think. The surprising result is that a cup of sugar contains only about one twenty-fifth as many molecules as there are in a cup of water. That means that in your two-cups-of-sugar-in-one-cup-of-water solution, there is only one molecule of sugar for every twelve molecules of water. Not such a big deal, after all.

TWO KINDS OF BROWNING

Recipes sometimes tell me to caramelize chopped onions, meaning to sauté them until they are soft and lightly browned. Does "caramelize" mean simply to brown something? And what's the connection, if any, to caramel candy?

. . . .

The word *caramelize* is used for the browning of a variety of foods, but strictly speaking, caramelizing means the heat-induced browning of a food that contains sugars, but no proteins.

When pure table sugar (sucrose) is heated to about 365°F it melts into a colorless liquid. On further heating it turns yellow, then light brown and in quick succession darker and darker browns. In the process it develops a unique, sweetly pungent, increasingly bitter taste. That's caramelization. It is exploited in making a wide range of sweets, from caramel syrups to caramel candies to peanut brittle.

Caramelization entails a series of complex chemical reactions that still aren't completely understood by chemists. But they begin when the sugar is dehydrated and end with the formation of polymers—large molecules made up of many smaller molecules bound together into long chains. Some of these large molecules have bitter flavors and are responsible for the brown color. If the heating is carried too far, the sugar decomposes into water vapor and black carbon, as when you get too impatient while toasting a marshmallow. (Hey, kids: It should *not* catch fire.)

On the other hand, when small amounts of sugars or starches (which, remember, are made up of sugar units) are heated in the presence of proteins or amino acids (the building blocks of proteins), a different set of high-temperature chemical reactions takes place: the Maillard reactions, named after the French biochemist Louis Camille Maillard (1878–1936), who characterized the first step in the process. Part of the sugar molecule (Techspeak: its aldehyde group) reacts with the nitrogen part of the protein molecule (Techspeak: an amino group), after which follow a series of complex reactions that lead to brown polymers and many highly flavored, as-yet unidentified chemicals. Food scientists are still having international research conferences to figure out the Maillard reactions in detail.

Maillard reactions are responsible for the good flavor of heat-browned, carbohydrate- and protein-containing foods such as grilled and roasted meats (yes, there are sugars in meats), bread crusts, and onions. "Caramelized" onions do indeed taste sweet, because in addition to the Maillard reactions, heating makes some of their starch break down into free sugars, which can then truly caramelize. Moreover, many recipes for caramelized onions prime the pump by including a teaspoonful of sugar.

The moral of the story is that the word *caramelization* should be reserved for the browning of sugar—any kind of sugar—in the absence of protein. When sugars or starches occur together with proteins, as they do in onions, breads, and meats, the browning is mostly due to Monsieur Maillard, not to caramelization.

The "caramel color" that you see on the labels of cola soft drinks, low-quality soy sauces, and many other foods is made by heating sugar solutions with an ammonium compound. Ammonium compounds act just like the amino groups in proteins. So in a sense, the "caramel color" is really a sort of Maillard color.

CORNY, BUT SWEET

So many prepared foods list "corn sweeteners"
or "corn syrup" on the label. How do they get all
that sweetness out of corn?

. . . .

I know what you're thinking. The corn that you bought at the farmers' market the other day wasn't really "as sweet as sugar," as the vendor promised, was it?

"Sweet corn" does indeed contain more sugar than "cow corn," but even in the new sugar-enhanced and supersweet varieties it's precious little compared with sugar cane or sugar beets. Why is it that corn-derived sugar is so widely used instead of cane or beet sugar?

Two reasons, one economic and one chemical.

We don't produce nearly enough cane or beet sugar in the United States to satisfy our 275 million sweet teeth, so we have to import some. In fact, we import about sixty times more sugar then we export. But much of this imported sugar comes from countries that have never won awards for crop reliability, political stability, or love for Uncle Sam, so sugar importing has always been a bit of a gamble. On the other hand, right here at home we produce enormous amounts of corn—ton for ton, more than six thousand times as much corn as sugar cane. So if we could only get our sugar fix from home-grown corn, the problem would be solved.

Well, we can. But we're not limited to corn's meager allotment of sugar. Through the magic of chemistry, we can actually make sugar out of cornstarch. There's lots more starch than sugar in corn.

What do we find inside the corn kernel's cupboard? If we take away the water from a kernel of corn, the remainder will be about 84 percent carbohydrates, a family of biochemicals that includes sugars, starches, and cellulose. The cellulose is in the kernel's hull. But starch is the main component of all the other stuff outside the cob.

Starches and sugars are two families of chemicals that are very closely related. In fact, a starch molecule is made up of hundreds of smaller molecules of the simple sugar glucose, all tied together (see page 6). In principle, then, if we could chop cornstarch molecules up into small pieces, we could make hundreds of molecules of glucose. If the chopping-up isn't quite complete, there will also be some maltose, another sugar that consists of two glucose molecules, still bonded together (a disaccharide). There will also be some even bigger fragments, consisting of dozens of glucose molecules, still bonded together (a polysaccharide). Because these bigger molecules can't slide around past one another as easily as small molecules can, the final mixture will be thick and syrupy. Corn syrup. And that includes the bottled corn syrup in your supermarket. The dark syrup has a more intense, molasses-like flavor than the light syrup because it contains some refiners' syrup, which is . . . well, molasses.

Almost any acid, as well as a variety of enzymes from plants and animals, can perform the trick of breaking starch molecules down into a syrup of mixed sugars. (An enzyme is a biochemical that helps a specific reaction to take place rapidly and efficiently. [Techspeak: It's a natural catalyst.] Without enzymes, many essential life processes would be uselessly slow or just wouldn't work at all.)

The common sugar contained in sugar cane, sugar beets, and maple syrup is sucrose. But a sugar by any other name may not taste as sweet. That is, the glucose and maltose in corn syrup are only about 56 percent and 40 percent as sweet, respectively, as sucrose. So if cornstarch is broken down, it may average out to perhaps 60 percent of the sweetness of sucrose.

Food manufacturers get around this by using yet another enzyme to convert some of the glucose into its alternative molecular form, fructose, a sugar that is 30% sweeter than sucrose. That's why "high-fructose corn syrup" often appears on the labels of foods that need to be really sweet, such as sodas, jams, and jellies.

Corn sweeteners don't taste quite the same as good old sucrose, because different sugars have slightly different kinds of sweetness. The flavors of fruit preserves and soft drinks, for example, just ain't what they used to be before the food manufacturers pretty much abandoned cane sugar for corn sweeteners. As a label-reading consumer, all you can do is to choose products sweetened with the highest proportion of sucrose, which is listed on the label as "sugar." (If there are other sugar ingredients in a product, they will be listed on the label as "sugars.")

Next time you find yourself in a tropical, sugar-cane-producing country, buy some Coca-Cola. It is undoubtedly still made there with cane sugar, instead of the corn sweeteners that most U.S. bottlers have been using for more than a decade. Bring some home and compare its flavor with the contemporary American "Classic."

But when the customs agent aks what's in your bag, for heaven's sake don't say "Coke."

BROWN AMBROSIA

Besides the amount of sugar, is there any difference between unsweetened chocolate, semisweet chocolate, and sweet chocolate?

. . . .

Yes. Let's look at how chocolate is made.

Cacao beans, which are really seeds, are found inside melon-shaped seedpods attached directly to the trunk or thick branches of the tropical cacao tree. The beans are first separated from the pulpy mass inside the pod and allowed to ferment, usually by piling them up in heaps and covering them with leaves. Microbes and enzymes attack the pulp, kill the germs of the seeds (the parts that would germinate or grow), remove some of the bitter flavor, and darken the beans' color from off-white to light brown.

The dried beans are then shipped off to Willy Wonka at the chocolate factory, where they are roasted to further improve their flavor and color, separated from their shells, and milled or ground. The frictional heat of grinding melts the beans' substantial content—

about 55 percent—of vegetable fat, euphemistically known as cocoa (not cacao) butter. The result is a thick, brown, bitter liquid called chocolate liquor: the ground-up solids suspended in melted fat. This is the starting material for making all chocolate products.

When cooled, chocolate liquor solidifies into the familiar unsweetened, or bitter, chocolate that's sold in one-ounce "squares" for baking. The FDA requires that this basic unsweetened chocolate contain between 50 and 58 percent fat.

The fat and the solids can be separated, however, and mixed in various proportions with sugar and other ingredients to make hundreds of different chocolates with a wide range of flavors and properties.

One of the wonderful things about chocolate is that its fat melts at 86° to 97°F, which is just below body temperature, so that at room temperature it is relatively hard and delightfully brittle, but it literally melts in the mouth, releasing maximum flavor and producing a smooth, velvety sensation.

Semisweet or bittersweet chocolate is a prepared mixture of chocolate liquor, cocoa butter, sugar, an emulsifier, and sometimes vanilla flavoring. When melted, it is more fluid than unsweetened chocolate and has a satin gloss, both of which qualities make it ideal for dipping. It is sold in "squares" or bars for cooking, but because it may contain only 35 percent fat (the presence of the sugar reduces the percentage of fat), it will have different cooking characteristics from the fattier unsweetened chocolate.

Thus, you can't substitute unsweetened chocolate plus sugar for semisweet or bittersweet chocolate in a recipe. To further complicate things, there are significant variations among brands, and chocolates labeled bittersweet are likely to have a higher ratio of chocolate liquor to sugar than those labeled semisweet.

Moving up the sweetness scale, we encounter hundreds of kinds of semisweet and sweet chocolate confections containing at least 15 percent chocolate liquor and often much more. Milk chocolate generally contains less chocolate liquor (10 to 35 percent) than dark chocolate (30 to 80 percent) because the added milk solids reduce its percentage. That's why milk chocolate has a milder, less bitter flavor than dark chocolate. The FDA sets ingredient standards for all of these products manufactured in the U.S.: sweet chocolate, semisweet or bittersweet chocolate, and milk chocolate.

Before any high-quality chocolate product is ready for molding into bars or for enrobing (coating) various objects, it goes through two important processes: conching and tempering. In conching, the chocolate mixture is kneaded in heated tanks at a controlled temperature somewhere between 130° and 190°F (it varies) for as long as five days. This aerates the chocolate and drives off moisture and volatile acids, improving both its flavor and smoothness. Then it is tempered, kept at carefully controlled temperatures while it cools, so that the fat crystallizes into very tiny crystals (about 40 millionths of an inch), rather than bigger ones (as large as 2 thousandths of an inch) that would give the chocolate a grainy texture.

Today, there are many excellent chocolates available for cooking. The quality depends on many factors, including the blend of beans used (there are about 20 commercial grades); the type and extent of roasting; the degree of conching, tempering, and other processing; and, of course, the amounts of cocoa butter and other ingredients.

Chocolate with Olive Oil?

Chocolate Velvet Mousse

Because of its cocoa butter content, chocolate blends well with other fats such as butter and the butterfat in cream. That has led to the invention of dozens of rich, creamy chocolate desserts. But here's a non-dairy chocolate mousse using, of all things, olive oil.

Our good friend Basque Chef Teresa Barrenechea offers this silky mousse at her Manhattan restaurant, Marichu. "More and more people don't want to eat so much cream," she says. "I don't tell guests this dessert contains olive oil when I serve it. I wait until I hear them murmuring, 'Mmmmh-mmmmmh.' " The chocolate flavor is intense, but in spite of the generous amount of extra-virgin olive oil, its flavor is subtle. Embellishment isn't necessary, but we serve the dessert with fresh raspberries.

- **6 ounces very good semisweet, dark chocolate (such as Lindt, Callebaut, or Ghirardelli), chopped**
- **3 large eggs, separated**
- **⅔ cup confectioners' sugar, sifted after measuring**
- **¼ cup double-strength coffee at room temperature or 1 tablespoon instant espresso powder**
- **2 tablespoons Chambord or Cointreau**
- **¾ cup extra-virgin olive oil**
- **Raspberries**

---

1. Melt the chocolate in a small bowl in the microwave oven or in a saucepan over very low heat. Let cool.
2. In a medium bowl, beat the egg yolks and confectioners' sugar until smooth with an electric mixer on medium speed. Beat in the coffee and Chambord just to combine. Then stir in the melted chocolate. Add the olive oil and mix well.

3. Wash the beaters thoroughly, so that they are completely free of oil. In another medium bowl, beat the egg whites until almost stiff. With a whisk, gently fold one-third of the egg whites into the chocolate mixture until all patches of white disappear. Fold in the remaining egg whites, ⅓ at a time, until the patches of white disappear. Do not overmix.

4. Transfer the mousse to a pretty bowl or individual dessert dishes, cover, and refrigerate until well chilled. Serve cold with raspberries.

No, it will not collapse. And no, it does not taste oily.

MAKES 6 SERVINGS

A DUTCH TREATMENT

*What is Dutch process cocoa? How is it used
differently from regular cocoa in recipes?*

. . . .

To make cocoa, unsweetened chocolate (solidified chocolate liquor) is pressed to squeeze out most of the fat, and the resulting cake is then ground to a powder. There are several types of "regular" cocoa powder, depending on how much fat remains. For example, "breakfast cocoa" or "high-fat cocoa," as defined by the FDA, must contain at least 22 percent cocoa butter. If labeled just plain "cocoa," it may contain anywhere between 10 and 22 percent fat. "Low-fat cocoa" must contain less than 10 percent fat.

In the Dutch process, invented in 1828 by Conrad J. van Houten in guess-what-country, either the roasted beans or the chocolate liquor cake is treated with an alkali (usually potassium carbonate), which darkens the color to a deep reddish brown and mellows the flavor. Hershey calls its Dutch-processed cocoa "European style."

Cocoa is naturally acidic, and the alkali used in the Dutch process neutralizes it. That can make a difference in a cake recipe, because acidic cocoa will react with any baking soda present to make carbon dioxide and increase leavening, but the neutralized Dutch process cocoa won't.

Devil's food cake is an interesting case because most recipes call for regular cocoa, yet the cake comes out with a devilish red color, as if it contained Dutch process cocoa. That's because baking soda is used for leavening, and the alkaline baking soda "Dutches" the cocoa.

In the U.S., the word *cocoa* makes us think of a hot, chocolaty beverage. But a cup of what we call cocoa or hot chocolate is to a cup of hot Mexican chocolate what skim milk is to heavy cream, because we have squeezed out all the fat from the cocoa powder. A cup of Mexican chocolate, on the other hand, is thick and unimaginably rich because it is made from the whole chocolate liquor, fat and all.

In Oaxaca, in southern Mexico, a few years ago, I watched as the fermented and roasted cacao beans were ground with sugar, almonds, and cinnamon, emerging from the grinder as a glistening, thick brown paste—a sweetened and flavored chocolate liquor. It was then cast into round or cigar-shaped molds, cooled to solid cakes and sold in that form.

In the kitchen, one or two cakes of this Mexican chocolate are beaten into boiling-hot water or milk to make a rich, frothy nectar. In Oaxaca, it is served in widemouthed cups made specifically for dunking the egg-rich Mexican bread, *pan de yema* (yolk bread). In Spain, I have dunked *churros*, lengths of deep-fried pastry, into the same rich chocolate beverage.

Of the treasures that the Spanish *conquistadores* brought home from the New World, many would agree that in the long run, the chocolate was more valuable than the gold. Mexican chocolate is available in the United States under the brand names Ibarra and Abuelita.

Baking Soda Makes the Devil Blush

Devil's Food Cupcakes

The deep color of devil's food develops when regular cocoa is "Dutched" by the alkaline baking soda. You can substitute Dutch process cocoa for an even deeper color and a more mellow flavor. There will be no difference in texture.

½ **cup unsweetened cocoa**

1 **cup boiling water**

2 **cups all-purpose flour**

1 **teaspoon baking soda**

½ **teaspoon salt**

½ **cup unsalted butter, softened**

1 **cup sugar**

2 **large eggs**

1 **teaspoon vanilla**

1. Preheat the oven to 350°F. Spray enough cupcake pans to hold 18 cupcakes with nonstick baking spray, or line with cupcake papers.

2. Place the cocoa in a small bowl. Add the water slowly, stirring with a spoon until well blended into a smooth paste. Set aside until lukewarm.

3. In a small bowl, mix the flour, baking soda, and salt. In a medium bowl, cream the butter and sugar with an electric mixer on medium speed until fluffy. Beat in the eggs one at a time until well incorporated. Add the cooled chocolate mixture all at once and stir well until blended.

4. Add the flour mixture all at once and stir until smooth and all patches of white disappear. Do not overmix.

5. Using a ⅓-cup measure, scoop out the batter and turn into pans. The pan's depressions should be about three-quarters full. Bake for 15 minutes or until a cake tester or toothpick comes out clean when inserted into the centers of the cupcakes.

MAKES EIGHTEEN 2½-INCH CUPCAKES

Mocha Cocoa Frosting

3 cups confectioners' sugar

½ cup unsweetened cocoa

⅓ cup unsalted butter at room temperature

½ teaspoon vanilla

Pinch of salt

About ⅓ cup cold, strong coffee

---

1. Remove the lumps from the confectioners' sugar and cocoa by placing the measured ingredients into a sieve set over a bowl; push and rub with the back of a spoon or a rubber spatula. Mix the sugar and cocoa together with a spatula.

2. Using an electric mixer, cream the butter until smooth. Add the vanilla and salt. Add the sugar-cocoa mixture all at once and mix until almost blended. Beat in as much of the coffee as needed to make a smooth, spreadable frosting.

MAKES 1¾ CUPS OR ENOUGH TO FROST 18 CUPCAKES GENEROUSLY

THE UN-CHOCOLATE CHOCOLATE

Is white chocolate caffeine-free?

. . . .

Yes. It's also chocolate-free.

White chocolate is simply the fat from the cacao bean (the cocoa butter) mixed with milk solids and sugar. It contains none of those wonderful, though inauspiciously brown, cocoa-bean solids that give chocolate its unique character and rich flavor. If you choose a white-chocolate–topped dessert to avoid chocolate's caffeine, bear in mind that cocoa butter is a highly saturated fat. You can't win 'em all.

To add insult to perjury, some so-called white-chocolate confections aren't even made with cacao fat; they're made with hydrogenated vegetable oils. Be sure to read the ingredient list on the label.

Chocolate Turns Pale

White Chocolate Bars

If chocolate can be white, what's to stop us from making white brownies? When made chewy with coconut and crunchy with nuts, these bars will tempt any chocoholic in spite of their pale color.

- 2 **cups all-purpose flour**
- ½ **teaspoon baking soda**
- ¼ **teaspoon salt**
- ¾ **cup (1½ sticks) unsalted butter, at room temperature, cut into tablespoons**
- 1 **cup dark brown sugar, lightly packed**
- 2 **large eggs**
- ½ **cup sweetened, flaked coconut**
- 2 **teaspoons vanilla**
- 10 **ounces white chocolate, coarsely chopped**
- 1 **cup coarsely chopped walnuts**
  Confectioners' sugar

1. Preheat the oven to 300°F. Spray a 9- by 13-inch baking pan with nonstick baking spray.
2. In a medium bowl, whisk together the flour, baking soda, and salt. In another medium bowl, using an electric mixer, cream the butter and sugar. Beat in the eggs one at a time until well incorporated, then the coconut and vanilla, and blend. Stir in the flour mixture, and mix with a wooden spoon until all

patches of white disappear. Stir in the chopped chocolate and nuts until evenly dispersed. It will have the texture of a heavy cookie dough.

3. Scrape the dough into the prepared pan. Push the dough completely into the corners and level the surface with a spatula. Bake for 40 to 45 minutes, or until the center is set, the top is golden, and a cake tester or toothpick inserted into the cake comes out clean. Remove from the oven and place the pan on a wire rack to cool to room temperature. Dust with confectioners' sugar and cut into bars 2 by 3 inches. The bars will keep several days at room temperature, or freeze them.

MAKES ABOUT 18 BARS

HOW SWEET THEY ARE!

Those little envelopes of artificial sweeteners on restaurant tables: What's different about the different brands?

. . . .

I never use them myself because I don't view the 15 calories in a teaspoonful of sugar as a serious threat to my existence. But artificial sweeteners are a boon to diabetics and others who want to limit their intake of real sugar.

Artificial sweeteners, also called sugar substitutes, must be approved by the FDA before they can be marketed in the United States. The four that are currently approved for a variety of food uses are aspartame, saccharin, acesulfame potassium, and sucralose. Others are being evaluated. Aspartame is a nutritive sweetener, meaning that it supplies the body with energy in the form of calories, while the others are non-nutritive, that is, devoid of calories.

Aspartame, which is 100 to 200 times sweeter than sucrose, is the main ingredient in NutraSweet and Equal. It is a combination of two proteins, aspartic acid and phenylalanine, and therefore contains the same four calories per gram as any protein and, for that matter, the same four calories per gram as sugar. But since it's so much sweeter than sucrose, only a tiny amount does the trick.

Because an estimated one in 16,000 people suffers from the genetic disease phenylketonuria (PKU), in which the body cannot produce the enzyme necessary to digest phenylalanine, sweeteners that contain aspartame must carry a warning label stating: "Phenylketonuric: contains phenylalanine." Other than for PKU sufferers, and in spite of e-mail and Internet campaigns to link aspartame with a whole flock of serious diseases from multiple sclerosis to brain damage, the FDA gives aspartame its no-strings-attached approval of safety in all but massive doses.

Saccharin, which has been known for more than 120 years and is about 300 times sweeter than sucrose, is the artificial sweetening agent in Sweet'n Low.

Over the years, saccharin has had an on-again-off-again history of government approvals and bannings. The last round began in 1977, when the FDA proposed banning saccharin because of a Canadian study indicating that it causes bladder cancer in rats. But because saccharin has never been shown to cause cancer in humans, public opposition led the U.S. Congress to pass a moratorium on removing it from the market. The moratorium has been renewed several times, but products containing saccharin still had to carry a warning label saying, "Use of this product may be hazardous to your health. This product contains saccharin, which has been determined to cause cancer in laboratory animals." Then early in 2001, following extensive studies commissioned by the U.S. Department of Health and Human Services, which found insufficient evidence that saccharin is a human carcinogen, President Bush repealed the warning requirement.

Acesulfame potassium, sometimes written as *acesulfame K*, 130 to 200 times sweeter than sucrose, is the sweetening ingredient in Sunett and Sweet One. It is used in combination with other sweeteners in thousands of products worldwide. While approved by the FDA since 1988, it has been under attack by consumer watchdogs because it is chemically similar to saccharin.

Sucralose, known also by its trade name Splenda, is 600 times sweeter than sucrose and was approved by the FDA in 1999 as a general-purpose sweetener for all foods. It is a chlorinated derivative of sucrose itself (Techspeak: Three hydroxyl groups in the sucrose molecule have been replaced by three chlorine atoms), but because it doesn't break down significantly in the body, it provides no calories. Because tiny amounts are so potently sweet, it is usually bulked up with maltodextrin, a starchy powder.

All of these artificial sweeteners can be deleterious to health if ingested in very large doses. But in spite of the fact that the same statement can be made about every substance on Earth, including all our foods (ten pounds of popcorn, anyone?), each of these sweet chemicals carries as baggage a vociferous group of opponents.

Before we leave sugar substitutes, you may have noticed (if you read labels the way I do) the ingredient *sorbitol* in sugar-free candies and other foods. It's neither a sugar nor a synthetic substitute, but a sweet-tasting alcohol found naturally in berries and certain fruits. It's about half as sweet as sucrose.

Sorbitol has the property of holding on to water, and is used to keep many processed foods, cosmetics, and toothpastes moist, stable, and soft-textured. But because of that same property, too much sorbitol can act as a laxative by retaining water in the bowel. People who have overindulged in sugar-free candy have had cause to regret their intemperance.

Chapter Two

The Salt
of the Earth

. . . .

ENEATH THE SURFACE OF Hutchinson, Kansas, and
thousands of square miles of its environs lies an enormous
deposit of a precious rock-like mineral called halite. There, several
huge mining operations extract almost 1 million tons per year,
and that's less than one-half percent of the world's annual halite
production.

What do we do with all that halite? Among other things, we eat it;
it is the only natural rock consumed by humans. The other name for
this crystalline mineral is rock salt. And unlike the crystals that some
people carry around for their supposed healing powers, this is one
crystal that really does keep us alive and healthy.

Common salt—sodium chloride—is probably our most precious
food. Not only are its sodium and chloride parts (Techspeak: ions)
nutrients that we can't live without, but saltiness is one of our fundamental taste sensations. In addition to its own flavor, salt has the
seemingly magical ability to enhance other flavors.

The word *salt* doesn't describe a single substance. In chemistry,
it is a generic term for a whole family of chemicals. (Techspeak: A salt

is the product of reaction between an acid and a base. Sodium chloride, for example, results from the reaction of hydrochloric acid with the base sodium hydroxide.) Some other salts of gastronomical importance are potassium chloride, used as a salt substitute in low-sodium diets; potassium iodide, added to common salt to supply iodine in the diet; and sodium nitrate and sodium nitrite, used in curing meats. In this book, unless I indicate otherwise, I'll do what everyone else does outside of the chemistry lab: use the word *salt* to mean sodium chloride.

In the face of so many different salts, can what we call "salty" really be the unique flavor of sodium chloride? Undoubtedly not. Taste one of the potassium chloride "salt substitutes" and you'll describe it as salty, but it's a different saltiness from the familiar flavor of sodium chloride, just as the sensation of sweetness is slightly different among different sugars and artificial sweeteners.

In addition to its roles as a nutrient and a condiment, salt has been used for thousands of years to preserve meats, fish and vegetables for consumption long after the hunt or the harvest was over.

In this chapter, while I can't solve the mysteries of salt's nutritional or savory qualities, I *can* tell you about the physical and chemical roles it plays in our foods, including preservation.

SALT STICKS

What's so special about those expensive
"popcorn salts" and "margarita salts"
sold in my supermarket?

. . . .

Chemically speaking, absolutely nothing. They're plain old salt: sodium chloride. But physically speaking, they're either finer-grained or coarser-grained than ordinary table salt. And that's all.

The number of specialty salts on the wholesale market is astounding. Cargill Salt, Inc., one of the world's largest salt producers, makes about sixty kinds of food-grade salt for food manufacturing and consumer use, including flake, fine-flake, coarse, extra-fine, super-fine, fine-flour and at least two grades of pretzel. Chemically, all are 99-plus percent pure sodium chloride, but they possess special physical characteristics designed for use in everything from potato chips, popcorn, and roasted nuts to cakes, breads, cheeses, crackers, margarine, peanut butter, and pickles.

For margaritas, you want coarse crystals that will stick to the lime juice on the rim of the glass. (You do wet the rim with lime juice, don't you? Not, Heaven forbid, with water?) Finer grains of salt would just dissolve in the juice. On the other hand, for popcorn you want exactly the opposite: fine, almost powdered particles that will nestle into the kernel crannies and stay put. Grains of ordinary salt-shaker salt don't stick to dry foods; they bounce off like the fake boulders in an Indiana Jones avalanche.

But why pay a high price for ordinary sodium chloride with a come-hither label? Kosher salt is quite coarse enough to coat a margarita rim and works very well despite the ethnic mismatch. And for popcorn, I grind kosher salt into a powder with a mortar and pestle.

I get a particular kick out of the label on one brand of "popcorn salt" that sells for nearly $5 a pound. (Table salt sells for about 30 cents a pound). The label forthrightly declares: "Ingredients: Salt." Well, that's fair enough. But then it goes on to boast that it "also enhances the flavor of French fries and corn on the cob." Big surprise.

Pounding Salt

Tapas Almonds

In Spain, complimentary dishes of almonds fried in olive oil and salted are set out at bars. They are addictive. You can make them at home either by frying or, for less fat, toasting them in the oven. Both methods are given below. In either case, the best way to make the salt adhere to the almonds is to use kosher salt ground to a powder in a mortar. Or you can powder the salt in a spice grinder, as long as you clean it out well before using it again for spices.

---

1 teaspoon kosher salt

2 cups whole blanched almonds (¾ pound)

½ cup extra-virgin olive oil

TOP-OF-THE-STOVE METHOD

1. Pulverize the salt with a mortar and pestle or whirl in a spice grinder until fine. (Salt doesn't pulverize well in a food processor or blender.)
2. Pour ½ cup olive oil into a medium sauté pan and add the nuts. Place the cold pan on the stove burner and turn the heat to medium high. Cook, stirring constantly, until the oil begins to sizzle and the nuts begin to take on color.
3. As the nuts become tan, remove them with a slotted spoon to paper towels to drain. Do not let the nuts get dark brown. While the nuts are still warm, transfer to a serving bowl, sprinkle with the powdered salt, and mix gently.
4. Don't throw away the olive oil; it will not have been heated long enough to deteriorate substantially. Allow it to cool, pour into a jar, and store in a cool, dark place. Use it for sautéing.

MAKES ABOUT 2 CUPS OR 8 SERVINGS

OVEN METHOD:

1. Preheat the oven to 350°F. Place the almonds on a baking sheet with sides. Drizzle with about 1 tablespoon olive oil, and mix to coat evenly.
2. Bake until the nuts are tan, 12 to 14 minutes, stirring once about halfway through.
3. Remove the nuts from the oven, transfer to a serving bowl, sprinkle with the powdered salt, and mix gently to distribute uniformly.

A LITTLE TENDERNESS

*I read the label on a jar of meat tenderizer
and it was mostly salt. Does salt tenderize meat?*

. . . .

Only to a slight extent. But if you read further down the ingredient list, you'll find papain, an enzyme found in unripe papayas. That's what really does the job. All that salt is there primarily to dilute and spread out the relatively small amount of papain in the product on the assumption, I suppose, that it would be more welcome than sand.

Meat can be tenderized in several ways. A piece of fresh meat becomes more tender in the weeks following the moment at which it was transformed into fresh meat—to put it as delicately as possible. That's why meat is aged—hung at controlled humidity for two to four weeks at a temperature of about 36°F. Some meats are quick-aged at 68°F for only 48 hours. But all aging, obviously, takes time, and time is money, so not all meats are even quick-aged before being shipped from the packing company. That's a shame because aging not only tenderizes the meat but improves its flavor.

There are various enzymes in fruits, however, that have the property of breaking down protein and can be used to tenderize meat. They include bromelain from pineapples, ficin from fig trees, and papain from papayas. But they don't penetrate the meat very far and mainly tenderize the surface, which isn't much help to a steak. Also, they are destroyed by temperatures over 180°F, so are effective only before cooking.

The solution? Find a butcher who sells well-aged meat (very hard to find these days) or buy the naturally more tender cuts. Of course, they're more expensive.

And while you're in the spices and seasonings aisle of the supermarket, check the labels on all those "seasoning mixes," the Cajun seasonings, hamburger seasonings, pork seasonings, and the like. You'll find that the primary ingredient, the first-named ingredient on the labels, is salt. Read down the list, buy one or two of the spices listed, and season the food yourself while cooking. No need to pay spice prices for what is mainly salt.

WHEN IS SALT NOT SALT?

*What are all those salt substitutes that I see in the
market? Are they safer than real salt?*

. . . .

"Real" salt is sodium chloride. The issue of safety revolves around its sodium content; no one has ever blamed the chloride for anything. The aim of all the substitutes is to lower or eliminate the sodium.

Sodium in the diet has long been suspected as a possible cause of high blood pressure, but there appears to be little consensus among medical researchers. Some believe that sodium contributes to high blood pressure and some don't. While no smoking gun evidence has yet been uncovered, opinion seems to be swinging toward the sodium—is-bad side of the fence.

As in all health research, the worst that can be said of a dietary practice is that it increases the risk of something or other. That doesn't mean "eat it and die." Risk is only a probability, not a certainty. Nevertheless, cutting down on sodium may well be a prudent thing to do.

The medical uncertainties haven't stopped our vast national food mill from grinding out fear-of-sodium products. Salt substitutes are usually potassium chloride, a chemical fraternal twin of sodium chloride. It tastes salty, but with a different kind of saltiness. Both are members of a large chemical family called salts; we call sodium chloride "salt" as if it were the only one because it's by far the most common. But you can hear chemists laughing as they pass the supermarket shelf where NoSalt is sold; it is potassium chloride, an honest-to-god chemical salt, but its label claims that it is "salt-free." That's only because the FDA allows labels to use the word *salt* to mean sodium chloride and nothing else.

Morton's Lite Salt Mixture is a 50-50 mixture of sodium and potassium chlorides, for those who want to cut down on sodium but retain some of sodium chloride's unique flavor.

And finally, there is Salt Sense, which claims to be 100 percent "real salt" (meaning real sodium chloride), yet also purports to contain "33 percent less sodium per teaspoon." That statement is disconcerting to a chemist, because sodium chloride is made of one atom of sodium plus one atom of chlorine, which means that sodium chloride must always contain the same percentage of sodium by weight: 39.3 percent. (It's less than 50 percent because the chlorine atom is heavier than the sodium atom.) So there's just no monkeying around with how much or how little sodium "real salt" contains. It would be like claiming that a certain dollar contains less than 100 cents.

So what's the trick? It's in the word *teaspoon*. A teaspoon of Salt Sense does indeed contain 33 percent less sodium, because a teaspoon of Salt Sense contains 33 percent less salt. Salt Sense consists of salt crystals that are flaky and fluffy, so they don't settle down into the spoon as much as ordinary granulated table salt does. So if you use the same volume, or bulk, of Salt Sense that you do of ordinary salt, it's actually less weight and, hence, less sodium. It's just as if a brand of ice cream claimed to have 33 percent fewer calories per mouthful because it's frothed up with more air (yes, they do that) and there is therefore less ice cream in a mouthful.

In tiny print at the bottom of the Salt Sense label, there's a footnote: "*100 grams of either product [Salt Sense or regular salt] contains 39,100 milligrams of sodium." Right. When you take equal weights, rather than an equal number of teaspoonfuls, Salt Sense is nothing but salt with an additive: creative marketing. (Okay, you nitpickers, you've noticed that 39.1 isn't exactly 39.3. That's because Salt Sense is only about 99.5 percent pure.)

FASTA PASTA

Why do we have to put salt in the water before
boiling pasta in it? Does it make the pasta
cook faster?

. . . .

Virtually every cookbook instructs us to salt the water in which we cook pasta or potatoes, and we dutifully comply without asking any questions.

There is a very simple reason for adding the salt: It boosts the flavor of the food, just as it does when used in any other kind of cooking. And that's all there is to it.

At this point, every reader who has ever paid the slightest attention in chemistry class will object. "But adding salt to the water raises its boiling point, so the water will boil hotter and cook the food faster."

To these readers I award an A in chemistry but a D in Food 101. It's true that dissolving salt—or really anything else, for that matter

(I'll explain)—in water will indeed make it boil at a higher temperature than 212°F at sea level. But in cooking, the rise is nowhere near enough to make any difference, unless you throw in so much salt that you could use the water to melt ice on your driveway.

As any chemist will be happy to calculate for you, adding a tablespoon (20 grams) of table salt to five quarts of boiling water for cooking a pound of pasta will raise the boiling point by seven hundredths of 1°F. That might shorten the cooking time by half a second or so. Anyone who is in that much of a hurry to get the spaghetti onto the table may also want to consider rollerblading it from the kitchen to the dining room.

Of course, you know that as an incorrigible professor I now feel obliged to tell you *why* salt raises the boiling point of water, small as the effect may be. Give me one paragraph.

In order to boil off, that is, in order to become vapor or steam, water molecules must escape from the ties that bind them to their liquid fellows. Wresting themselves loose with the aid of heat is tough enough because water molecules stick together quite strongly, but if there happen to be any alien particles cluttering up the liquid, it's even tougher, because the particles of salt (Techspeak: the sodium and chloride ions) or other dissolved substances simply get in the way. The water molecules therefore require some extra oomph, in the form of a higher temperature, in order to make good their escape to airborne freedom. (For more, ask your friendly neighborhood chemist about "activity coefficients.")

Now back to the kitchen.

Unfortunately, there is even more mumbo jumbo surrounding the addition of salt to cooking water than the fallacy about boiling temperature. The most frequently cited fables, even in the most respected cookbooks, tell us precisely *when* we must add the salt to the water.

One recent pasta cookbook observes that "it is customary to add salt to the boiling water prior to adding the pasta." It goes on to warn that "adding the salt before the water boils may cause an unpleasant aftertaste." Thus, the recommended routine is (1) boil, (2) add salt, (3) add pasta.

Meanwhile, another pasta cookbook counsels us to "bring the water to the boil before adding salt or pasta," but leaves open the momentous question of salt-first or pasta-first.

The fact is that as long as the pasta cooks in salted water, it makes no difference whether or not the water had already been boiling when the salt was added. Salt dissolves quite easily in water, whether hot or merely lukewarm. And even if it didn't, the roiling of boiling would dissolve it immediately. Once dissolved, the salt has no memory of time or temperature—of precisely when it entered the water or of whether it took the plunge at 212°F or 100°F. It cannot, therefore, affect the pasta differently.

One theory I have heard from a chef is that when salt dissolves in water it releases heat, and that if you add the salt when the pot is already boiling the extra heat can make it boil over. Sorry, Chef, but salt doesn't release heat when it dissolves; it actually absorbs a little bit of heat. What you undoubtedly observed is that when you added the salt, the water suddenly erupted into livelier bubbling. That happened because the salt—or almost any other added solid particles—gives the budding bubbles many new places (Techspeak: nucleation sites) upon which to grow to full size.

Another theory (everybody has one, it seems; is boiling pasta such an Earth-shaking challenge?) is that the salt is added for more than flavor, that it toughens the pasta and keeps it from getting too mushy. I have heard some plausible but quite technical reasons for that, but I won't trouble you with them. Let's just add the salt whenever and for whatever reason we wish. Just make sure we add it or the pasta will taste blah.

OH SAY, CAN YOU SEA?

Please tell me about sea salt. Why are so many
chefs and recipes using it these days? How is it
better than regular salt?

. . . .

The terms *sea salt* and *regular salt* or table salt are often used as if
they denote two distinctly different substances with distinctly different properties. But it's not that simple. Salt is indeed obtained from
two different sources: underground mines and seawater. But that fact
alone doesn't make them inherently different, any more than water
obtained from wells and springs are inherently different because of
their sources.

Underground salt deposits were laid down by ancient seas that
ultimately dried up at various times in Earth's history, from a few
million to hundreds of millions of years ago. Some of the deposits
were later thrust upward by geologic forces and are quite near the
surface in the form of "domes." Other salt deposits lie hundreds of
feet below ground, creating a bigger challenge to mining.

Rock salt is chopped out by huge machines within caverns carved
into the salt. But rock salt isn't suitable for food use because the
ancient seas trapped mud and debris when they dried up. Instead,
food-grade salt is mined by pumping water down a shaft to dissolve
salt, pumping the salt water (brine) up to the surface, settling out the
impurities, and vacuum-evaporating the clear brine. That creates the
familiar, tiny crystals of table salt in your salt shaker.

In sunny coastal regions, salt can be obtained by allowing sun-
shine and wind to evaporate the water from shallow ponds or "pans"
of contemporary seawater. There are many kinds of sea salt, harvested from waters around the world and refined to various degrees.

There are gray and pinkish-gray sea salts from Korea and France,
and black sea salt from India, all of which owe their colors to local
clays and algae in the evaporation ponds, not to the salt (sodium

chloride) that they contain. Black and red sea salts from Hawaii owe their colors to deliberately added powdered black lava and red baked clay. These rare and exotic boutique salts are used by adventurous chefs. They have undeniably unique flavors, of course; they taste like salt mixed with various clays and algae. Each one has its fervent partisans.

In what follows, I am not writing about these rare, expensive ($33 or more per pound) multicolored boutique salts, which are not easily available to the home cook. I am writing about the wide variety of relatively white salts obtained by one means or another from seawater, and which *for that fact alone* are revered because they are believed to be rich in minerals and universally superior in flavor.

MINERALS

If you evaporate all the water from a bucket of ocean (fish previously removed), you will be left with a sticky, gray, bitter-tasting sludge that is about 78 percent sodium chloride: common salt. Ninety-nine percent of the other 22 percent consists of magnesium and calcium compounds, which are mostly responsible for the bitterness. Beyond that, there are at least 75 other elements in very small amounts. That last fact is the basis for the ubiquitous claim that sea salt is "loaded with nutritious minerals."

But cold, hard chemical analysis tells the tale: The minerals, even in this raw, unprocessed sludge, are present in nutritionally negligible amounts. You'd have to eat two tablespoons of it to get the amount of iron, for example, contained in a single grape. Although people in the coastal regions of some countries do use this raw material as a condiment, the FDA requires that in the U.S. food-grade salt be at least 97.5 percent pure sodium chloride. In practice, it is invariably much purer.

That's only the beginning of the Great Mineral Deception. The sea salt that winds up in the stores contains only about one-tenth of the mineral matter in raw sea sludge. The reason for that is that in the production of food-grade sea salt, the sun is allowed to evaporate much of the water in the ponds, but by no means all of it—and that's a critical distinction. As water evaporates, the remaining water becomes more and more concentrated in sodium chloride. When the concentration of salt in the ponds gets to be about nine times what it was in the ocean, it begins to separate out as crystals, because there isn't enough water left to hold the salt in its dissolved form. The crystals are then raked or scooped out for subsequent washing, drying and packaging. (How do you wash salt without dissolving it away? You wash it with a solution that is already holding as much salt as possible and cannot dissolve any more. In Techspeak, a saturated solution.)

The vital point here is that this "natural" crystallization process is in itself an extremely effective refining step. Sun-induced evaporation and crystallization make the sodium chloride about 10 times purer—freer of other minerals—than it was in the ocean.

Here's why.

Whenever you have a water solution containing a preponderance of one chemical (in this case, sodium chloride) along with a lot of other chemicals in much lesser amounts (in this case, the other minerals), then as the water evaporates away, the preponderant chemical will crystallize out in a relatively pure form, leaving all the others behind. It's a purification process that chemists use all the time. Madame Curie used it repeatedly to isolate pure radium from uranium ore.

Salt harvested by the solar evaporation of ocean water, known as solar salt, is therefore about 99 percent pure sodium chloride right off the bat, with no further processing. The other 1 percent consists almost entirely of magnesium and calcium compounds. Those other 75-or-so "precious mineral nutrients" are virtually gone. To get that single grape's worth of iron, you'd have to eat about a quarter of a pound of solar salt. (Two pounds of salt can be fatal.)

Incidentally, the notion that sea salt arrives naturally iodized is a myth. Just because certain seaweeds are rich in iodine, some people think of the oceans as vast pots of iodine soup. In terms of the chemical elements in seawater, there is 100 times more boron, for example, than there is iodine, and I've never heard anybody tout sea salt as a source of boron. Un-iodized commercial sea salts contain less than 2 percent of the amount of iodine in iodized salt.

IS "SEA SALT" SEA SALT?

Actually, the "sea salt" sold in markets might not even have been taken from the sea, because as long as they satisfy the FDA's purity requirements manufacturers don't have to specify their sources, and according to industry insiders I have talked with, fibbing does occur. Two batches of salt may have been taken from the same bin at the mine plant and one of them labeled for sale as "sea salt." Well, of course it is. It just crystallized a few million years earlier. Conversely, on the West Coast of the U. S. the common table salt in the salt shaker is most likely to have come from the sea, rather than from a mine.

The point is that *a salt's characteristics depend on how the raw material has been processed, rather than on where it came from.* You can't generalize. Thus, when a recipe specifies simply "sea salt," it is a meaningless specification. It might as well be specifying "meat."

ADDITIVES

Sea salt is often specified to avoid the "harsh-flavored additives" in shaker salt. Whether from a mine or a sea, shaker salt does indeed contain anti-caking additives to keep its grains flowing smoothly, because they are tiny cubes and their flat surfaces tend to stick together. But the FDA limits the total amount of all additives to a maximum of 2 percent, and it is invariably much less than that. Morton's table salt, for example, is more than 99.1 percent pure sodium chloride and contains only 0.2 to 0.7 percent of the anti-caking agent calcium silicate. Because calcium silicate (and all the other anti-caking agents) are insoluble in water, shaker salt makes a slightly cloudy solution.

Other common anti-caking additives are magnesium carbonate, calcium carbonate, calcium phosphates, and sodium aluminum silicates. *These are all completely tasteless and odorless chemicals.*

But even if they weren't, even if expert tasters could detect subtle flavor differences among solid salts due to an additive of less than one percent, the 50,000-fold dilution factor that occurs when the salt is used in a recipe would certainly wipe them out. Just do the math. One percent of a 6-gram teaspoon of salt is 0.06 gram of additive in 3 quarts or more than 3,000 grams of stew: 3,000 ÷ 0.06 = 50,000.

FLAVOR

There is no denying that some of the finer (read more expensive) sea salts—even below the boutique level—have interesting flavor characteristics. But that depends on how they are used and on what your definition of "flavor" is.

A food's flavor consists of three components: taste, smell, and texture. With salt, we can pretty much eliminate smell because neither sodium chloride nor the calcium and magnesium sulfates that may be present in some of the less purified sea salts have any odor. (Techspeak: They have exceedingly low vapor pressures.) Nevertheless, our sense of smell is very sensitive, and it is possible that a smell of algae in these less purified salts might be detected. Also, when any kind of salt is inhaled nasally as a fine dust, some people report a slight metallic sensation high in the nose.

That leaves taste and texture: what the taste buds actually detect and how the salt feels in the mouth.

Depending on how they were harvested and processed, the crystals of different brands of sea salt can vary widely in shape, from flakes to pyramids to clusters of irregular, jagged fragments. (Check them out with a magnifying glass.) The sizes of the crystals also can range from fine to coarse, although virtually all of them are coarser than shaker salt.

When sprinkled on a relatively dry food such as a slice of tomato just before serving, the bigger, flakier crystals can deliver bright little explosions of saltiness as they hit the tongue and dissolve or as they are crushed between the teeth. That's why the savviest chefs value them: for those sensuous little bursts of saltiness. Shaker salt doesn't do that because its compact little cubes dissolve on the tongue much more slowly. Thus, it is the complex shapes of the crystals, not their nautical origin, that give many sea salts their sensory properties.

The reason that most sea salts have large, irregularly shaped crystals is that that's what slow evaporation produces, whereas the rapid vacuum-evaporation process used in making shaker salt produces tiny, regularly shaped grains designed to fit through the holes in the shaker. That's a phenomenon well known to chemists; the more rapidly crystals grow, the smaller they will be.

COOKING

Crystal size and shape are irrelevant when a salt is used in cooking, because the crystals dissolve and disappear completely in the food juices. And once dissolved, all textural differences are gone. The food doesn't know what shape the crystals were in before they dissolved. That's another reason why it's silly to specify sea salt in any recipe that contains moisture, and what recipe doesn't? Using it to salt the water in which vegetables or pasta are to be cooked makes even less sense.

But are sea salts perhaps still distinguishable from one another in flavor, even though dissolved in water? In a series of controlled taste tests reportedly conducted in 2001 under the auspices of the Leatherhead Food Research Association in England, panels of tasters attempted to distinguish among a number of different salts dissolved in water. The results, as reported in *Vogue* magazine, were wholly inconclusive.

One common assertion is that sea salt is saltier than shaker salt. But since they're both about 99 percent pure sodium chloride, that can't be true. The idea undoubtedly arose from the fact that in on-the-tongue taste tests, the flaky, irregularly shaped crystals of many sea salts dissolve instantly, giving a quicker rush of saltiness than do the small, compact, slow-dissolving little cubes of shaker salt. But again, it's not the ocean that made that difference; it's the shapes of the crystals.

The notion that sea salt is saltier has led to the claim that one can use less of it in seasoning. ("Good for those watching their sodium intake," trumpets one sea salt manufacturer.) Obviously, because sea salts generally have big, complexly shaped crystals that don't pack down as tightly, a teaspoonful will contain less actual sodium chloride than a teaspoonful of tiny, compact shaker grains. Teaspoon for teaspoon, therefore, sea salt is actually *less* salty than shaker salt. Weight for weight, of course, they're identical, because any gram of sodium chloride is precisely as salty as any other. You can't cut down on salt by eating the same weight of salt in a different form.

MAKING THE MOST OF IT

At home in your kitchen, which coarse, complexly grained sea salt should you sprinkle on your *foie gras* or venison *carpaccio* just before serving? The ones that earn the most frequent praise from chefs are the (surprise!) French salts harvested from the coastal waters of southern Brittany at Guérande or on the île de Noirmoutier or île de Ré. You will find them in several forms. *Gros sel* (big salt) and *sel gris* (gray salt) are the heavy crystals that fall to the bottom of the salt ponds and may therefore be gray with clay or algae.

In the battle of the sea salts, most connoisseurs agree that the champion is *fleur de sel* (flower of salt), the delicate crust of crystals that forms on the surface of the French ponds when the sun and wind are exactly right. Because it forms in very limited amounts and must be carefully hand-skimmed from the surface, *fleur de sel* commands the highest price and is (as a consequence, perhaps?) most highly regarded by leading chefs. Because of its fragile, pyramidal crystal shape, it does indeed produce a delightfully crunchy salt-burst when sprinkled on relatively dry foods just before serving or at the table.

But cooking with it is pointless.

YOU DON'T HAVE TO BE JEWISH

So many chefs and recipes specify the use of kosher
salt. What's different about it?

. . . .

Kosher salt is misnamed; it should be called koshering salt because it is used in the koshering process, which involves blanketing raw meat or poultry with salt to purify it.

Kosher salt may be either mined or taken from the sea; nobody seems to care. Its crystals, however, must always be coarse and irregular, so they will cling to the surface of the meat during koshering. Ordinary granulated table salt would fall right off. Besides the rabbinical supervision of its manufacture, its crystal size is the only distinction between kosher salt and other salts.

Because of its coarseness, kosher salt is better used by the pinch, rather than by the shake. Pinching lets you see and feel exactly how much you're using. That's why most chefs use kosher salt. I keep it ever handy in a small ramekin, not only in the kitchen but on the table. I use my shaker mainly for sprinkling salt on the tails of birds.

Some people believe that kosher salt contains less sodium than granulated table salt. That's nonsense. They're both virtually pure sodium chloride, and sodium chloride always contains 39.3 percent sodium. Gram for gram, every edible salt is precisely as salty as any other.

There really is a difference, however, in the amount of kosher salt to use in cooking. When a recipe specifies simply "salt," it almost always means granulated table salt: salt that consists of crystals tiny enough to fit through the holes in a saltshaker. But kosher salts, having bigger, irregularly shaped grains, don't settle down into a teaspoon measure as compactly as table salt does. So a teaspoonful of kosher salt will contain less actual sodium chloride and you must therefore use a larger volume of it to get the same degree of saltiness.

That's what's behind the "less sodium" myth; if you use the same number of teaspoonfuls, you are, of course, getting less salt, and hence less sodium, than in granulated salt.

By carefully weighing a cupful of each kind, I have determined the following conversion factors: For Morton's Coarse Kosher Salt, use 1¼ times the specified volume of granulated table salt. For Diamond Crystal Kosher Salt, use exactly twice the specified volume.

It is often said that kosher salt contains no additives. And indeed, because its crystals aren't tiny cubes like shaker salt's, they don't tend to stick together and don't generally need shaker salt's anti-caking additives. But read the labels. Diamond Crystal Kosher Salt has no additives, but Morton's Coarse Kosher Salt does contain a tiny amount—limited by the FDA to less than thirteen ten-thousandths of 1 percent—of the anti-caking agent sodium ferrocyanide.

Ferro- what? Relax. Even though ferrocyanide is a totally different chemical from poisonous cyanide, the labels play it safe by listing it by its less alarming name, yellow prussate of soda.

Any salt, whether from mine or sea and whether kosher or secular, may be iodized. A maximum of one-hundredth of 1 percent of potassium iodide is added as protection against the iodine-deficiency disease goiter. Iodized salt does require a special additive, however, because potassium iodide is somewhat unstable and in a warm, humid or acidic environment will decompose, its iodine content wafting off into the air. (Techspeak: The iodide is oxidized to free iodine.) To prevent this, a tiny amount—four-hundredths of 1 percent—of dextrose is often added.

Sugar in salt? Yes. Dextrose is what is known as a reducing sugar, and it prevents oxidation of the iodide to free iodine. But at the high temperatures used in baking, some of the iodide can nevertheless be oxidized to iodine, which has an acrid flavor. Many bakers therefore won't use iodized salt in their doughs and batters.

THE OLD MILL SCHEME

*Why is freshly ground salt supposed to be better
than granulated salt?*

. . . .

It's better for the people who sell those fancy salt mills and combination salt-and-pepper grinders in so-called gourmet shops. The idea seems to be that if freshly ground pepper is so much better than the powdered stuff in cans, then why not use freshly ground salt as well?

That's a delusion. Unlike pepper, salt contains no volatile, aromatic oils to be released by grinding. Salt is solid sodium chloride through and through, so a small chunk will be absolutely identical to a large chunk in everything but size and shape. The fun of a salt grinder is that it deposits coarse little chunks, instead of tiny grains, on your food, and therefore delivers a burst of saltiness when you bite them. But it doesn't matter how "freshly" they were ground.

WHOOPS!

*When making soup, I accidentally put in too
much salt. Was there anything I could have done
about that? I've heard that raw potato will
absorb the excess.*

. . . .

Almost everyone has heard that advice: Throw in some chunks of raw potato, simmer them for a while, and they will absorb some of the extra salt. But as with so many common beliefs, this one, to my knowledge, has never been tested scientifically. I took that as a challenge and set up a controlled experiment. I simmered raw potato in salty water and with the help of a chemistry professor colleague's laboratory assistant, measured the amount of salt in the water, both before and after the potato treatment.

Here's what I did.

I made up a couple of too-salty mock soups—actually, just plain salt water, so there would be no other ingredients to mess things up with their own saline predilections. But how salty should I make my samples? Many recipes begin with about a teaspoon of salt in four quarts of soup or stew, with more salt added "to taste" at the finish. So I made my soup sample No. 1 with one teaspoon of table salt dissolved in each quart of water, while soup No. 2 contained one tablespoon of table salt per quart of water. That's about four and twelve times the usual recipe-starting saltiness, respectively, and perhaps two and six times the saltiness of a soup that had already been salted "to taste."

I heated each of the two mock-soup samples to boiling, added six ¼-inch-thick slices of raw potato, simmered gently for 20 minutes in a tightly covered pan, removed the potato, and allowed the liquid to cool.

Why did I use slices of potato rather than chunks? Because I wanted to expose as much surface area to the "soup" as possible, giving the spuds every opportunity to live up to their salt-sucking reputation. And I used the same amount of potato surface area (300 square centimeters, if you must know) in both samples. Of course, I also simmered the same amounts of the two liquids in the same covered pot on the same burner. Scientists, as you must be thinking by now, are absolute maniacs about controlling all conceivable (and even some inconceivable) variables except the one they're comparing. Otherwise, they'd never know what caused any differences they might observe. It always annoys me when a person tries something once under completely uncontrolled circumstances and then goes running around saying, "I tried it and it works."

The concentrations of salt in the four samples—the two salt waters both before and after being simmered with the potato—were determined by measuring their electrical conductivities. The idea is that salt water conducts electricity, and the conductivity can be directly related to the salt content.

And what were the results? Did the potatoes really reduce the concentrations of salt? Well . . .

First let me tell you about the taste tests. I reserved the potato slices after they had been simmered in the salty waters. I had also simmered potato slices in plain water (same amounts of potato and water). My wife, Marlene, and I then tasted all of them for saltiness. She didn't know which samples were which. Sure enough, the potato simmered in plain water was bland, the potato simmered in the one-teaspoon-per-quart water was salty, and the potato simmered in the one-tablespoon-per-quart water was much saltier. Does this mean that the potato actually absorbed salt from the "soups?"

No. All it means is that the potatoes soaked up some salt water; they didn't selectively extract the salt from the water. Would you be surprised if a sponge placed in salt water came out tasting salty? Of course not. The *concentration* of salt in the water—the amount of salt per quart—would not be affected. So the salty taste of the potatoes proved nothing, except that for more flavor we should always boil our potatoes—and our pasta, for that matter—in salted water rather than in plain water.

Okay, now, what were the results of the conductivity measurements? Are you ready? *There was no detectable difference in the salt concentrations before and after being simmered with potato.* That is, the potato did not lower the concentration of salt at all, either in the one-teaspoon-per-quart or in the one-tablespoon-per quart "soup." The potato trick just doesn't work.

There are other saltiness-reduction dodges that one hears about, such as adding a little sugar, lemon juice, or vinegar to reduce the *perception* of saltiness. Are there, then, any reactions between saltiness and either sweetness or sourness that could diminish the sensation of saltiness? After all, it's the salty *taste* that we want to diminish, even if the salt is still there.

It was time for me to go to the taste experts—the scientists at the

Monell Chemical Senses Center in Philadelphia, an institution devoted to research in the complex field of human taste and smell.

First, as far as potato effects are concerned, no one I spoke with could think of any reason that a potato or its starchiness would reduce the perception of saltiness. But Dr. Leslie Stein helpfully supplied me with a 1996 review paper in the journal *Trends in Food Science & Technology* by Paul A. S. Breslin of the Monell Center on the interactions among flavors.

Can one flavor suppress another? Yes and no. It depends on both the absolute amounts and the relative amounts of the interacting flavors. "In general," Dr. Breslin writes, "salts and acids [sour flavors] enhance each other at moderate concentrations but suppress each other at higher concentrations." That might indicate that adding a fair amount of lemon juice or vinegar to a quite salty soup could indeed make it taste less salty. But, Breslin points out, "there are exceptions to . . . these generalities." In the particular case of salt and citric acid (the acid in lemon juice), he quotes the results of one study in which citric acid reduced the perceived saltiness, one study in which the saltiness was unaffected, and two studies in which the perceived saltiness was actually increased.

So whatcha gonna do? Add lemon juice? Vinegar? Sugar? There is really no way to predict how they will act in your particular soup containing your particular amounts of salt and other ingredients. But by all means try any one of these measures before feeding the stuff to your dog.

It appears that there's only one sure way to rescue a too-salty soup or stew: Dilute it with more stock—unsalted, of course. It would skew the flavor balance toward that of the pure stock, but that can be corrected.

EPILOGUE

There were a few interesting sidelights to this experiment that I'll record for you science buffs. (The rest of you may go on to the next question.)

First, it turned out that the conductivities of the salt waters after simmering with potato were slightly higher than—not lower than—those of the untreated waters. So potatoes alone must contribute some electrical conductivity to the water in which they are boiled. That took me by surprise, because on first blush one would think that only starch comes out of the potatoes into the water, and starch doesn't conduct electricity. But potatoes contain a lot of potassium, about two-tenths of a percent in fact, and potassium compounds do conduct electricity, just as sodium compounds do. At any rate, I corrected for that effect by subtracting the potato's conductivity contribution from the conductivities of the potato-simmered salt waters.

Second, if, in spite of the tight cover and gentle simmering, any substantial amount of water had been lost from the pots by evaporation while cooking the potatoes, the conductivity of the water would have gone up, not down, and no such effect was found after correcting for the conductivity provided by the potato itself.

I think it's an airtight case, don't you?

HOLD THE SALT

Why does a recipe tell me to use unsalted butter,
and then later to add salt?

. . . .

It sounds silly, but there's a reason.

A quarter-pound stick of typical salted butter may contain 1½ to 3 grams, or up to half a teaspoon, of salt. Different brands and regional products may contain very different amounts. When you're following a carefully formulated recipe, especially one that uses a lot of butter, you can't afford to play Russian roulette with something as important as salt. That's why serious, high-quality recipes will specify unsalted or "sweet" butter and leave the salt for a separate seasoning step.

Many chefs prefer unsalted butter also because it is often of higher quality. Salt is added partially for its preservative effect, and butter that is used promptly, as in a restaurant kitchen, doesn't need it. Also, in unsalted butter any "off"-flavors, such as incipient rancidity, are more readily detected.

Never Gamble with a Cookie

Butter Cookie Stars

You don't want to gamble on the amount of salt in these butter cookies, so we use unsalted butter and add just the right amount of salt to the dough. This is the kind of crisp sugar cookie you want for cutouts. Make them plain, sugar-topped, or decorated with sprinkles and colored icings. They're easiest to handle when you roll the dough between sheets of waxed paper.

2¼ cups all-purpose flour, plus flour for dusting
1 teaspoon cream of tartar
½ teaspoon baking soda
¼ teaspoon salt
½ cup (1 stick) unsalted butter
1 cup sugar
2 large eggs, lightly beaten
½ teaspoon vanilla
1 egg yolk mixed with 1 teaspoon water
   Sugar for topping

---

1. In a medium bowl, stir together the flour, cream of tartar, baking soda, and salt. In a large mixing bowl, cream the butter and sugar with an electric mixer. Beat in the eggs and vanilla until combined. Add the dry ingredients and, using a wooden spoon, mix until a dough is formed.

2. Divide the dough into 3 parts. Place one-third of the dough between two sheets of waxed paper on a flat surface. With a rolling pin, roll it out to a uniform thickness of about ⅛ inch. Transfer the dough "sandwich" to a refrigerator shelf and store flat. Repeat with the other two pieces of dough, rolling each between sheets of waxed paper, and stack them on top of each other in the refrigerator. The dough may be refrigerated for up to 2 days in advance of baking.

3. Preheat the oven to 350°F. Remove one sheet of dough from the refrigerator. Peel off the top sheet of waxed paper but do not discard. Lightly dust the surface of the dough with flour, spreading it on the whole surface with the palm of your hand. Replace the top sheet of waxed paper loosely, and flip the sandwich over. Peel off the second sheet of waxed paper and discard. Dust the second side of the dough with flour, and spread with the palm of your hand.

4. With floured cookie cutters, cut out desired shapes and place on cookie sheets that have been sprayed with nonstick baking spray. Brush with the egg yolk–water mixture and sprinkle with a light coating of sugar or colored sprinkles. The cookies may also be left plain or decorated after baking.

5. Bake for 10 to 12 minutes or until lightly browned. Allow the cookies to rest on the sheet for 2 minutes before using a wide metal spatula to transfer them to racks to cool. The cookies will keep several weeks when stored in airtight containers. Keep them in the freezer for longer storage.

MAKES ABOUT 4 DOZEN, DEPENDING ON THE ROLLING THICKNESS AND THE SIZE OF THE CUTTER

Chapter Three

The Fat
of the Land

....

THE THREE MAJOR COMPONENTS of our foods are proteins, carbohydrates, and fats. But judging by the flood of ink
spent on fats in newspapers, magazines, and official dietary guidelines these days, one might think that fat is the only one we need be
concerned about—not about eating enough of this essential nutrient,
but about eating too much and/or the wrong kinds.

There are two major concerns: the caloric content of all fats,
which is about nine calories per gram, compared with only four calories per gram of either protein or carbohydrate; and the unhealthful
effects of eating certain kinds of fat.

I am not a nutritionist and am therefore not qualified to address
the health aspects of various fats—not that even the experts can agree
on many issues. Instead, I will focus on what fats are and how we use
them. Understanding these basics should enable you to interpret and
evaluate that flood of ink more intelligently.

ON FATS AND ACIDS

Whenever I read about saturated and unsaturated fats, the article starts off talking about "fats" and then switches without warning from "fats" to "fatty acids," and then back and forth almost randomly between these two terms as if they were the same thing. Are they? If not, what's the difference?

. . . .

I have read this kind of inaccurate writing probably far longer than you have. In fact, as a chemist I cannot help but harbor the suspicion that many writers just don't know the difference. And there is indeed a difference.

Every molecule of fat incorporates three molecules of fatty acids. The fatty acids may be either saturated or unsaturated, and they thereby impart those qualities to the fat as a whole.

First, let's see what a fatty acid is.

Fatty acids are the acids that are found as components of fats. They are members of a larger family that chemists call carboxylic acids. As acids go, they are very weak—unlike sulfuric acid, for example, which is the highly corrosive battery acid in your car.

A fatty acid molecule consists of a long chain of as many as sixteen or eighteen (or more) carbon atoms, each one of which carries a pair of hydrogen atoms. (Techspeak: The chain is made up of CH_2 groups.) If the chain contains its full complement of hydrogen atoms, the fatty acid is said to be saturated (with hydrogen). But if somewhere along the chain one pair of hydrogen atoms is missing, the fatty acid is said to be monounsaturated. If two or more pairs of hydrogen atoms are missing, it is said to be polyunsaturated. (Actually, one hydrogen atom is missing from each of two adjacent carbon atoms, but let's not quibble.)

Some common fatty acids are stearic acid (saturated), oleic acid (monounsaturated), and linoleic and linolenic acids (polyunsaturated).

To chemists, and apparently to our bodies as well, the exact positions of the unsaturated parts of the fatty acid molecules (Techspeak: the double bonds) matter. You've heard that the "omega-3" fatty acids found in fatty fish may play a role in preventing coronary heart disease and strokes? Well, "omega-3" is the chemist's way of telling exactly how far the first missing pair of hydrogen atoms (the first double bond) is from the end of the polyunsaturated molecule: it is three places from the end. (Omega is the last letter—the end—of the Greek alphabet.)

Fatty acids are generally bad-tasting and foul-smelling chemicals. Fortunately, they don't usually exist in foods in their free, yucky forms. They are tamed by being chemically fastened to a chemical called glycerol, in the ratio of three fatty acid molecules to each glycerol molecule. *Three fatty acid molecules tied to a glycerol molecule constitute one molecule of fat.* Chemists draw the fat molecule's structure schematically on paper as a short flagpole (the glycerol molecule) with three long banners (the fatty acids) flying from it. They call the

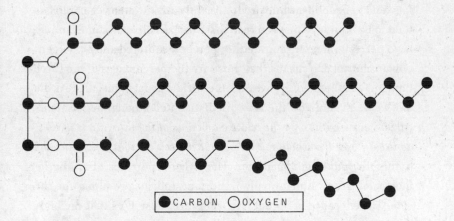

CARBON   OXYGEN

Representation of a fat (triglyceride) molecule, showing three fatty acid chains attached to a glycerol molecule at left. (Hydrogen atoms are not shown.) The top two fatty acid chains are saturated; the bottom one is monounsaturated—that is, it contains one double bond.

resulting molecule a triglyceride (*tri-* indicating that it contains *three* fatty acids), but its common name is simply a "fat" because by far the majority of natural fat molecules are triglycerides.

The fatty acids (I'll call them FA's) in any given fat molecule can be all of the same kind or any combination of different kinds. For example, they might be two saturated FA's plus one polyunsaturated FA, or they might be one monounsaturated FA plus one polyunsaturated FA plus one saturated FA, or all three might be polyunsaturated FA's.

Any real-life animal or vegetable fat is a mixture of many different fat molecules containing various combinations of FA's. In general, shorter-chain and less saturated FA's make softer fats, while longer-chain and more saturated FA's make harder fats. That's because in an unsaturated FA, wherever a pair of hydrogen atoms is missing (Techspeak: wherever there is a double bond), the FA molecule has a kink in it. As a result, the fat molecules can't pack together as tightly to make a hard, solid structure, and the fat is likely to be more liquid than solid. Therefore, predominantly saturated animal fats tend to be solids, while predominantly unsaturated vegetable fats tend to be liquids. When you read that a certain olive oil, for example, is 70 percent monounsaturated, 15 percent saturated and 15 percent polyunsaturated, it means that those are the percentages of the three kinds of FA's, added up over all the different fat molecules in the oil. We don't care how the FA's are distributed among the fat molecules, because *it is only the relative amounts of the three kinds of FA's, added up over the whole mixture of fat molecules, that determine the healthful or unhealthful qualities*. The glycerol portions of all the fat molecules aren't nutritionally important and just go along for the ride. The so-called essential fatty acids are those FA's that the body needs in order to manufacture the important hormones called prostaglandins.

While we're talking about fatty acids and triglycerides, let's straighten out some other fat-related terms you may have heard.

Monoglycerides and diglycerides are like triglycerides but, as you may guess, have only one (mono-) or two (di-) FA molecules attached to the glycerol molecule. They exist in very minor amounts along with the triglycerides in all natural fats, and their FA's are incorporated into the saturation/unsaturation profiles of the fats. They are also used as emulsifiers (substances that help oil and water to mix) in many prepared foods. But are they considered fats themselves? Sort of. Triglycerides are broken down into mono- and diglycerides during digestion, so their nutritional effects are essentially the same.

Finally, there is the word *lipid*, from the Greek *lipos*, meaning fat. But we use the word much more broadly than that. Lipid is a catchall term for anything and everything in living things that's oily, fatty, or oil-loving, including not only mono-, di- and triglycerides but such other chemicals as phosphatides, sterols, and fat-soluble vitamins. When your blood chemistry report comes back from the medical lab it may contain a *lipid panel*, listing not only the amount of triglycerides (fat blood isn't good) but also the amounts of the various forms of cholesterol, which is a fatty alcohol.

WHAT CAN BE DONE to minimize the confusion between "fats" and "fatty acids" in food writing?

First of all, we have to recognize that although the word *fat* strictly means a specific kind of chemical—a triglyceride, as distinguished from a protein or a carbohydrate—in common usage the word *fat* is used to refer to mixtures of fats, such as butter, lard, peanut oil, and so on. (Each of these products is referred to as "a fat" in the diet.) There is little a reader can do about that ambiguity, except to try to determine whether the word is being used in the context of a specific chemical substance or a category of food.

Second, we can implore food writers to be more careful about switching indiscriminately back and forth between "fat" and "fatty acid." Here are some suggestions·

The relative saturation and unsaturation of a fatty food can be expressed without using either term. For example, we can just say that it is x percent saturated, y percent monounsaturated, and z percent polyunsaturated, without adding the object (fatty acid) that these adjectives in truth modify.

Instead of saying, as I have seen many times, "a saturated (or unsaturated) fat," which is meaningless, we should say "a fat high in saturates (or high in unsaturates)" or "a highly saturated (or highly unsaturated) fat." Those are shorthand ways of saying "high in saturated (or unsaturated) fatty acids."

In general, the less often the term fatty acid is used the better, because people already understand the term *fat* (or think they do), and that word is less intimidating. But if individual fatty acids must be discussed, the term should be defined the first time it is used as something like "the building blocks of fats."

WHEN GOOD FATS GO BAD

What makes fats turn rancid?

. . . .

Free fatty acids. That is, fatty acid molecules that have been broken off from their fat molecules. Most fatty acids are foul-smelling and bad-tasting chemicals, and it doesn't take much of them to give a fatty food an off flavor.

There are two main ways in which the fatty acids can become disconnected: the fat's reaction with water (hydrolysis) and its reaction with oxygen (oxidation).

You might think that fats and oils won't react with water because they are so loathe to mix. But given time, enzymes that are naturally present in many fatty foods can make the reaction happen. (Techspeak: They catalyze the hydrolysis.) So foods like butter and nuts can turn rancid by hydrolysis simply by being stored for a long time. Butter is particularly vulnerable because it contains short-chain fatty acids, and these smaller molecules can fly off into the air more easily (Techspeak: They are more volatile) and produce a bad smell. In rancid butter, butyric acid is the main culprit.

High temperatures also speed up the rancidity of an oil by hydrolysis, such as when wet foods are deep-fried in it. That's one reason why deep-frying oil begins to smell bad when overused.

The second major cause of rancidity, oxidation, happens most readily in fats containing unsaturated fatty acids, with polyunsaturates being oxidized more readily than monounsaturates. The oxidation is speeded up (catalyzed) by heat, light, and trace amounts of metals, which may be present from the machinery that processed the food. Preservatives such as ethylenediaminetetraacetic acid, mercifully nicknamed EDTA, prevent metal-catalyzed oxidation by imprisoning (sequestering) the metal atoms.

Moral: Because rancidity reactions are catalyzed by heat and light, cooking oils and other fatty foods should be kept in a cool, dark place. Now you know why the labels always tell you that.

ENOUGH IS ENOUGH

On food labels I often see "partially hydrogenated" vegetable oil. What is hydrogenation, and if it's so good why don't they go all the way with it?

. . . .

Oils are hydrogenated, that is, hydrogen atoms are forced into their molecules under pressure to make them more saturated, because saturated fats are thicker—more solid and less liquid—than unsaturated fats. The hydrogen atoms fill in hydrogen-poor gaps (Techspeak: double bonds, which are more rigid than single bonds) in the oil molecules, and that makes them more flexible. They can then pack together more closely and stick to each other more tightly, so they won't flow as easily. Result: The fat becomes thicker, less liquid and more solid.

If the oils in your margarine hadn't been partially hydrogenated, you'd be pouring it instead of spreading it. But partial hydrogenation may fill in only about 20 percent of the missing hydrogen atoms in the molecules. If your margarine were 100 percent hydrogenated, it would be like trying to spread candle wax on your toast.

Unfortunately, saturated fats are less healthful than unsaturated fats. Food manufacturers therefore walk a tightrope between minimum hydrogenation for health and enough hydrogenation to produce desirable textures.

FAT MATH

How come the amounts of fat on food labels don't add up? When I add the numbers of grams of saturated, polyunsaturated, and monounsaturated fats, they come to less than the number of grams of "total fat." Are there other kinds of fat that aren't listed?

. . . .

No, all fats fall into those three categories.

I had never noticed the funny arithmetic you mention, but as soon as I received your question I ran to my pantry and grabbed a box of Nabisco Wheat Thins. Here's what I saw in the Nutrition Facts panel for the amounts of fat per serving: "Total Fat 6g. Saturated Fat 1g. Polyunsaturated Fat 0g. Monounsaturated Fat 2g."

I got out my calculator. Now, let's see. One gram of saturated fat plus zero grams of polyunsaturated fat plus two grams of monounsaturated fat makes three grams of total fat, not six. What happened to the other three grams?

Next, I grabbed a box of Premium Original Saltine Crackers. Worse yet! The two grams of total fat are supposedly made up of zero grams of saturated fat, zero grams of polyunsaturated fat, and zero grams of monounsaturated fat. Since when does zero plus zero plus zero equal two? I didn't even need my calculator to know that something was wrong with that one. Something very strange was going on here. I hurried to my computer and pulled up the Web site of the FDA, the agency that made the rules for the nutrition labeling of prepared foods. The FDA's site has a page that answers frequently asked questions about food labeling. Here's what I found.

"Question: Should the sum of saturated, monounsaturated, and polyunsaturated fatty acids equal the total fat content?

"Answer: No. The sum of the fatty acids generally will be lower than the weight of total fat, because the weights of components of fat such as trans fatty acids and glycerol are not included."

Aha! So that's it!

Still not clear? Lemme 'splain it to ya.

A fat molecule consists of two parts, a glycerol part and a fatty acid part. Although the number of grams of "Total Fat" on the label is indeed the weight of the whole fat molecules, glycerol parts and all, the amounts of "Saturated Fat," "Polyunsaturated Fat," and "Monounsaturated Fat" are the weights of the fatty acid parts alone. Part of the missing weight is the combined weights of the glycerol parts of all the fat molecules. (I'll get to the trans fatty acids later.)

Why, then, are these amounts called "fats" on the labels instead of what they really are: fatty acids? According to Virginia Wilkening, deputy director of the FDA's Office of Nutritional Products, Labeling and Dietary Supplements, there are two reasons: (1) the general public wants to know only the relative amounts of saturated and unsaturated stuff in their fats, and it's the fatty acid parts alone that determine that; (2) space is at a premium on food labels, and the words "fatty acids" take up more space than "fats."

Okay, I guess, but the inaccurate wording still annoys nitpickers like me.

As the FDA's Q&A page admits, there is even more fudging in the Nutrition Facts panel, because the weights of the trans fatty acids are not included in the list. In fact, they usually account for even more of the missing weight than the glycerols do.

Trans fatty acids are the latest villains to appear in the Frightening Fat Follies; they seem to raise the levels of LDL ("bad") cholesterol in the blood just about as much as naturally saturated fatty acids do. Trans fatty acids don't occur naturally in vegetable oils, but are formed when they are hydrogenated. The two added hydrogen atoms may attach themselves to opposite sides of the carbon chain (Techspeak: in the trans configuration) instead of both on the same side (Techspeak: in the cis [pronounced *sis*] configuration). That changes the molecular shape of the fatty acid from kinked to straight, thus making them resemble and behave like saturated fatty acids.

Partially hydrogenated vegetable oils may contain substantial amounts of trans fatty acids but, largely because of difficulties in determining their amounts, they are not currently reported separately on food labels.

In your own pursuit of longevity, you will still want to pay attention to the amount of "Total Fat" listed on the label. But to learn whether it is primarily "good fat" or "bad fat," disregard the exact numbers of grams and pay attention to the *relative* amounts of saturated, polyunsaturated, and monounsaturated fat(ty acids). That's what counts. And remember that at this writing the villainous trans fatty acids are still lurking somewhere off the label. The FDA is considering listing them together with the saturated fatty acids.

Oh, and what about those "zero grams of fat(ty acids)" in my Premium Crackers that mysteriously add up to 2 grams of total fat? Are there some kinds of fat that have no fatty acids attached to them at all? No. Then they wouldn't be fats. It's that the FDA permits manufacturers to list "zero grams" of either a fat or a fatty acid when the amount is less than 0.5 gram per serving.

The rules of arithmetic that we learned in first grade are not in jeopardy.

IS THAT PERFECTLY CLEAR?

I have a recipe that calls for clarified butter.
How do I do that? And what does clarifying but-
ter accomplish besides, well, making clear butter?

. . . .

That depends on your point of view. Clarifying butter gets rid of everything but that delicious, artery-clogging, highly saturated butterfat. But when we use it in sautéing instead of whole butter, we avoid eating the browned proteins, which could also be unhealthful because of possible carcinogens. Name your poison.

Some people think of butter as a block of fat surrounded by guilt. But guilt or no guilt, it isn't all fat. It's a three-part mixture of fat, water, and protein solids. When we clarify butter, we're separating out the fat and throwing everything else away. Using the pure fat, we can sauté at a higher temperature without any burning or smoking, because the water in whole butter holds the temperature down and the solids do indeed tend to burn and smoke.

When heated in a frying pan, the solid proteins in whole butter begin to turn brown and smoke at around 250°F. One way to minimize these goings-on is to "protect" the butter in the pan with a little cooking oil, which might have a smoking temperature of around 425°F. But you'll still get a little browning of the proteins in the butter.

Or, you can use clarified butter. It's the pure oil without the proteins, and it won't set off your smoke alarm until about 350°F.

Clarified butter will keep much longer than whole butter will, because bacteria can work away at protein, but not at pure oil. In India, where refrigeration can be scarce, they make clarified butter (*usli ghee*) by melting it slowly and then continuing to boil off the water, whereupon its proteins and sugars become slightly burned, producing a pleasant, nutty flavor.

Eventually, clarified butter will turn rancid. But rancidity is only a sour flavor, not bacterial contamination. Tibetans, in fact, prefer their clarified yak butter on the rancid side. *Chacun à son goût.*

To clarify butter, whether salted or unsalted, all you have to do is melt it slowly at the lowest possible temperature, keeping in mind that it scorches easily. The oil, the water, and the solids will separate into three layers: a froth of casein on the top; the clear, yellow oil in the middle; and a watery suspension of milk solids on the bottom. If you're using salted butter, the salt will be distributed between the top and bottom layers.

Skim off the top froth and pour or ladle off the oil—the clarified butter—into another container, leaving the water and sediment behind. Or use a gravy separator to pour off the watery layer. Better yet, refrigerate the whole mess, after which the top froth can be scraped off the solidified fat, which in turn can be lifted away from the watery layer.

Don't throw away the casein froth; it contains most of the buttery flavor. Use it to flavor steamed vegetables. It's superb on popcorn, especially if you've used salted butter.

I clarify a couple of pounds at a time and pour the clarified butter into plastic ice cube trays, making approximately two-tablespoon portions. After they're frozen, I remove the "butter cubes," place them in a plastic bag in the freezer and take out what I need when I need it.

One cup (two sticks) of whole butter will yield about three-quarters of a cup when clarified. You can use clarified butter measure for measure with whole butter in recipes.

And by the way, the watery layer contains all the milk sugar or lactose. People who can't eat butter because they are lactose intolerant can still cook with clarified butter. That may be one of the major reasons for clarifying it.

No Smoking

Crusty Potatoes Anna

Using clarified butter in this classic dish allows the potatoes to cook up golden brown and crisp. Even though the oven temperature is high, the fat won't burn or smoke because the milk solids are absent. A cast-iron skillet works best.

4	medium potatoes, preferably Yukon Golds
2 to 4	tablespoons clarified butter
	Coarse salt
	Freshly ground pepper

1. Preheat the oven to 450°F. Select an 8½-inch cast-iron skillet and a lid to fit, and butter the skillet generously. Wash the potatoes, pat dry, and cut them into ⅛-inch slices; to peel or not is your choice.

2. Arrange a single layer of potato slices on the bottom of the skillet in a circular or spiral pattern, starting at the middle of the pan and working outward with overlapping slices. Brush this layer with butter and sprinkle with salt and pepper. Continue building layers and buttering them in this way until all the potato slices are used.

3. Pour the remaining butter over the top. On the stove top, bring the potatoes to a sizzle over medium-high heat. Cover with a lid, transfer to the oven, and bake for 30 to 35 minutes, or until the potatoes are golden brown on top and tender when tested with a fork or toothpick. A light crust should be visible on the bottom when the edge is lifted with a table knife or fork. If not, bake a little longer.

4. Give the skillet a good shake to loosen any pieces that may be stuck. Slide a wide metal spatula underneath if necessary. Turn the skillet upside down onto a platter or large plate to serve the potatoes crusty side up.

MAKES 4 SERVINGS

BETTER BUTTER

*In France, I had the most marvelously flavorful
butter—better than anything I've had in the
States. What makes it so different?*

. . . .

More fat.

Commercial butter is 80 to 82 percent milk fat (also called butterfat), 16 to 17 percent water, and 1 to 2 percent milk solids (plus about 2 percent salt if salted). The United States Department of Agriculture (USDA) sets the lower limit of butterfat content for American butter at 80 percent, while most European butters contain a minimum of 82 or even as much as 84 percent.

That may not sound like much of a difference, but more fat means less water and hence a richer, creamier product. Pastry chefs often refer to European butter as "dry butter." Moreover, higher-fat butter makes smoother sauces and flakier and more flavorful pastries. (Compare the croissants you had in France with those *anything-that's-bent-in-the-middle* American imitations.)

Butter, as you know, is made by churning cream or whole, unhomogenized milk. The agitation of churning breaks up the emulsion (tiny globules of fat suspended in water) in the cream, so that the fat globules are free to coalesce into granules the size of rice grains. These then mat together and separate from the watery part of the milk, called the buttermilk. (Today's cultured buttermilk products have been processed further.) The fat is then washed with water and "worked" to squeeze out more buttermilk. European butter is generally made in small batches, allowing for more complete removal of the buttermilk.

Some American brands of European-style butter are Keller's, formerly known as Plugrá, a pun on the French *plus gras*, meaning "more fat"; Land O' Lakes Ultra Creamy; and Challenge. European butters imported from France and Denmark are available in specialty stores. Bring lots of *euros*.

THE BIG SQUEEZE

I think of corn as a low-fat food. So how do they
get all that corn oil out of it?

. . . .

They use a lot of corn.

Corn is indeed a low-fat food—containing about 1 gram per ear until you slather it with all that butter. But it is by far the biggest crop in the United States, grown in 42 states to the tune of more than 9 billion bushels per year. Nine billion bushels of corn contain some 3 billion gallons of oil, and that's enough to deep-fry Delaware.

The oil resides in the germ of the grain, where Mother Nature stores it as a concentrated form of energy—9 calories per gram—to fuel the everyday miracle of creating whole new plants from seeds. In corn, the germ makes up only about 8 percent of the kernel and only about half of that is oil, so an ear of corn isn't exactly a gusher.

As you can imagine, it takes some doing to get the oil out. At the mill, the kernels are steeped in hot water for a day or two, then coarsely ground to break the germ loose. The germ is then separated by a floating or spinning process, after which it is dried and crushed to press out the oil.

UP IN SMOKE

How do the various cooking oils differ in their
boiling points, and what are the consequences
for the cook?

. . . .

I don't think you mean boiling point, because in spite of the poetic and sadistic appeal of the expression "boiled in oil," oil doesn't boil.

Long before it becomes hot enough to think about bubbling, a cooking oil will decompose, breaking down into disagreeable chemicals and carbonized particles that will assault your taste buds with a burnt flavor, your nostrils with an acrid smell, and your ears with a shrieking smoke alarm. If you mean the highest practical cooking temperature for an oil, it is limited not by a boiling point but by the temperature at which the oil begins to smoke.

The smoke points of common vegetable oils, which come mostly from plant seeds, can range anywhere from 250°F to more than 450°F. But in spite of the ostensibly precise values listed in some books, exact smoke-point temperatures cannot be given because a particular type of oil can vary quite a bit, depending on its degree of refinement, the seed variety, and even the climate and weather during the plant's growing season.

Nevertheless, according to the Institute of Shortening and Edible Oils (there's one for everything, isn't there?), the approximate Fahrenheit smoke-point ranges of some common cooking oils are: safflower oil, 325–350°; corn oil, 400–415°; peanut oil, 420–430°;

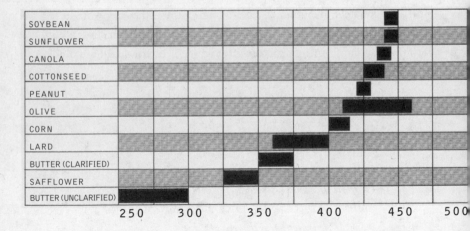

The approximate smoke-point ranges of some fresh cooking oils, plus lard.
The exact smoke points depend on how the oil was refined and can be sub-
stantially lower in used oil.

Source, except lard: Institute of Shortening and Edible Oils.

cottonseed oil, 425–440°; canola oil, 435–445°; and sunflower and soybean oils, 440–450°. Olive oils may vary from 410° to 460°, depending on the type; extra-virgin oils are generally lower, while light olive oil is the highest because it has been filtered. Animal fats generally smoke at lower temperatures than vegetable oils, because saturated fatty acids break down more easily.

When heated to around 600°F, most cooking oils will reach their flash points, the temperatures at which their vapors can be ignited by a flame. At even higher temperatures, around 700°F, most oils will reach their fire points and burst into flame spontaneously.

With the exception of a few specialty oils, most oils are valued by American cooks for their blandness, for their lack of any intrusive flavor. Olive oil, on the other hand, is prized for its complex flavors, which can range from nutty to peppery and grassy to fruity, depend-ing on the country and region from which it comes, the variety of olive, and its growing conditions. The cuisines of the Mediterranean owe their unique qualities largely to the almost exclusive use of olive oil, which is a flavor component of the recipes, not just a cooking medium. It is used in everything from baking to deep frying. And I've yet to hear a Spaniard or an Italian complain about a wisp of smoke in the kitchen.

Fortunately, the smoke points of several common cooking oils are higher than the most desirable range of temperatures for deep frying, which is 350–375°. If you're not careful to control it, though, fat for deep frying can reach close to 400°, so there isn't much leeway there. Except for the lowest-smoke-point cooking fat of all, unclari-fied butter, which begins to smoke at only 250–300°, smoke shouldn't be a problem in sautéing unless you have a very heavy hand on the burner control.

It's important to note that all of the smoke points quoted above are for fresh oils. When oils are either heated or oxidized, they break down into free fatty acids, which both lower the smoke point and taste acrid. Reused deep-frying oil, or any oil that has been exposed significantly to heat or air, will therefore smoke more readily and take on a disagreeable flavor. Moreover, hot oils tend to polymerize—their molecules join together into much bigger molecules that give the oil a thick, gummy consistency and a darker color. And finally, hot oils can break down into unhealthful chemicals such as those highly reactive molecular fragments called free radicals.

All things considered, then, the safest and best idea for both health and palate is to discard deep-frying oil after one or at most two uses—or immediately, if it has been allowed to smoke appreciably.

Deep-Fried Dessert

Ricotta Fritters

Deep-fried food doesn't have to be heavy, and the kitchen can remain a smoke-free zone. These dessert fritters are light and crisp, and there's no olive oil flavor or oiliness if the frying temperature remains between 355 and 365°F. Drizzled honey is a traditional finishing touch, but any fruit syrup is good, especially strawberry.

---

1 cup plus 2 tablespoons (8-ounce carton) ricotta cheese

2 large eggs, lightly beaten

1½ tablespoons unsalted butter, melted

1 tablespoon sugar

Zest of one lemon

⅛ teaspoon nutmeg, freshly ground

¼ teaspoon salt

⅓ cup all-purpose flour

Olive oil

Fruit syrup or honey

---

1. Place the ricotta in a medium bowl. Whisk in the beaten eggs until well mixed. Add the butter, sugar, lemon zest, nutmeg, and salt; mix well. Stir in the flour until well combined. Set the mixture aside to rest for 2 hours.

2. Pour the olive oil into a small, deep saucepan to a depth of 1 inch and turn the heat to medium-high. (We use a heavy, 7-inch-diameter saucepan.) Heat the oil to 365°F, as measured by a deep-frying thermometer. To test the oil without a thermometer, drop a bit of batter into the fat and if it floats immediately to the surface, the temperature is about right.

3. Gently drop in the batter one tablespoon at a time, using a second spoon to push it off. Do not crowd the pan. The fritters will puff up and brown. Use a chopstick or the handle of a wooden spoon to flip them over for browning on the other side. As the fritters are finished, remove them from the oil with a

slotted spoon and place them on paper towels to drain. Repeat until all the batter is used.

4. Serve the fritters hot and pass the fruit syrup or honey.

MAKES ABOUT 30, 4 TO 6 SERVINGS, UNLESS THE COOK'S HELPER LIKES TO SAMPLE

GET RID OF UNSIGHTLY FAT

After I fry foods, how do I throw the used fat away? It's an environmental no-no, isn't it?

. . . .

Yes. While edible fats and oils are ultimately biodegradable, they can gum up the works in a landfill for years. They're not as bad as petroleum oils, however, which are digestible by only one or two species of bacteria and stay around essentially forever.

Small amounts of fat can be absorbed in a couple of paper towels and thrown in the trash. I pour slightly larger amounts into an empty food can that I keep in the freezer, where the oil freezes solid. When the can is full, I seal it in a plastic bag and put it into the trash, hoping that it won't melt and leak out until it's far, far away and untraceable back to me. That's unconscionable, I know, but it's vastly preferable to pouring it down the drain. Moreover, it makes a jolly flame when the garbage is incinerated.

Large amounts of used deep-frying fat are a bigger problem. Restaurants often subscribe to a disposal service that collects their gallons of used "grease" and sells it to soap and chemical companies. But what can you do with it at home, short of gift-wrapping it, leaving it in your unlocked car in a rough neighborhood, and hoping it gets stolen?

A hydrogeologist (he studies how liquids flow through soils) I consulted at the Department of Environmental Protection advises that unless your house is on a septic system, you can mix the oil with a liberal amount of dishwashing liquid, which has a prodigious appetite for grease, stir or shake it thoroughly to homogenize it, and then slowly feed the mixture to the garbage disposer along with lots of cold running water, to be scattered down the drain and ultimately dealt with by the local wastewater treatment plant. I'm not recommending that, however, so if you plug up your plumbing or shut down your local sewage plant, don't blame me.

Even better would be to turn an environmental liability into a conservation asset: Use the oil as an alternative fuel for your diesel-powered Volkswagen, Mercedes, or pickup truck. After all, when Rudolf Diesel demonstrated his new engine at the World Exhibition in Paris in 1900, he ran it on peanut oil. But don't try it until you read Joshua Tickell's book, *From the Fryer to the Fuel Tank* (Greenteach Publications, 2000), which tells how to do it.

If you use this suggestion, I advise that you stop feeding fat to your car when it starts getting too big for the garage.

WHEN IS AN OIL NOT AN OIL?

How do those nonstick cooking sprays work? Their labels say the contents are nonfat and low calorie, but when I spray it on the pan it sure looks like oil to me. Is there such a thing as a non-fat oil? Or does it contain some kind of chemical substitute for oil?

. . . .

No, there is no such thing as a nonfat edible oil. Fats are a family of specific chemical compounds, and an oil is just a liquid fat. Nor do the sprays have to contain a substitute for oil, because—are you ready?—they *are* oil.

Those handy little cans, so great for coating baking pans and muffin tins instead of greasing them, contain primarily a vegetable oil, usually with some lecithin and alcohol added. Lecithin is a fat-like substance (Techspeak: a phospholipid) found in egg yolks and soy beans, among other places, and helps to keep food from sticking. But the sprays are still almost entirely oil.

Their main virtue is that they put you more in control of your calories and fat usage. Instead of pouring a heavy-handed glug of oil into your skillet, you just give the pan a quick spritz from the can. The alcohol evaporates and the oil and lecithin remain behind, coating the pan. You'll still be cooking on a layer of oil, but it's a very thin and therefore low-calorie one.

In the manufacturers' effort to earn that highly profitable "non-fat" claim, the cooking spray labels can engage in some pretty bizarre arithmetic. The label on a can of Pam, for example, boasts that it contains "only two calories per serving." But what is a "serving"? The label defines it as a one-third-of-a-second spray which, the label advises, is just long enough to cover one-third of a 10-inch skillet. (Just right, we must presume, for making one-third of an omelet.) In the race to claim even fewer calories, the label of one oil spray advises that a "serving" is a spritz that lasts for only one-quarter of a second.

If you don't have the finely calibrated trigger finger of Billy the Kid, or even if you throw caution to the winds and defiantly spray your pan for an entire second, you'll still be getting by with fewer than six calories. But even so, a little bit of fat isn't *no* fat. So how small must an amount of fat be before a label can legally call it "none?"

According to the FDA, any product that contains less than 0.5 gram of fat per serving may be labeled as containing "zero grams of fat." A one-third-of-a-second "serving" of cooking spray contains around 0.2 gram of fat; hence, it is legally "nonfat." If they had defined a serving as a whole second's worth of spritz, they'd be over the 0.5-gram limit and couldn't call it nonfat. Cute dodge, eh?

By the way, if you're a belt-and-suspenders type, spritz a little nonstick spray onto your nonstick frying pan. The food will brown better than it would without the fat. Excuse me—I mean without the nonfat.

Pouring olive oil out of a bottle in a neat stream can be difficult. Every brand seems to have a different kind of pouring spout. And those "oil-can" dispensers are a pain to keep refilling. I leave my oil in the original bottle but replace the top with one of those pouring-spout stoppers sold for liquor bottles. It fits almost all olive oil bottles and dispenses the oil in a reproducible, thin stream with no dripping.

A pouring spout for olive oil.

CAUTION: FAT NOODLES AHEAD

I enjoy eating ramen noodles, but I've noticed
that they contain a lot of sodium and fat per
serving. Is it the noodles or the flavor mix that
contains the fat?

. . . .

The ingredients in the noodles and in the package of flavorings are listed separately, so you can easily find out which contains what. The salt (usually lots of it) is in the flavorings. You might not expect the noodles to contain fat, but surprisingly, that's where most of it is hiding.

I know you've always wondered how they make that compact, rectangular block of perfectly intertwined curlicues, and so have I, so here's what your question has stimulated me to find out.

The dough is first extruded through a row of nozzles to make a ribbon of long, side-by-side wavy strands. The ribbon is then cut to length and folded over onto itself, after which it is held in a mold while being deep-fried, which dries out the noodles so that the block will hold its convoluted shape ever after. The deep frying, of course, adds fat to the noodles, and although there may be a small amount of oil in some seasoning mixes, virtually all of the fat is therefore in the noodles.

A few brands of ramen noodles are air-dried instead of being fried, but unless it says so on the package, the only way to tell is the absence of fat in the noodles' ingredient list. A little arithmetic applied to the Nutrition Facts charts on the labels of four leading brands showed that, except for the hot water, the ingredients in a bowl of ramen soup ranged from 17 to 24 percent fat. So if you think that ramen noodles are "just pasta," you may want to think again.

A SURE-THING BAR BET

*A friend wanted to bet me that heavy cream
weighs less than light cream. Should I have
taken the bet?*

. . . .

No. You would have lost.

Heavy cream contains a higher percentage of milk fat (usually called butterfat, because butter can be made from it) than light cream does: 36 to 40 percent fat in heavy whipping cream versus only 18 to 30 percent in light cream. (And, if you're interested, the heavy cream can contain up to twice as much cholesterol.) But volume for volume, fats weigh less than water; they're less dense. So the higher the percentage of fat in a water-based liquid, the lighter the whole liquid will be.

It's not a huge difference. In my kitchen laboratory, a pint of heavy whipping cream weighed 475.0 grams, while a pint of light cream weighed 476.4 grams: three-tenths of a percent heavier.

The names "heavy" and "light" as related to cream were never meant to signify weight; they apply to richness or thickness. Fattier substances are thicker—more viscous—and therefore feel more substantial or "heavier" on the tongue.

CUTTING FAT

How do they homogenize milk?

. . . .

Some of my older readers may remember milk delivered to the doorstep in bottles. (I've read about it in my history books.) The milk had a separate layer of cream at the top. Why? Because cream is just milk with a higher proportion of butterfat and, because fat is lighter (less dense) than water, it floats to the top. We—I mean, those old-timers—had to shake the bottle vigorously to distribute the creaminess uniformly.

If the fat globules could be chopped up into small enough "globulettes"—around 80 millionths of an inch in diameter, they wouldn't rise; they would be kept suspended in place because water molecules would be bombarding them from all directions.

To accomplish this, the milk is shot out of a pipe at a pressure of 2500 pounds per square inch at a metal sieve, coming out the other side as a fine spray containing fat particles tiny enough to stay suspended.

Yogurt and ice cream are usually made from homogenized milk, but butter and cheese are not, because we want the butterfat globules to be able to join together into a separate fraction.

PASTEUR REVISITED

All the milk and cream in my supermarket these days claim to be "ultra pasteurized." What happened to plain, old "pasteurized"? Didn't it kill enough germs?

. . . .

welcome this question because it solves an old problem for me.

Back in 1986, during a six-month residence in the South of France, I saw something I had never seen in the U.S. The supermarkets kept their milk on the shelves without refrigeration. Instead of bottles or cartons, it was packaged in brick-shaped, cardboard-like boxes.

How can they do that, I wondered. Granted, milk is not the preferred beverage in France, but how do they get away with treating it in such a cavalier manner? Doesn't it spoil? I promised myself to find out as soon as I returned to the States, but I seem to have procrastinated a bit.

The glass milk bottle, invented in 1884, began to be replaced after World War II by wax-coated paperboard cartons. The wax has since been replaced with a plastic coating, and today the coated paper carton competes with all-plastic, translucent jugs, especially in the larger sizes. Those brick-shaped, non-refrigerated containers are called aseptic packaging, which means, of course, germ-free packaging.

But isn't all the milk that we buy in this country germ-free? Surprisingly, no, even though it has all been pasteurized in one way or another. There is a difference between killing all the germs dead and keeping the few that survive from multiplying.

The objective of pasteurization is to kill or deactivate all disease-causing microorganisms by "cooking" them. Just as you can roast a chicken at a relatively low temperature for a long time or at a higher temperature for a shorter time, effective pasteurization can be accomplished at a variety of time-and-temperature combinations. Traditional pasteurization, originally intended primarily to kill tuberculosis bacilli, involved heating the milk to 145–150°F and holding it there for 30 minutes. Traditional pasteurization isn't used much anymore, because it doesn't kill and deactivate heat-resistant bacteria such as Lactobacillus and Streptococcus. That's why ordinary pasteurized milk still has to be refrigerated.

Then came flash pasteurization, which keeps the milk at 162°F for only 15 seconds. But today, modern dairy processing machinery can achieve sterilization by flash-heating it to 280°F for a mere two seconds. It's done by passing the milk through the thin spaces between hot, parallel plates, and then chilling it rapidly to 38°F. That's ultra pasteurization. Ultra pasteurized milk and cream still have to be refrigerated, but their shelf life is increased from 14 to 18 days to 50 to 60 days, depending on the refrigerator temperature. (It should never be higher than 40°F.)

Did I say that ultra pasteurization heats the milk to 280°F? Yes. But wouldn't the milk boil first? Yes, it would, if it were in a container open to the atmosphere. But just as a pressure cooker raises the boiling point of water, the pasteurization equipment heats the milk under a high gas pressure that keeps it from boiling normally.

Europe has been ahead of us in adopting ultra pasteurization, and it is ahead of us in adopting aseptic packaging—those milk bricks I saw in France. In aseptic packaging, the milk is sterilized at high temperature for a short time as in ultra pasteurization, and then sent to the containers and the packaging machinery, both of which had been sterilized separately with steam or hydrogen peroxide. The filling and sealing are done under sterile conditions. The resulting product has an unrefrigerated shelf life of several months or even up to a year. Moreover, because the package is hermetically sealed with no air inside, the butterfat won't turn rancid from oxidation.

In our American markets, we rarely see aseptically packaged milk or cream. We see aseptic packaging mainly in soy milk products and tofu in the organic and "health food" sections, and in those little "drink boxes" of juice. In Europe, aseptic packaging is more widely used, perhaps because it is more energy-efficient. The foods don't have to be refrigerated during transportation and the packages are lighter than if steel cans or glass bottles had been used. Another reason, industry sources tell me, is that American consumers just don't trust milk that isn't refrigerated. But many consumers have told me that high-temperature pasteurized milk has an unpleasant, cooked flavor.

No matter how your milk or cream has been pasteurized or packaged, it does have an expiration date, even as you and I. Always check the date printed on the package.

Chapter Four

Chemicals in the Kitchen

. . . .

I T'S A THREADBARE CLICHÉ that cooking is chemistry. True, the application of heat to foods causes chemical reactions to take place, resulting in chemical changes that we devoutly hope will enhance flavor, texture, and digestibility. But the art of cooking, as distinguished from the craft, lies in knowing which "reactant" ingredients to combine, and how to combine and manipulate them to produce the most gratifying chemical changes.

Is that still too unromantic a characterization of one of life's greatest pleasures? Of course. But the fact remains that all foods are chemicals. Carbohydrates, fats, proteins, vitamins, and minerals are all made up of those tiny chemical units called molecules and ions. A vast variety of different molecules plays a vast number of different roles in the mélange of almost infinitely complex chemical reactions we call cooking, metabolism, and indeed, life itself.

Besides the primary nutrients, there are many other substances—chemicals—that we encounter in cooking. In this chapter we look at some of the "chemicals in our foods," not with the frightening implications that are sometimes attached to that phrase by opponents of food additives but in recognition of the fact that ultimately our foods are nothing *but* chemicals. Pure water or H_2O is, of course, the most important chemical of all.

CLEARING UP WATER FILTERS

What, exactly, do water filters do? I bought a Brita pitcher and it claims to eliminate things like lead and copper with "ion exchange resins," whatever they are. Do they also remove useful things like fluoride?

. . . .

The name "water filter" is misleading. The word *filtered* literally means only that the water has passed through a medium containing tiny holes or fine passageways that screen out suspended particles. When traveling in a country whose water supply is suspect and you ask a waiter whether the water is filtered, an affirmative reply may mean little more than that you can see through it.

Here at home, *filter* has become a generic word for a device that does more than clarify the water; it purifies it by removing tastes, odors, toxic chemicals, and pathogenic microorganisms. The idea is to make sure the water is safe and palatable.

Your nose and palate will tell you whether you want to remove odors and tastes. As far as toxic chemicals and pathogens are concerned, an analysis can be provided by many local water companies or independent labs. Depending on your degree of paranoia, you may feel like searching for a filter that will remove everything from the water but its wetness. Keep in mind, though, that it's a waste of money to buy a device to remove things that aren't there. Continually replacing the cartridges can be expensive.

What kinds of "bad stuff" can contaminate water? Industrial and agricultural chemicals; chlorine and its byproducts; metal ions; and cysts, which are tiny chlorine-resistant capsules of protozoan para-sites such as cryptosporidium and giardia that can cause abdominal cramping, diarrhea, and even more serious symptoms in people with weakened immune systems.

Cryptosporidium and giardia cysts are generally bigger than one micron or 40 millionths of an inch, so any barrier with holes smaller than that will screen them out. But not all filter devices contain such particle filters, so if these contaminants are of concern to you, check the product's literature to see if the performance claims include cyst reduction.

Commercial water filters, which may be either batch-at-a-time pitchers or attachments to faucets or supply lines, remove other con-taminants in three ways: with charcoal, with ion exchange resins, and with actual particle filters.

The workhorse of most water filters is activated charcoal, a mate-rial that has a prodigious and indiscriminate appetite for chemicals in general and gases (including chlorine) in particular. Charcoal is made by heating organic matter such as wood in a limited supply of air, so that it decomposes into porous carbon but doesn't actually burn. Depending on how it is manufactured, the charcoal can contain an enormous amount of microscopic internal surface area. An ounce of so-called activated charcoal—the best kind is made from coconut shells—can contain some 2,000 square feet of surface area. That surface area makes a highly attractive landing field for wandering molecules of impurities in water or air, and when they land they stick.

Activated charcoal is used to adsorb colored impurities from sugar solutions and to adsorb poisonous gases in gas masks. (That wasn't a misprint. *Adsorption*, with a "d," is the sticking of individual molecules to a surface, while *absorption*, with a "b," is the wholesale soaking up of a substance. Charcoal adsorbs; sponges absorb.) In water filters, the charcoal removes chlorine and other odoriferous gases and a variety of chemicals such as herbicides and pesticides.

Now about those ion exchange resins. They're little plastic-like granules that remove metals such as lead, copper, mercury, zinc, and cadmium. These are, of course, not present in the water as chunks of metal but as *ions*.

When a chemical compound of a metal dissolves in water, the metal goes into solution in the form of ions: positively charged atoms. We can't just pluck these ions out of the water with charcoal, for example, because removing positive charges would leave the water with a surplus of negative charge, and Nature makes that a very costly operation in terms of expended energy; she vastly prefers that the world remain electrically neutral.

What we *can* do is exchange those positive ions for other, more harmless positive ions: sodium ions or hydrogen ions, for example. That's what an ion exchange resin does. It contains loosely bound sodium or hydrogen ions that can swap places with metal ions in the water, leaving the metals effectively trapped in the resin. The resin (as well as the charcoal) eventually becomes fully loaded with contaminants and must be replaced. How long it continues to work depends on how contaminated your water is. If your water is hard, the ion exchange resin will also remove calcium and magnesium ions, and you'll have to replace it sooner.

Most domestic water filters contain both activated charcoal and an ion exchange resin, usually mixed together into a single cartridge. They therefore remove metals and other chemicals, but not necessarily pathogenic cysts. As I've said, check the claims about cysts in the product literature.

Do the purification filters remove fluoride? Generally, no. Fluoride is a negatively charged ion, not a positively charged one. So it is ignored by the ion exchange resin, which has only positive ions to swap. But when a filter cartridge is new, some fluoride may be removed from the first gallon or two, presumably by adsorption on the charcoal. After that, however, the filter doesn't remove fluoride.

THE WHITE POWDER TWINS

*Some recipes call for baking soda, some for baking
powder, and some even call for both.
What's the difference?*

. . . .

It's all in the chemicals.

Baking soda (aka bicarbonate of soda) is a single chemical: pure sodium bicarbonate, whereas baking powder is baking soda combined with one or more acid salts, such as monocalcium phosphate monohydrate, dicalcium phosphate dihydrate, sodium aluminum sulfate, or sodium aluminum phosphate.

Now that I've warmed the hearts of chemistry fans and confounded the rest of my readers, let me try to win the latter back.

Both baking soda and baking powder are used for leavening (from the Latin *levere*, meaning to raise or make light): making baked goods rise by producing millions of tiny bubbles of carbon dioxide gas. The gas bubbles are released within the wet batter, after which the heat of the oven expands them until the heat firms up the batter and traps them in place. The result is (hopefully) a light, spongy cake instead of a dense, gummy mess.

Here's how these two confusingly named leavening agents work.

Baking *soda* releases carbon dioxide gas as soon as it comes in contact with any acidic liquid, such as buttermilk, sour cream, or, for that matter, sulfuric acid (not recommended). All carbonates and bicarbonates do that.

Baking *powder*, on the other hand, is baking soda with a dry acid already mixed in. It is used when a recipe contains no other acid ingredients. As soon as the powder gets wet, the two chemicals begin to dissolve and react with each other to produce carbon dioxide. To keep them from "going off" prematurely, they have to be protected zealously from atmospheric moisture by being kept in a tightly closed container.

Baking soda keeps almost indefinitely, although it can pick up acidic odors and flavors; that's why people put an open box of it in the refrigerator. Baking powder, on the other hand, can lose its potency over a period of a few months because its chemicals react slowly with each other, especially if exposed to humid air. Test your baking powder by adding some of it to water. If it doesn't fizz vigorously it's lost its potency and will do a poor job of leavening. Throw it away and buy a new can.

In most cases, we don't want our baking powder to release all its gas as soon as we mix the batter—before it has been baked enough to trap the bubbles in place. So we buy a "double-acting" baking powder (and most of them are, these days, whether the label says so or not), which releases only a portion of its gas when it gets wet and releases the rest only after reaching a high temperature in the oven. Generally, two different chemicals in the powder are responsible for the two reactions.

But why would a recipe call for *both* baking soda and baking powder? In this case the cake or cookie is actually being leavened by the baking powder, which contains exactly the right proportions of bicarbonate and acid to react completely with each other. But if there happens to be an acid ingredient such as buttermilk present that would upset that balance, some extra bicarbonate in the form of baking soda is used to neutralize the excess acid. (Ask any chemist about this, but walk briskly away if he or she utters the word *titration*.)

Commercial bakers mix up their own witch's brews of leavening chemicals, designed to release just the right amounts of gas at just the right times and temperatures during the baking process. At home, the safest course is simply not to tamper with a well-tested recipe; use the prescribed amount(s) of whatever leavening agent(s) it calls for.

DOES ALUMINUM CAUSE
WHAT'S-HIS-NAME'S DISEASE?

*The label on my baking powder can says it
contains sodium aluminum sulfate. But isn't
aluminum dangerous to eat?*

. . . .

Sodium aluminum sulfate and several other aluminum compounds
are listed by the FDA as GRAS: Generally Regarded as Safe.

About twenty years ago, one study found increased levels of aluminum in the brains of deceased Alzheimer's victims. Ever since
then, suspicions have been circulating that aluminum, whether in
food or water or dissolved from aluminum cookware by acidic foods
such as tomatoes, causes Alzheimer's, Parkinson's, and/or Lou
Gehrig's diseases.

A great deal of subsequent research has been done, with conflicting and contradictory results. At this writing, the Alzheimer's
Association, the FDA, and Health Canada, the Canadian federal
department of health, all agree that there is as yet no verifiable scientific evidence for a relationship between aluminum ingestion and
Alzheimer's disease, and that there is therefore no reason for people
to avoid aluminum. In the words of the Alzheimer's Association,
"The exact role (if any) of aluminum in Alzheimer's disease is still
being researched and debated. However, most researchers believe
that not enough evidence exists to consider aluminum a risk factor
for Alzheimer's or a cause of dementia."

As one of millions of people afflicted with chronic heartburn, I
swallowed large doses of Maalox (MAgnesium ALuminum hydrOXide) and similar aluminum-containing antacids for many years
before the new anti-reflux drugs were invented. Yet I have no signs
whatsoever of Alzheimer's disease.

Now, what was your question?

> Aluminum foil has a shiny side and a dull side. Some people believe that one side or the other should be used for certain purposes. Not true. It makes no difference which side is up. The only reason the two sides look different is that in the final stages of rolling out the metal, two sheets are rolled together as a sandwich to save time. Where they contact the polished rollers they come out shiny; where they contact each other they come out somewhat duller.

AMMONIA, WE'VE HARDLY KNOWN YA

*I have an old recipe that calls for baking
ammonia. What is it?*

. . . .

Ammonia itself is an acrid-smelling gas, usually dissolved in water and used for laundry and cleaning purposes. But baking ammonia is ammonium bicarbonate, a leavening agent that when heated breaks down into three gases: water vapor, carbon dioxide, and ammonia. It isn't used much anymore—if you can even find it—because the ammonia gas can impart a bitter taste if it isn't all driven off during baking. Commercial cookie bakers can use it because flat cookies have a large surface area for the gas to escape from.

SOUR POWER

My mother's recipe for stuffed cabbage calls for
sour salt. None of the stores I've tried knows what
it is. Come to think of it, neither do I.
What is it and where can I get some?

. . . .

Sour salt is misnamed. It has nothing to do with table salt or sodium chloride. In fact, it isn't a salt at all; it's an acid. They're two different classes of chemicals.

Every acid is a unique chemical having properties that distinguish it from all other acids. But it can have dozens of derivatives called salts; every acid is the parent of a whole brood of salts. So-called sour salt is not one of those offspring salts but rather a parent acid in its own right: citric acid. It has an extremely sour flavor and is added for tartness to hundreds of prepared foods, from soft drinks to jams and frozen fruits.

In addition to its tartness, citric and other acids retard the browning of fruits by enzymes and oxidation. It is obtained from citrus fruits or fermented molasses and is used in Middle Eastern and Eastern European dishes, commonly in borscht. You can find it by the name *sour salt* in kosher markets or in the ethnic foods section of the larger supermarkets, or as *lemon salt* in Middle Eastern markets.

Citric acid is not alone in its sourness, by any means. All acids are sour. In fact, *only* acids are sour, because of their unique property of producing so-called hydrogen ions, which make our taste buds shriek "sour" to our brains. The strongest acids in your kitchen are vinegar and lemon juice. But sour salt, being 100 percent citric acid in crystalline form, is much more sour than vinegar, which is only a 5 percent solution of acetic acid in water, or lemon juice, which contains only about 7 percent citric acid.

Citric acid is unique in that it contributes sourness virtually without any other flavor, whereas the assertive flavors of lemon juice and vinegar must be factored into the overall balance of any dish. American chefs could well benefit by experimenting with sour salt in dishes that need a touch of tartness without any accompanying lemony or vinegary flavors.

A BAD RAP FOR THE TARTARS

What is cream of tartar? Is it related to
tartar sauce or steak tartare?

. . . .

Not at all. The words *tartar* and *tartare* come to us from two different directions.

"Tartar" or "Tatar" was the Persian name for Genghis Khan's horde of Mongols who stormed through Asia and Eastern Europe in the Middle Ages. The Tartars were viewed by Europeans as being, shall we say, culturally challenged, or at the very least politically incorrect, inasmuch as they wore the whole skins of animals and often ate their meat raw. One of our contemporary, semi-barbaric delicacies was therefore given the name steak tartare: ground or minced raw beefsteak mixed with chopped raw onion, raw egg yolk, and salt and pepper, with *ad lib* touches of Tabasco, Worcestershire, Dijon mustard, anchovies and capers. (James Beard ventured to civilize his with cognac.)

Tartar sauce is mayonnaise with chopped pickles, olives, chives, capers, and such mixed in. It is traditionally served with fried fish. Classic tartar sauce may contain vinegar, white wine, mustard, and herbs, so it may have been dubbed "tartar" because of its potency and pungency. In fact, the French refer to a variety of highly seasoned dishes as *à la tartare*. The Tartars apparently take the rap for almost anything that's raw, pungent, or crude.

The "tartar" in cream of tartar is quite another story. It comes to us via old Latin from the Arabic *durd*, meaning the dregs or sediment that form in a cask of fermenting wine. Today's winemakers use the word *tartar* specifically for the brownish-red, crystalline deposits left in the bottoms of casks after the wine has been drawn off. Chemically, it is impure potassium hydrogen tartrate (aka potassium bitartrate or potassium acid tartrate), a salt of tartaric acid. "Cream of tartar" is the fancy name given to the white, highly purified potassium hydrogen tartrate that's sold in food stores.

The tartar that forms in wine casks comes from the tartaric acid present in grape juice. Tartaric acid is what gives wine about half of its total acidity. (Malic acid and citric acid contribute most of the rest.) The salt called tartar was known long before its parent acid was discovered, and when tartaric acid was ultimately nailed down by chemists they named it after the tartar in the wine casks. It's a case of the parent chemical being named after its offspring.

The most common use for cream of tartar in the kitchen is for stabilizing beaten egg whites. It accomplishes this trick because it is somewhat acidic, even though it is a salt. (Techspeak: It lowers the pH of the mixture.) A stable egg-white foam depends on the coagulation of its several kinds of proteins, among which the best foam producers are known as globulins. The right acid conditions make the globulin proteins lose their mutually repulsive electric charges, thus making it easier for them to coagulate in the bubbles' walls and make them stronger, like balloons made of stronger rubber.

Quite a few books mistakenly state that cream of tartar is tartaric acid instead of its salt, potassium hydrogen tartrate. That's an easy error to make because, as I've said, cream of tartar is slightly acid even though it is a salt.

Without Cream of Tartar, This Would Be Soup

> ### *Portuguese Poached Meringue*

This unusual, gently cooked dessert from Portugal may seem like a flourless angel food cake, but it is a different kind of angel food and although made in a Bundt pan, it is not a cake. It's a meringue sponge with an uncommonly light and airy texture that will surprise you. Without the half-teaspoon of cream of tartar, the egg whites would break down and revert to their liquid state.

The Portuguese are famous for their egg-yolk-and-sugar sweets, *ovos moles*, of which there are literally thousands of varieties. This meringue might have been created by a frustrated cook who wanted to use up the resulting hoard of leftover egg whites. After making this recipe, you'll have the opposite problem: what to do with 10 yolks. The solution? Make lemon curd twice (see page 285).

About 2 tablespoons sugar for sprinkling
10 egg whites (1½ cups), at room temperature
½ teaspoon cream of tartar
1 cup sugar
½ teaspoon vanilla
¼ teaspoon almond extract, optional
Sliced and sweetened fresh fruit, berries, or fruit sauce

---

1. Bring 2 quarts of water to a boil and keep it at a simmer for later use. Grease a 12-cup Bundt cake pan with nonstick baking spray and wipe out any excess with a paper towel. Sprinkle with sugar and tilt to coat all inner surfaces. Tap out the excess sugar. Arrange the oven rack at its lowest position and preheat the oven to 350°F.

2. Beat the egg whites and cream of tartar with an electric mixer on medium speed in a large bowl until foamy. Beat in the sugar, 1 tablespoon at a time. Continue beating until the beaters begin to leave a track and soft peaks

form. Beat in the vanilla and almond extract, if used. Do not overbeat or the mixture will overrise, or "soufflé," in the oven.

3. Transfer the egg white mixture into the pan, cutting gently through the mixture with a knife or metal spatula to release any large air bubbles. Place the Bundt pan in a shallow roasting pan on the lowest oven rack. Pour simmering hot water into the roasting pan to a depth of 1 inch to create a *bain-marie* or double-boiler effect. Bake until the meringue is set and the top is golden brown, about 45 minutes. If it overrises, don't worry; it will settle.

4. Remove from the oven and immediately loosen the meringue from the edges of the pan with a spatula if it appears to be stuck. Usually, it will slide right out. Invert onto a large, brightly colored serving plate. Cool to room temperature before cutting. It can be served at room temperature or cold. Store in the refrigerator, but for the freshest flavor use within 24 hours. To serve, cut the meringue into wedges and top with sweetened fresh fruit, berries, or fruit sauce.

MAKES ABOUT 12 SERVINGS

JEKYLL AND HYDE IN A BOTTLE

Why does vanilla extract smell so good and make food taste so good, yet taste so awful from the bottle?

. . . .

Vanilla extract is around 35 percent ethyl alcohol, which has a harsh, biting flavor. Whiskeys and other distilled beverages contain even more alcohol, of course (usually 40 percent), but they are lovingly produced by time-honored flavoring and aging processes that soften the harshness.

"Pure vanilla extract," in order to be labeled as such, must be extracted from real vanilla beans. But the chemical that gives the beans most of their great flavor and aroma is vanillin, and chemists can make vanillin a lot more cheaply than the vanilla plant (an orchid) can. Synthetic vanillin is used commercially to flavor baked goods, candies, ice creams, and such. It's identical to the natural chemical, and is the main ingredient in imitation vanilla flavoring.

Real vanilla extract is so much more complex than just plain vanillin, however, that it doesn't pay to buy the imitation stuff, especially since you use so little of it and it keeps forever. More than 130 distinct chemical compounds have been identified in true vanilla extract.

Even better for some applications is a whole vanilla bean, obtainable for a few dollars in an airtight glass or plastic test tube. The bean should have a flexible, leathery texture, rather then being dried out and hard. (The vanilla "bean" is not a bean, by the way; it's a pod. Beans are seeds, whereas pods are fruits that contain seeds.) The vanilla flavor and aroma are mostly concentrated in the pod's seeds and especially in the oily liquid that surrounds them, so for the most intense flavor as a recipe ingredient, slit the pod lengthwise with a sharp knife and use the seeds, scraping them out with the back of the knife blade.

The pods are also aromatic and flavorful, however, and should not be discarded. Bury them in granulated sugar in a tightly sealed jar for a few weeks, shaking the jar periodically. The sugar becomes infused with the flavor of vanilla and is great in coffee or for flavoring baked goods.

PERCHANCE TO ENHANCE

*What is MSG, and does it really
"enhance flavors"?*

. . . .

It certainly does sound mysterious that these innocent-looking fine, white crystals with no really distinctive taste of their own should be able to boost the inherent flavors of such a wide variety of foods. The mystery lies not in whether MSG really works—nobody doubts that—but in *how* it works. As is the case with so many ancient, stumbled-upon practices, a lack of scientific understanding hasn't stopped people from enjoying the benefits of MSG for more than two thousand years.

What makes MSG's reputation as a flavor enhancer so hard to swallow is that the terminology is somewhat misleading. Flavor enhancers don't enhance the flavors of foods in the sense of improving them; that is, they don't necessarily make things taste better. What they seem to be doing is intensifying, or magnifying, certain flavors that are already present. The food processing industry likes to call them potentiators; I call them flavor boosters.

At this point, I'm obliged to acknowledge the debate about its effects on sensitive individuals.

Everyone has heard of Chinese Restaurant Syndrome or CRS, an unfortunate and politically incorrect label that was applied in 1968 to a diffuse collection of symptoms, including headaches and burning sensations, reported by some people after consuming their selections from column A and column B. The culprit behind CRS appeared to be MSG, which is short for its chemical name, monosodium glutamate (gluTAMate). And thus began a thirty-year battle over its safety.

In one corner sits the National Organization Mobilized to Stop Glutamate, whose uncomplicated solution to the problem is expressed in its acronym. According to NOMSG, glutamates in their many guises (see below) are responsible for at least twenty-three afflictions, from runny noses and bags under the eyes to panic attacks and partial paralysis.

In the other three corners, predictably, are the manufacturers of prepared foods, who find MSG and similar compounds to be enormously valuable in enhancing the consumer appeal of their products.

The official referee is the FDA who, after many years of evaluating data, remains convinced that "MSG and related substances are safe food ingredients for most people when eaten at customary levels." The trouble is that all people are not "most people," and the

FDA is still struggling to regulate the labeling of glutamate-containing foods so as to be most useful to all consumers.

Monosodium glutamate was first isolated from kombu seaweed by a Japanese chemist in 1908. The Japanese call it *aji-no-moto*, which means "essence of taste" or "at the origin of flavor." Today, 200,000 tons of pure MSG is produced every year in fifteen countries. It is sold by the carload to manufacturers of prepared foods and by the ounce to consumers as Ac'cent and Zest.

Monosodium glutamate is a salt of glutamic acid, one of the most common amino acids that proteins are made of. The flavor-boosting properties reside in the glutamate part of the molecule, so any compound that releases free glutamate can perform the same trick. The monosodium version is merely the most concentrated and convenient form of glutamate.

Parmesan cheese, tomatoes, mushrooms, and seaweed are rich sources of free glutamate. That's why a little bit of any of these ingredients can give a big boost to the flavor of a dish. The Japanese have traditionally made use of seaweed's glutamate in subtle, delicate soups.

Our sense of taste involves some very complex chemical and physiological reactions. Exactly how glutamates fit in has been hard to pin down. But there are a couple of ideas that have been kicking around.

It is known that different-tasting flavor molecules stick to the receptors in our taste buds for different lengths of time before detaching. One possibility, then, is that glutamates make certain molecules stick around longer, and therefore taste stronger. Also, it is probable that glutamates have their own distinct set of taste receptors, separate from the receptors for the traditionally quoted quartet of sweet, sour, salty, and bitter. To further complicate matters, quite a few substances other than glutamates have "flavor enhancing" properties.

The Japanese long ago invented a word to describe the unique effects of seaweed's glutamates on taste: *umami*. Today, *umami* is acknowledged to represent a separate family of savory tastes that are stimulated by glutamates, similar to the family of sweet tastes that are stimulated by sugar, aspartame, and their saccharine relatives.

Many proteins contain glutamic acid, which can be broken down into free glutamate in several ways, including bacterial fermentation and our own digestion. (There are about four pounds of glutamate in the proteins of the human body.) The chemical breakdown reaction is called hydrolysis, so any time you see "hydrolyzed protein" of any kind—vegetable, soy, or yeast—on a food label, it probably contains free glutamate. Hydrolyzed proteins are the most widely used flavor boosters in prepared foods.

While a food product may not contain MSG as such and may even say "No MSG" on the label, it may well contain other glutamates. So if you suspect that you are one of the small number of people who are hypersensitive to glutamates, watch also for these euphemisms on the labels of soups, vegetables, and snacks: hydrolyzed vegetable protein, autolyzed yeast protein, yeast extract, yeast nutrient, and natural flavor or flavoring.

What's a "natural flavor," you ask? It's a substance derived from something in Nature, rather than made from scratch in a laboratory or factory. To be called "natural," it doesn't matter how chemically complex or convoluted the processes may be that ultimately isolated the flavor substance, as long as those processes began with something untouched by human hands.

As The U.S. Code of Federal Regulations 1o1.22(a)(3) puts it: "The term natural flavor or natural flavoring means the essential oil, oleoresin, essence or extractive, protein hydrolysate, distillate, or any product of roasting, heating or enzymolysis, which contains the flavoring constituents derived from a spice, fruit or fruit juice, vegetable or vegetable juice, edible yeast, herb, bark, bud, root, leaf or similar plant material, meat, seafood, poultry, eggs, dairy products, or fermentation products thereof, whose significant function in food is flavoring rather than nutritional. Natural flavors include the natural essence or extractives obtained from plants listed in Secs. 182.1o, 182.20, 182.40, and 182.50 and part 184 of this chapter, and the substances listed in Sec. 172.51o of this chapter."

Got that?

NEW MATH: ZERO ≠ 0

Why does the label on my cream cheese package
say it contains no calcium? After all,
it's made from milk, isn't it?

. . . .

If you'll pardon the double negative, cream cheese doesn't contain "no calcium. In the jabberwocky world of food labeling, zero is not the same as none.

When you come right down to it, there's no such thing as a zero amount of anything. All anyone can say is that the amount of something is too small to be detected by whatever detection method is being used. If you can't find any of a certain substance, that doesn't mean that there aren't a couple of zillion molecules of it lurking somewhere below your sensitivity threshold.

With that fundamental principle in mind, the FDA was faced with the problem of what upper limits to place on certain ingredients before allowing food producers to claim in the labels' Nutrition Facts chart that a food contains "none" or "0 percent," or is "not a significant source" of a given nutrient. It wasn't an easy task, especially for such loaded questions as when a food may claim to be "fat-free." (I'm always amused when a label says "97 percent fat-free" instead of "3 percent fat.")

Cream cheese is a particularly interesting case, because its calcium content falls right smack on the edge of "zero."

First of all, being made as it is from cream or a blend of milk and cream, the cheese contains less calcium than you might think. The surprising reason for this is that cream contains substantially less calcium than an equal weight of milk. In the same 100 grams, whole milk contains an average of 119 milligrams of calcium, whereas heavy cream contains only 65. That's because milk is less fatty and more watery than cream, and most of the calcium resides in the watery parts. It may therefore be left largely behind in the watery whey when the cheese curds are coagulated. That's especially true of cream cheese, whose whey is relatively acidic (Techspeak: pH 4.6–4.7) and can therefore retain more calcium.

As a result, cream cheese winds up with only 23 milligrams of calcium per ounce compared, for example, with the 147 milligrams in an ounce of mozzarella. Even 23 milligrams is still *some* calcium, of course, not none. So how come it's listed on the label as "o percent"?

Pay attention, now, because here's where it gets a bit complicated. The percentage of a nutrient that's listed in the Nutrition Facts chart is not the percentage of that nutrient in the product; it's the percentage of the Reference Daily Intake or RDI for that nutrient. The RDI, which used to be called the Recommended Daily Allowance or RDA and now often appears on the labels as Percent Daily Value or % DV (got it?), is the percentage of a person's recommended daily intake of that nutrient that each serving provides.

For example, according to the label, a two-tablespoon (32-gram) serving of Jif Creamy Peanut Butter supplies 25 percent of your daily value for fat. But that 32-gram serving contains 16 grams of fat, so the product is actually 50 percent fat.

Now back to the cream cheese. The RDI for calcium is a whopping 1,000 milligrams, so the 23 milligrams of calcium in an ounce of cream cheese is only about 2 percent of the RDI. And guess what? The FDA permits an amount of 2 percent or less per serving to be listed as "o percent."

The moral of the story:

If Little Miss Muffet had sat on her tuffet
Eating just curds, no whey,
She'd become an old crone,
Quite weak in the bone,
All her calcium wasted away.

FOILED AGAIN

*The last time I made lasagne, I put the leftovers
in the refrigerator, covered with aluminum foil.
When I took it out of the fridge to reheat, I noticed
that wherever the foil touched the lasagne there
were tiny holes in the foil. Is something chemical
going on? If so, what is the lasagne doing to our
stomachs?*

. . . .

As you feared, your lasagne is actually eating holes in the metal. (No
reflection on your cooking.) Aluminum is what chemists call an
active metal, easily attacked by acids such as the citric and other
organic acids in tomatoes. In fact, you shouldn't cook tomato sauce or
other acidic foods in aluminum pots because they can dissolve
enough metal to make them taste metallic. Stomach linings, on the
other hand, contain a much stronger acid (hydrochloric) than the
acids found in any foods, and are even immune to office coffee.

But in your case, something else was going on besides the simple
dissolving of a metal by an acid. It turns out that tomato sauce can eat
holes in the aluminum foil covering a leftover container only if the
container is made of metal, not glass or plastic. So without even asking you, I know that your leftover lasagne must have been in a stainless steel pan or bowl, right? (Elementary, my dear Watson.)

When aluminum metal is in simultaneous contact with a different metal and an electrical conductor such as tomato sauce (you
knew, of course, that tomato sauce conducts electricity, didn't you?),
the combination of the three materials actually constitutes an electric
battery. Yes, an honest-to-goodness electric battery. An electrical
(more accurately an electrolytic) process, not a simple chemical one,
is what chews up the foil. While it would be difficult, not to mention
messy, to run your Walkman on lasagne power, it could in principle
be done.

Here's what was going on.

Your stainless steel bowl is, of course, mostly iron. Now, iron atoms hold onto their electrons much more tightly than aluminum atoms hold onto theirs. So if given an opportunity, the iron atoms in the bowl will steal electrons away from the aluminum atoms in the foil. The sauce provides that opportunity by offering a conductive path through which the electrons can get from the aluminum to the iron. But an aluminum atom that has lost electrons is no longer an atom of metallic aluminum; it is an atom of an aluminum compound that is capable of dissolving in the sauce. (Techspeak: The aluminum has been oxidized to an acid-soluble compound.) So what you see is that the aluminum foil has been dissolved only where the sauce makes the aluminum-to-iron transfer of electrons possible.

If the lasagne had been put into a nonmetallic bowl, none of this would have happened because glass and plastics have no desire to suck electrons away from other substances. You'll have to either take my word for that or sign up for Chemistry 202.

You can test this for yourself. Put a tablespoon or so of tomato sauce (ketchup will do) in each of three bowls—stainless steel, plastic, and glass. Lay a strip of aluminum foil on each blob of sauce, making sure that the foil also makes good contact with the bowl. After a couple of days, you'll see that the foil in the stainless-steel bowl has been eaten away wherever it touched the sauce, while the foil in the other two bowls will be unchanged.

There are a few practical morals to this story.

First of all, your leftover sauce—and it doesn't have to be tomato sauce; it can be any acidic sauce such as a wine reduction or one containing lemon juice or vinegar—can be kept in any kind of container and covered with anything you wish. But if it's in a metal bowl covered with aluminum foil, just make sure that the foil isn't in contact with the sauce.

Second, don't hesitate to use those aluminum lasagne pans sold in supermarkets. They're inexpensive, and disposable, and they work just fine. Even if you cover them with aluminum foil, it's just aluminum against aluminum; no two different metals, so no electrolytic corrosion.

VINEGAR HAPPENS!

I have read so much about the powers of vinegar
for everything from cleaning coffeepots to relieving
arthritis pain and promoting weight loss.
What's so special about vinegar?

. . . .

Vinegar has been known for thousands of years. No one even had to make it in the first place, because it actually makes itself. Wherever there happens to be some sugar or alcohol lying around, vinegar is on the way.

Any chemist will tell you without a moment's hesitation that vinegar is a solution of acetic acid in water. But we may as well define wine as a solution of alcohol in water. Vinegar is so much more than that. The most popular vinegars are made from grapes (red or white wine vinegar), apples (cider vinegar), malted barley or oats (malt vinegar), and rice (. . . uh, rice vinegar). All retain chemicals from their sources that give them unique flavors and aromas. Beyond that, there are vinegars that have been deliberately flavored with raspberries, garlic, tarragon, and virtually anything else that can be stuffed into the bottle and allowed to steep for a few weeks.

At the high end of the purity spectrum is the familiar distilled white vinegar, which is indeed nothing but pure 5 percent acetic acid in water and is just as well kept in the laundry as in the kitchen. Having been made from industrial alcohol and purified by distillation, white vinegar contains no fruit, grain, or other flavors.

Finally, there is balsamic vinegar. True balsamic vinegar has been made for almost a thousand years in Italy's region of Emília-Romagna, and particularly in and near the town of Módena in the province's Réggio nell'Emília region. There, trebbiano grapes are crushed into *must* (the juice and skins), then fermented and aged in a succession of wooden barrels for at least twelve years and perhaps as many as one hundred. The result is a thick, brown brew with a complex sweet-tart, oaky flavor. It is used in small quantities as a condiment, rather than in the familiar ways in which we use ordinary vinegar.

Unfortunately, no one regulates the printing of the word *balsamic* on a label, and the term is sometimes affixed to small, fancy-shaped bottles of sweetened, caramel-colored vinegar and sold for whatever the traffic will bear. Even if the label on a bottle says *Aceto Balsamico di Módena*, there is no real way of judging what's inside. As Lynne Rossetto Kasper puts it in her book *The Splendid Table* (William Morrow, 1992), "Buying balsamic vinegar poses all the hazards of Russian roulette" (well, maybe not all) and "price is no indicator of quality." Her advice: For the real thing, made in Italy by the slow, traditional artisanal method, look for the words *Aceto Balsamico Tradizionale di Módena* or the curiously bilingual *Consortium of Producers of Aceto Balsamico Tradizionale di Réggio-Emília* on the label. And bring your checkbook.

But hey, if you find a bottle of vinegar labeled "balsamic" that you like, no matter how modest the price, stick with it and use it however you like.

HERE'S HOW ALL VINEGAR "happens," whether spontaneously in Nature or induced deliberately by humans.

There is a two-step sequence of chemical reactions: (1) sugar is broken down into ethyl alcohol and carbon dioxide gas, and (2) the ethyl alcohol is oxidized to acetic acid. The first transformation, called fermentation, is what makes wine out of grape sugars and innumerable other alcoholic beverages out of innumerable other carbohydrates in the presence of enzymes from yeast or bacteria. In the second transformation, bacteria known as *Acetobacter aceti* help the alcohol to react with oxygen in the air to form acetic acid. Wines can become oxidized, and therefore sour, without *Acetobacter*, but it's a slower process. The word *vinegar*, in fact, comes from the French *vin aigre*, meaning sour wine.

You can make vinegar at home from wine or other alcoholic liquid by adding a small amount of vinegar containing a mass of vinegar bacteria, called mother of vinegar, to start the reaction. For everything else you need to know about making vinegar, visit Vinegar Connoisseurs International at www.vinegarman.com.

Commercial vinegars range from 4.5 to 9 percent acetic acid, with most of the common ones at 5 percent. At least that strength is necessary for preserving foods by pickling, which is one of vinegar's most venerable uses, since most bacteria cannot thrive in acids of this strength or stronger.

A few words about acids, while I'm in the neighborhood. People tend to think of the word *acid* as being almost synonymous with *corrosive*. They're undoubtedly thinking of the mineral acids, such as sulfuric acid and nitric acid, which could indeed dissolve a Volkswagen. But we can eat acetic acid with no ill effects for two reasons: One, it is a weak acid and two, vinegar is a pretty dilute solution of it. One hundred percent acetic acid is quite corrosive, actually, and you wouldn't want to get any of it on your skin, much less on your salad. Even at 5 percent, vinegar is the second strongest acid in the kitchen, after lemon juice.

What does vinegar do? What *doesn't* it do, at least ostensibly? Folk medicine abounds with claims that it cures headaches, hiccups, and dandruff; soothes sunburn and bee stings; and, to quote an advertisement that I found on the Internet for a Chinese rice wine vinegar, "is the secret to longevity, tranquility, balance, and strength." Believers in these and similar folk remedies will zealously inform you that science has been unable to prove that they don't work. The reason, of course, is simply that scientists have better ways to spend their time than chasing after such will-o'-the-wisps.

After cutting raw meat or poultry on your cutting board or butcher block, it's a good idea to wipe it down with a disinfectant solution, such as a tablespoon or two of chlorine bleach in a quart of water. But the bleach leaves the board with a long-lasting chlorine smell that is very hard to wash off.

Vinegar will remove it. Rinse the board with any kind of vinegar; its acetic acid neutralizes the alkaline sodium hypochlorite of the bleach and kills the smell.

Not to encroach on Heloise's territory, but if you add some distilled white vinegar to the final rinse water when washing your white clothes with chlorine bleach, your hankies won't smell like a chemistry lab.

BEWARE OF BUDS ON SPUDS

Will a potato with green skin eventually ripen?

. . . .

No, no, no. It's not green because it's unripe; potatoes are ready to eat at any stage of growth. And they're not flaunting the green because they're a traditionally Irish food. The green color is Mother Nature's Mr. Yuk sticker, warning us of poison.

Potato plants contain solanine, a bitter-tasting member of the notorious alkaloid family, a group of powerful and toxic plant chemicals that includes nicotine, quinine, cocaine, and morphine. Most of the solanine in potato plants is in the leaves and stems, but smaller amounts are found in and under the skin of the tuber and to a lesser extent in the eyes.

If an underground-dwelling potato is accidentally uncovered during growth, or even if it's exposed to light after its disinterment, it thinks it's time to wake up and start photosynthesizing. So it manufactures chlorophyll and becomes tinged with green on the surface. It also manufactures solanine in the same location.

While solanine won't hurt you unless you eat a lot of it, it's always prudent to cut away and discard the green parts; the rest of the potato will be perfectly okay. Or, because the solanine is concentrated near the surface, you can get rid of most of it by peeling the potatoes rather heavy-handedly. But don't buy a bag of potatoes that has more than a few green areas, because it's a nuisance to cut them all away.

The solanine level goes up when the potato has seen better days and is wrinkled or spongy. So by all means toss out those sad-sack spuds that you've been storing too long. As for the sprouted ones, the sprouts are particularly rich in solanine, especially when they start to turn green.

Potatoes keep best in a dark, dry, and cool place, but not too cool. At refrigerator temperatures, they tend to manufacture solanine. They also convert some of their starch into sugar, which produces a peculiar sweetness and makes them turn brown when fried.

GREEN AROUND THE FRILLS

Why do some potato chips have green edges?
Are they okay to eat?

. . . .

Those chips were sliced from green-surfaced potatoes, and they therefore contain small amounts of toxic solanine, which is not destroyed by frying. It's okay to eat them, because in order to experience any ill effects you'd have to eat so many bags of chips that you'd turn greener around the gills than they are around the frills.

Oh, and if you think you can check out the potato chips in the store to see how many green-edged ones there might be in a package before buying it, think again. Have you ever noticed that potato chip bags are always opaque, unlike the bags of pretzels and other snacks that often let you see the contents? That's not to foil prying eyes, but to keep out ultraviolet light, which speeds up oxidation of the fat in the chips, turning it rancid. All fats and cooking oils, in fact, should be kept out of strong light.

Bags of potato chips are also usually filled with nitrogen gas to displace oxygen-containing air. That's why they are puffed out like balloons. Of course, cynic that I am, I must point out that opaque, ballooned-out packages take up more display space and prevent us from realizing that they may be only about half full.

AVOIDING THE EVIL EYE

*Whenever I peel potatoes I feel I'm flirting
with death, ever since a well-meaning friend
told me that the eyes are poisonous and that I'd
better be careful to get them all out.
How dangerous are they?*

. . . .

Not as dangerous as some well-meaning friends who spread scary stories. But there is a small grain of truth to the story.

When potatoes were introduced into Europe in the second half of the sixteenth century, they were suspected of being either poisonous or aphrodisiac or—an intriguing thought—both. (What a way to die!) Europeans tended to think the same of any exotic food from the New World, including tomatoes. (Their scarlet color no doubt helped to provoke the French into calling them *pommes d'amour*, or love apples.)

But we must let the suspicious Old Worlders off lightly, because both potatoes and tomatoes are indeed members of the same family, the nightshade, whose most infamous and deadly poisonous member is the belladonna plant.

I can't help pointing out here that in Italian, *bella donna* means "sweetheart" or "good-looking woman." Why was the plant so named? Because it contains atropine, an alkaloid that dilates the pupils of the eyes. It was used (the story goes) by sixteenth-century Italian women as a cosmetic to simulate sexual arousal.

Fast-forward to the twenty-first century and your well-meaning friend. The toxic alkaloid solanine, normally present in small amounts in potatoes, does build up in the eyes when they sprout. So eyes that are beginning to sprout should certainly be excised, and most especially if they have started to turn green. But even then, the solanine doesn't lie very deep, and an ordinary gouge with the paring knife will take care of it.

> ## HOMINY GRITS DOES IT TAKE
> ## TO EDUCATE A YANKEE?

*Here in the South, the starch on our plates is often
hominy grits instead of potatoes or rice. But I
understand that they're made with lye. Isn't lye a
very corrosive chemical used in drain cleaners?*

. . . .

Yes, but it has been thoroughly washed out before the grits ever get near your breakfast plate.

The word *lye* is related to the Latin for *wash*, and originally referred to the strong alkaline solution obtained by soaking, or washing, wood ashes in water. (The alkaline material in wood ashes is potassium carbonate, and because alkalis and fats react to form chemicals called soaps, early soaps were made from wood ashes plus animal fat.)

Today, lye refers most often to caustic soda, which chemists call sodium hydroxide. It certainly is nasty stuff. Not only is it poisonous, but if given the chance will dissolve your skin. It opens drains both by converting grease into soap and by dissolving hair.

If you soak corn kernels in a weak solution of lye, it loosens the tough cellulose hulls. It also separates the oil-containing germ, leaving only the starchy part or endosperm, which is then washed and dried and christened hominy. The anxiety-alleviating step in all of this is the thorough washing, which removes all the excess lye. The dried hominy is then coarsely ground into hominy grits, which are boiled and consumed below the Mason-Dixon Line.

A less powerful alkali than caustic soda is lime (calcium oxide), which also can be turned loose upon corn kernels to break them down, such as in making hominy. Lime is so easy to make by heating limestone or seashells (calcium carbonate) that it has been known and used for thousands of years. Natives of the Americas used it for centuries to treat or cook corn. In Mexico and Central America today, corn is boiled in lime water, then washed, drained, dried, and ground into masa, the flour from which tortillas are made.

Unknowingly, the early Americans were improving both the flavor and the nutritional value of corn by treating it with lime. Corn is deficient in certain essential amino acids, and the alkali makes them more available. Lime reacts with the amino acid tryptophan, producing a very flavorful chemical (2-aminoacetophenone) that gives tortillas their unique flavor. Lime also adds calcium to the diet, and perhaps most importantly, increases our absorption of niacin, an essential B vitamin.

A deficiency of niacin in the diet causes pellagra, a debilitating disease characterized by three D's: dermatitis, diarrhea, and dementia. Pellagra was rampant in societies whose diets consisted primarily of corn, such as in polenta-consuming Italy and the rural American South, until 1937, when the disease was recognized as being caused by a deficiency of niacin. Because of their lime treatment, Mexicans and Central Americans have always been quite free of pellagra.

But back to the gritty details: Having been raised in the grits-deprived North, but being acutely aware of the fact that this book is being offered for sale also in the South, I hasten to praise a memorable brunch that I once enjoyed in the Cajun country west of New Orleans. It consisted of mimosas, fried eggs, grits, andouille sausage, grits, biscuits, grits, and *café au lait*. I was converted.

Want to know more about grits? Go to (where else?) www.grits.com. And that's no lye.

The Baking Soda Blues

Blueberry Blue Corn Pancakes

Blue corn is common in the American southwest and has a rich and nut-like flavor. It is treated with wood ashes, which are alkaline and, like lime and lye, make certain amino acids more available. Many people value blue cornmeal for its superior nutritional value. The alkali treatment also intensifies its blue color, as does the alkaline baking soda in this recipe.

You'll find the cornmeal to be a disappointing grayish color. Don't despair. As the pancakes cook, the cornmeal's blue color intensifies by reaction with the baking soda. The blueberries, of course, add even more blueness.

Since blue cornmeal is not a standardized product, you may find various degrees of milling, from fine to quite coarse. No matter. The coarse kind gives these pancakes a nice crunch.

You can find blue cornmeal at specialty grocery stores that sell Mexican or Southwestern ingredients. If not, feel free to substitute a yellow or white cornmeal, but the color and texture may be different.

---

1   **cup blue cornmeal**

1   **tablespoon sugar**

2   **teaspoons baking powder**

1   **teaspoon baking soda**

½   **teaspoon salt**

1   **cup milk**

2   **large eggs, lightly beaten**

3   **tablespoons melted unsalted butter**

½   **cup all-purpose flour**

1   **cup fresh blueberries**

   Butter or oil for greasing griddle

   Butter and syrup

---

1. Mix the cornmeal, sugar, baking powder, baking soda, and salt together in a large bowl. In a small bowl, mix the milk, eggs, and butter well. Add the wet ingredients to the dry ingredients and mix just enough to make a thin, homogeneous batter. Allow the batter to rest for 10 minutes.

2. Stir in the flour and mix the batter until patches of white disappear. Do not overmix. Fold in the blueberries.

3. Heat the griddle until it feels hot to the palm of a hand held a few inches above it. Grease it lightly by brushing with butter or oil. Using a ¼-cup measure, drop pancake portions of batter onto the griddle.

4. When bubbles form on top, the edges are firm, and the bottoms are brown (1 to 2 minutes), turn and cook the cakes until they are lightly browned on the second side. Serve with butter and syrup.

MAKES FOURTEEN TO SIXTEEN 4-INCH PANCAKES

Chapter Five

Turf and Surf

....

W E *HOMO SAPIENS* A R E an omnivorous lot, with teeth and digestive systems well adapted to eating both plant and animal foods. But animal rights activists notwithstanding, it's an undeniable fact that in our society, meat and fish are most often the center of the plate, the star players in our main dishes.

Of the virtually unlimited number of animal species on Earth, perhaps only a few hundred have been routinely hunted, trapped, or fished by humans for food, and only a small handful of those have been domesticated. In our contemporary Western society, we routinely consume even fewer. Walk through the meat department of a supermarket and you'll rarely see more than four general kinds of meat: beef or veal, lamb, pork, and poultry.

On the other hand, some five hundred species of fish and shellfish are available in the United States, with more than twice as many available worldwide. The seas contain an unimaginable variety of edible species, yet we have only scratched the surface (the depths?) in domesticating them, that is, in "farming" them in commercially significant numbers.

Our relative dearth of choice, then, is not because of any lack of diversity in Nature, but because of self-imposed cultural and economic limitations. Many of us have sampled such other-cultural delicacies as grasshopper, rattlesnake, alligator, cockle, sea urchin, and sea cucumber, while many more of us have begun to enjoy rabbit, bison, venison, ostrich, and emu because of their growing commercial availability.

Nevertheless, it is still possible to classify our everyday animal foods into two categories: meat and fish. Or, as some restaurants put it for expense-account customers who can't make up their minds which expensive dish to order, Surf and Turf—a combination of lobster tail and steak that goes together about as well as anchovies and ice cream.

In this chapter, we'll see what makes animal protein from the land and from the sea look and cook differently.

ON THE LAND

RED, WHITE, AND BLEU

*I like my steaks and roast beef rare. But often
there'll be someone at the table who makes a nasty
crack about my eating "bloody" meat.
What can I say in my defense?*

. . . .

Nothing. Just smile and continue to carve away, because they're wrong. There is virtually no blood in red meat. Most of the blood that circulates through a cow's veins and arteries never makes it to the butcher shop, much less to the dinner table.

Not to get too graphic about it, but down at the slaughterhouse, just after the critter is dispatched, most of the blood is drained out, except for what remains trapped in the heart and lungs which, you will agree, are of minimal gastronomic interest.

Blood is red because it contains hemoglobin, an iron-containing protein that carries oxygen from the lungs to the muscle tissues, where it is needed for movement. The color of red meat, however, doesn't come primarily from hemoglobin. It is mainly due to another red, iron-containing, oxygen-carrying protein called myoglobin. Myoglobin's job is to store oxygen right in the muscles, where it will be available for instant use whenever a muscle receives a call to action. If it weren't for that on-the-spot myoglobin, the muscle would quickly run out of oxygen and have to wait for more blood to get there. Prolonged, strenuous activity would therefore be impossible.

When cooked, myoglobin turns brown, just as hemoglobin does. Well-done beef will therefore be grayish brown, while rare beef will still be red. But in France, when you want your steak to be very rare, ask that it be *bleu*. Yes, that means blue, but since when do the French have to be logical?

(Okay, to be fair, fresh, raw beef is actually the somewhat purplish color of myoglobin.)

Various animals contain various amounts of myoglobin in their muscle tissue, because they have varying degrees of need for a reservoir of strenuous-activity oxygen. Pork (those lazy pigs) contains less myoglobin than beef, which allows the pork pushers to advertise it as "the other white meat," even though it's really pink.

Fish contains even less. So animal flesh can be inherently red, pink, or white, depending on the evolutionary need for sustained muscular activity in different species. Tuna meat, for example, is fairly red, because tunas are strong, fast swimmers who migrate for vast distances across the world's oceans.

Now you know why chickens' breast meat is white, while their necks, legs, and thighs are darker. They exercise their necks by pecking and their legs by walking, but that huge breast is nothing but excess baggage. It has been bred into them because compared with the rest of the world, Americans have a stronger preference for white meat. In fact, unless they are given free range, today's American-bred chickens are so pampered that even their "dark meat" is as white as their breasts.

> When I have leftover rare meat such as steak, roast beef, or lamb, I want to warm it up the next day but I don't want it to cook any further. Even a quick shot in the microwave oven would kill its rareness because microwaves penetrate deeply. Instead, I put it in a sealed zipper-top plastic bag with all of the air squeezed out and soak it in a bowl of hot water from the tap. The water will warm the meat, but it isn't hot enough to cook it.

HOW NOW, BROWN COWBURGER?

The ground beef in my supermarket is bright red on the outside and dull-looking on the inside. Are they spraying it with some sort of dye to make it look fresh?

. . . .

No, they're probably not playing games.

A freshly cut meat surface isn't bright red; it's naturally purplish because it contains the purplish-red muscle protein, myoglobin. But when myoglobin is exposed to oxygen in the air, it quickly turns into bright, cherry-red oxymyoglobin. That's why only the outer surface of your ground beef is that nice, bright red color that we generally associate with freshness; the inner parts haven't been exposed to enough air.

Freshly cut, purplish beef is shipped from the packing house to the markets in airtight containers. After being ground at the market, it is usually wrapped in a plastic film that permits the passage of oxygen, and the surface of the meat then "blooms" with the red color of oxymyoglobin. But on longer exposure to oxygen, the red oxymyoglobin gradually oxidizes to brownish metamyoglobin, which not only looks bad but gives the meat an "off"-flavor. It's this metamyoglobin-brown color that signals over-the-hill meat. In reality, however, this transformation happens long before the meat becomes actually unwholesome.

Retail markets use plastic packaging materials (either low-density polyethylene or polyvinyl chloride) that allow just enough oxygen to penetrate to keep the surface of the meat at the bright red oxymyoglobin stage.

To sum it up: If your beef, whether cut or ground, is a dull purple, it's really very fresh. But even if it has gone brown with metamyoglobin, it can still be good for several days. Your nose, not your eyes, is ultimately your best sense organ for determining whether your hamburger is *too* brown.

PRIME RIB, NO FIB

What does the "prime" really mean in "prime rib"? I thought it was the best and most expensive kind of beef, but in some restaurants the prime rib is really pretty bad.

. . . .

USDA Prime is indeed the finest and most expensive grade of beef. But we have all at one time or another been subjected to a $5.95 (salad bar included) slab of tough, dry "prime rib" rimmed with vulcanized-rubber fat that clearly deserved to be stamped "USDA Inedible." Is there some misrepresentation going on here?

Not necessarily. It's true that in almost any context, the word *prime* implies first or top quality. But in this case it has nothing to do with quality: It refers only to the cut: where in the animal it came from. A prime rib roast can be of any USDA quality grade at all.

Before they are butchered, the USDA grades beef carcasses into eight quality categories, based on such characteristics as maturity, texture, color and fat distribution—characteristics that result in tenderness, juiciness and flavor on the plate. In descending order of desirability, they are Prime, Choice, Select, Standard, Commercial, Utility, Cutter, and Canner. (Select used to be called Good until 1987.)

When a carcass is butchered—regardless of its USDA grade—it is first divided into eight "primal" cuts: chuck, rib, short loin, sirloin, round, brisket and shank, short plate, and flank. The primal rib cut consists of rib numbers six to twelve of the steer's thirteen ribs. After the tips of the ribs (the short ribs) are chopped off, what remains is what in butcherese shorthand is known as "prime rib." Again, the name has nothing at all to do with the USDA Prime quality grade, so don't be enticed by the words on the menu. Judge the roast's probable quality by the quality of the restaurant.

DEM BONES

What do bones contribute to a stock? I can understand how meat and fat impart their flavors, but do the bones break down somehow? Or do we just put them in for the marrow?

. . . .

Dem bones are an essential ingredient in making a soup, stock, or stew, every bit as essential as the meat, vegetables, and seasonings. Their purpose may not be obvious, however, if we think of them as hard, nonreactive mineral matter. Yes, their structural material is mineral: calcium phosphates, to be specific. But calcium phosphates don't dissolve or decompose in hot water, so if that were all they were made of, we might as well add stones as bones. They wouldn't contribute any flavor to a stock.

But bones also contain organic, as opposed to mineral, materials, most notably cartilage (gristle) and collagen. In young animals, the bones can actually contain more cartilage than mineral matter, and cartilage contains collagen, a protein that breaks down into soft gelatin when cooked. So bones actually contribute a rich and unctuous mouth feel to the stock.

Shin and thigh bones, together with their connecting knuckle joints, are particularly rich in collagen. If you really want a stock or stew that will jell almost like Jell-O when cooled, add a collagen-rich calf's foot or a couple of pigs' feet. Cooked pigs' feet cooled in their jelly is an old-fashioned country treat. If you make it, tell your guests it's a fancy French dish called *Pied de Cochon*.

The hard parts of bones appear to be solid, but they contain a surprising amount of water, nerve fibers, blood vessels, and other stuff that would make an instant vegetarian out of you if I told you. In Bones 101 you would learn that a typical bone is made up of three layers. The inner core is a spongy material containing lots of yummy organic matter and, in the hollows of the long bones, the even yummier marrow. That's why—and this is important—we cut or crack open the bones before putting them in the stockpot. Outside the core is the hard, largely mineral layer followed by a tough, fibrous outer membrane called the periosteum.

But the bones we throw into the stockpot have hangers-on, too. Outside of a Halloween skeleton or an anatomy lab, have you ever seen a perfectly clean bone, without any meat, fat, gristle, or other connective tissue clinging to it? Not likely. All those bits contribute greatly to the stock's flavor. Moreover, they brown beautifully when we roast our veal bones before committing them to the pot when making a brown stock.

So save all your bones in the freezer for stock-making day. Or take advantage of the last thing in the world besides advice that is free or nearly free: bones from your butcher.

Thin Skins and Gelatins

Greek Lamb Shanks

The shin bones of young animals such as lambs are surrounded by an abundance of collagen-containing cartilage, which cooks down into lots of mouth-watering gelatin in the meat and contributes, along with the meat juices, fat, and bone marrow, to a rich brown sauce. (You may not be able to get the marrow out of the rather thin bones—*osso buco*, it's not— but as it cooks its flavorful fat drips into the sauce.)

Success here depends to a great degree on the choice of cooking vessel. For best results, use an enameled cast-iron Dutch oven, which holds its heat to ensure even cooking and browning. When done, the meat will be brown, glistening, flecked with herbs, and falling-off-the-bone tender.

You can make this dish a day in advance. Refrigerate the shank and vegetables in a separate container from the sauce, so that the solidified fat can be lifted off from the sauce.

---

4   **lamb shanks, ¾ to 1 pound each**

2   **tablespoons olive oil**

   Salt and freshly ground pepper

2   **large carrots, coarsely chopped (or 12 baby-cut)**

2   **ribs celery, coarsely chopped**

1   **large onion, coarsely chopped**

4 to 6   **cloves garlic, coarsely chopped**

½   **cup dry red wine**

½   **cup water**

1   **cup (8-ounce can) tomato sauce**

1   **teaspoon dried oregano, preferably Greek**

½   **teaspoon dried thyme leaves or 1 tablespoon fresh leaves**

---

1. Preheat the oven to 350°F. Trim the lamb shanks of excess fat. Place the olive oil in a heavy Dutch oven on medium-high heat. Working in two batches if necessary, brown the lamb shanks well on all sides. Salt and pepper them generously. Using tongs, remove to a plate.

2. In the same pan over medium heat, sauté the carrots, celery, and onion until soft but not browned, about 5 minutes. Add the garlic and cook for 2 minutes longer. Place the lamb shanks on the bed of vegetables in the pan.

3. In a glass measuring cup, stir together the wine and water and pour over and around the lamb. Pour the tomato sauce over and around the lamb. Sprinkle with oregano and thyme. Heat until the liquid comes to a simmer.

4. Cover with a tight lid or crimped aluminum foil and bake in the oven for 2 hours or until the meat is tender and almost falling off the bone.

5. Using tongs, remove the shanks to a serving dish and cover with foil to keep warm. Remove the vegetables with a slotted spoon and arrange them around the meat. Pour the sauce into a measuring cup, remove the excess fat (see page 134) and discard. There should be about 1 cup of sauce. Correct its seasoning if necessary and serve over the lamb or in a sauceboat.

MAKES 4 SERVINGS

WHEN NOBODY'S WATCHING . . .

Why do people say that the meat nearest the bone is always the sweetest?

. . . .

We can take that remark with a grain of . . . sugar, because the word *sweet* is both overused and misused in gastronomic parlance. It is often used just to mean pleasant tasting and not meant to be taken literally. Perhaps that's because, of the fundamental tastes that have been identified in humans, sweetness is the one that seems to give us the most pleasure.

Nevertheless, the meat nearest the bone really is tastier for several reasons.

First, because it's buried down inside the meat, the bone and its surroundings don't get as hot and cook as fast as the outer parts do. When you grill a T-bone steak, for example, the meat near the bone ends up rarer than the rest, and the rarer the meat, the juicier and more flavorful it is.

Another effect arises from the abundance of tendons and other connective tissue that anchor the meat to the bone. The collagen protein in these tissues breaks down when heated and turns into gelatin, a much softer protein. Gelatin has the further property of being able to hold huge amounts of water, up to ten times its own bulk. So in general, wherever there is the most collagen—and that's usually next to the bone—the meat will be both more tender and juicier.

A third meat-near-the-bone effect is more obvious. In certain cuts, notably in ribs and chops, there is a lot of fat near the bone. So when no one's looking and you're gnawing away like Henry VIII at one of those bones, you can't help but get a large dose of fat. And much to our regret and that of our arteries, highly saturated animal fat is delicious.

THERMOMETRY GEOMETRY

Cookbooks caution that when I use a meat
thermometer to test the done-ness of a roast,
I should never let it touch the bone. Nowhere
have I seen an explanation of why.
Does the roast explode or something?

. . . .

I hate warnings without reasons, don't you? All they do is dispense anxiety without information. Whenever I see an "open other end" warning on a box, I open the wrong end just to see what will happen. I'm still alive.

Bone is a lesser conductor of heat than meat is. For one thing, bone is porous, and the air cells are heat insulators. Also, bones are relatively dry, and much of the heat transfer through a roast is due to the water in the meat. So when most of the meat has reached a certain temperature, it's likely that the regions surrounding the bones will still be relatively cool. They will make the thermometer read too low and fool you into overcooking your chicken, turkey, or roast.

ODE ON A GREASY URN

When I make a meaty stock, soup, or stew, it
winds up with an oil slick on top: fat melted from
the meat. I want to skim it off, but it's messy and
I can never get all of it. Is there an easy way?

. . . .

Recipes tell you to "skim the fat" from soups and stews as if it were as easy as peeling a banana. Supposedly, you just grab a spoon and scoop off the layer of fat without removing any of the underlying solids or liquids. But the word *skim* is a scam.

For one thing, it's hard to know how deeply to scoop without removing a lot of the underlying liquid. If the pot or pan is wide, the fat may be spread out into such a thin layer that you can't remove it with a spoon. Moreover, there are probably lumps of meat and vegetables sticking up through the surface that impede your scavenging. And finally, there can still be a lot of fat hiding down among the solids.

If there's not too much liquid in the pot, you can pour it all into a gravy separator—one of those glass or plastic cups that look like miniature watering cans and dispense their contents from the bottom, like a crooked card dealer. The watery liquid flows out, leaving the top layer of fat behind.

Or, you can strain the liquids into a tall, narrow, heatproof glass container, so that the fat layer becomes deeper and can be sucked off the top with a rubber-bulb turkey baster.

The most tempting method is to put the whole pot in the refrigerator, so that the fat layer will solidify and you can then lift it off in pieces like ice from a frozen pond. But that's dangerous, because the pot can heat the contents of your fridge to a bacteria-friendly temperature. Cool hot foods in several small containers before refrigerating them.

A wonderfully quick and easy method involves a midget-size mop—yes, a mop—that literally mops up the fat. You swish it across the surface of your stock (or soup or stew) and it selectively soaks up the oil without absorbing the watery liquid. It goes by various unappetizing brand names, including Oil Mop, Fat Mop, and Grease Mop, and is available at kitchenware stores.

How, you may ask, can a mop distinguish between oily and watery liquids?

An ordinary mop absorbs water because the water wets—that is, sticks to—the fibers of the mop. There is an attraction between the water's molecules and the molecules of the cotton, or whatever the mop fibers are made of. Moreover, water will even climb up between the fibers by capillary attraction. Thus, when you dip an ordinary mop into water and withdraw it, a lot of water comes along with it.

But water doesn't wet all substances, by a long shot; its molecules just have too little attraction to certain other molecules. Dip a candle into water, for instance, and it will come out dry. Water won't stick to wax or to many plastics, but—and here's the thing—oils will. The Grease Mop is made of a plastic that is wetted by oil but not by water. It therefore sucks out only the oil.

Now that your mop is loaded with oil, and it can hold only so much per swish, how do you dispose of that oil before the next swish?

You can hold the mop under hot water and let the oil go down the drain, but it may eventually find a cool spot and solidify, clogging the pipes beyond the reach of any plumber, short of tearing the house down. Alternatively, you can step out the back door and flick the mop smartly. A little shower of oil won't hurt the grass, and it's biodegradable. The ants will even thank you for it. Then, back to the kitchen to swish and flick again, until all the fat is gone from your pot.

A fat mop or grease mop.

A HAM EXAM

Ever since I moved to Virginia, I've been
perplexed by the fact that "Virginia hams" are
never refrigerated, but are sold off-the-shelf at
roadside stands and in supermarkets.
What keeps them from spoiling?

. . . .

They don't spoil because they're "cured," which is a catch-all term for any process that inhibits bacterial growth, even at room temperature. But hams can be bewildering. How are they cured? Are all hams salted? Smoked? Do you have to soak them? Cook them?

There is no single set of answers to these questions because there are so many different kinds of ham, prepared in so many different ways. Few challenges to humankind seem to have evoked as much resourcefulness as how to eat the hind end of a hog.

In terms of cuts, you can find whole hams, half (shank end or butt end) hams, skin-on or skinless hams, and rolled and tied hams, not to mention bone-in, boneless, and the artlessly oxymoronic "semi-boneless" hams. ("Semi-boned" might be a tad more logical because in butcherese, "boned" actually means boneless!)

And then there are hams named not for the surgical procedures they have endured, but for their styles or places of production. Every region and culture outside of Israel and Islam seems to have its own ways of dealing with a hog's butt. Some of the best-known regional hams come from England, France, Germany, Poland, Italy, and Spain. And in the United States there are highly acclaimed hams from Kentucky, Vermont, Georgia, North Carolina, and . . . yes, Virginia. (I've always wanted to write "Yes, Virginia" in answer to a question.)

Now please don't write to tell me that I've left out "the best hams in the world." I do not argue politics, religion, or hams.

What classifies these many products under the common heading of "ham" is that they are all hogs' hind legs, treated—except for "fresh" ham, which is untreated—by one or more of five processes: salting, smoking, drying, spicing, and aging. There are almost as many different hams as there are combinations and permutations of these five procedures, except that salting is the one step common to all and is often called "curing" all by itself.

Salting, smoking, and drying all contribute to killing food-spoiling bacteria. Here's how they do it.

SALTING

MEATS HAVE BEEN preserved with salt for thousands of years. Salt preserves food because it kills or deactivates bacteria by osmosis.

A bacterium is essentially a blob of protoplasm inside a cell membrane, like a pillowcase full of Jell-O. The protoplasm contains water with dissolved stuff—proteins, carbohydrates, salts, and a lot of other chemicals that are of vital interest to the bacterium but of no concern to us at the moment.

Now let's douse an unlucky bacterium in very salty water, so that there is a stronger, saltier environment outside its cell membrane than inside. Whenever there exists such an imbalance on opposite sides of a water-permeable barrier (the cell membrane), Mother Nature, who hates imbalances, tries to restore the balance. In this case she does it by forcing water out of the less-concentrated side (the bacterium's guts) and into the more concentrated side (the external salt water). The effect is to diminish the imbalance by making the strong solution weaker and the weak solution stronger. The unfortunate consequences for the bacterium are that it loses water, shrivels up, and dies. At the very least, it's no longer a threat to us because it is discouraged from reproducing. ("Not tonight, Dear; I'm dehydrated.")

This spontaneous movement of water through a membrane, driven by an imbalance of concentration between the solutions on either side, is called osmosis. It comes into play also in the brining of meats to improve their flavor and cooking properties (see page 143).

And by the way, a strong solution of sugar in water can have the same effect as strong salt water. That's why we can use lots of sugar to preserve fruits and berries to make, well, preserves. In principle, you could just as well make your strawberry jam with salt instead of sugar. Just don't invite me to breakfast.

These days, hams and other pork products may be cured with salt mixed with additional substances, including sugar ("sugar-cured hams"), seasonings, and sodium nitrite. Nitrites do three things: They inhibit the growth of *Clostridium botulinum* bacteria, the notorious source of botulin poison; they contribute flavor; and they react with myoglobin, the red color in fresh meat, to form a chemical called nitric oxide myoglobin, which turns the meat a bright pink color during the slow heating used in the curing process.

In the stomach, nitrites are converted to nitrosamines, which are cancer-producing chemicals. The FDA therefore places a limit on the amount of residual nitrite that can be present in cured meat products.

SMOKING

CURING A HAM DOESN'T cook it, so it usually has to be dealt with further. Smoking it over a wood fire also kills germs, partly because it dries out the meat, partly because it's a sort of low-temperature cooking, and partly because the smoke contains evil chemicals. (You don't want to know.) But it can also give the meat a wonderful range of flavors, depending on the type of wood, the temperature, the length of time, and so on.

Generally, hams that have been smoked, and that's most of them, need not be cooked any further before eating. Supermarket hams may be either partially or fully cooked. Ask the butcher or check the label, which will say something like "cooked" or "ready to eat" or "cook before serving."

To answer your question, then: Virginia hams, including the renowned Smithfields, have been thoroughly cured by both salting and smoking, so they don't need to be refrigerated or cooked. But that doesn't stop many people from soaking, simmering, roasting, glazing, and generally fussing over them once they get them home.

DRYING

LONG PERIODS OF hanging in dry air can also do the job of dehydrating and killing bacteria. Italian *prosciutto* and Spanish *serrano* are cured with dry salt and then dried by hanging, traditionally in wind-blown caves or attics. Not having been hot-smoked, they are still technically raw and are eaten that way, sliced paper-thin. There's nothing wrong with eating bacteria-free raw meat.

SPICING AND AGING

THIS IS WHERE real individuality comes into the picture. Hams can be coated with salt, pepper, sugar, and various secret concoctions of spices, and then aged for years. If cured and dried, they won't spoil from bacteria, but with age they may develop coatings of mold that must be scrubbed off before eating. So-called country hams are often in this category. The mold may look awful, but the meat inside can be superb. Again, there's no harm in eating it.

At the lowliest end of the ham spectrum are those pink, plastic-clad, square or round slices in the deli cases of supermarkets and convenience stores. They can be called ham because they contain cured pork, but all relationship to real hams ends there. (Have you ever seen a perfectly square hog's leg?) They are made by pressure-forming meat scraps into geometric loaves to fit between the slices of gummy, convenience store white bread that they so justly deserve. Even though smoked, they spoil easily because of all the water they contain, so they have to be kept in the refrigerator case.

Leave them there.

Preserving with Sugar and Salt

Gravlax

Hams and other meats are usually cured by salting, while fruits are usually preserved with sugar. The reason for the difference, obviously, has to do with flavor. But salt and sugar are equally effective at killing bacteria; they pull water out in the same way: by osmosis.

One classic cured meat—fish, actually—is gravlax or gravad lax, a Scandinavian cured salmon. Whether you spell it *lax* (Swedish), *laks* (Danish and Norwegian), *lachs* (German), or *lox* (Yiddish), the word means salmon, and gravlax means buried salmon. Medieval Scandinavians were in the habit of burying salmon and herring in holes in the ground to ferment.

Today, the salmon is cured by coating it with sugar and a dash of salt. The French sometimes do it with salt and a dash of sugar. This recipe uses half and half, because that's the way we like it, but you can vary the ratio of salt to sugar to suit yourself. Just make ½ cup total of the mixture.

Gravlax is a cinch to make, but you have to plan ahead because it takes two or three days. At the end of that time, you'll have one of the prettiest and most toothsome of appetizers. Serve it thinly sliced with Sweet Mustard Sauce (recipe below) and buttered rye bread.

---

3 to 3½   **pounds center cut salmon with skin intact, in one piece, as rectangular (not tapered in width) as possible**

1   **large bunch dill (about ¼ pound)**

¼   **cup coarse kosher salt**

¼   **cup sugar**

2   **tablespoons white or black peppercorns, crushed coarsely in a mortar or with a meat pounder**

---

1.   Rub a finger over the flesh side of the fish from head end to tail end, to feel for bones. Using needle-nosed pliers or tweezers, pull out the bones and discard. Rinse the dill and shake dry. Mix the salt, sugar, and crushed peppercorns in a small dish. Cut the salmon in half across the width and lay the two pieces skin side down, side by side on a work surface. Sprinkle the salt-sugar-pepper mixture evenly over the fillets and gently rub it onto all exposed flesh.

2. Place dill sprigs on one piece of fish, and top with the second piece, skin side up. It will look like a thick, whiskery sandwich.

3. Wrap the sandwich in 2 layers of plastic wrap, place in a shallow baking dish, and top with 5 to 10 pounds of weight. Canned goods or books in sealed plastic bags are good. (We use a plastic-wrapped lead brick, but most households are not so privileged.)

4. Refrigerate for 3 days, turning the salmon every 12 hours or so. Unwrap and scrape the fish clean with a knife or spatula, discarding the salty-sugary dill. To serve, slice very thinly on the diagonal, detaching each slice from the skin.

SERVES 10 OR 12

Sweet Mustard Sauce

Combine ¼ cup spicy brown mustard, 1 teaspoon dry mustard, 3 tablespoons sugar, 2 tablespoons red wine vinegar. Beat in ⅓ cup vegetable oil in a steady stream to reach the consistency of thin mayonnaise. Stir in 3 tablespoons finely chopped dill and refrigerate for 2 hours to mellow.

DEFINING BRINING

*Brining seems to be all the rage these days, as if
the world's chefs and food writers have suddenly
discovered salt water, like Balboa discovering the
Pacific Ocean. What, exactly, is it supposed to do?*

. . . .

Brining, soaking meat, fish or poultry in a solution of salt in water,
is far from new. Surely, at some time in maritime history, someone
discovered—accidentally, perhaps?—that meat that had soaked in
seawater was juicier and had better flavor when cooked.

How does brining work? What does a bath in salt water accomplish, besides making the food . . . well, wet and salty? Are the claims
of increased juiciness and tenderness justified?

First, let's get our terminology straight. The word *brining* is mistakenly used for everything from rubbing salt on a roast to soaking it in
a concoction of salt, sugar, pepper, vinegar, wine, cider, oil, spices,
and, oh, yes, water. But rubbing dry salt on meat isn't brining; it's
making a rub, which serves a completely different purpose. Some people call the soaking of meat in a liquid mixture of many ingredients
brining, although it's really marinating, which is a different ball game.
On the other hand, the meat industry refers to the injection of salt
water into pork as marinating, whereas it's really a form of brining.

To keep this section somewhat shorter than the briny *Moby-Dick*,
I'll limit my discussion to the effects of soaking meat in plain salt
water, although most brining liquids also contain sugar.

A typical meat (muscle) cell is a long, cylindrical fiber of protein
and liquid containing dissolved substances, all encased in a membrane that allows water molecules to pass through. When such a cell
is bathed in a brine that has a lot more free water molecules per cubic
inch than it has, Nature tries to even things up by forcing free water molecules through the membrane from where they are more plentiful—
in the brine—to where they are less plentiful—inside the cell. This

process, in which water moves from a solution that is water-rich into a solution that is relatively water-poor is called osmosis, and the pressure that forces the water through the membrane is called osmotic pressure. In this case, the result is a transfer of water from the brine into the cells, making a juicier piece of meat.

Meanwhile, what about the salt? There is very little dissolved salt (Techspeak: very few sodium ions and chloride ions) inside the cell, but there are tons of salt in the brine, usually from one to six cups per gallon. Again, Nature tries to even things up, this time by the process of diffusion: Some of the plentiful salt ions outside the cell diffuse or migrate through the membrane into the cell. There, by a mechanism that still isn't completely understood, it increases the protein's ability to hold water. The result is a seasoned, moister piece of meat. As a bonus, the meat may well be more tender, because protein structures that are binding more water tend to be swollen and softer.

Brining is therefore most effective for relatively flavorless, lean meats that tend to dry out when cooked, such as today's white-meat turkeys and fatless pork loins. But that, my friends, is where science ends and art takes over, because there are dozens of different ways to brine and cook various kinds of meat. There can be no general answer to how long and in how strong a salt solution one should brine a given kind of meat that is subsequently to be cooked in a certain way, at a certain temperature, for a certain length of time. That's where your confidence in the recipe developer must be the deciding factor, because trial and error rule. If you find a brining recipe that gives you tender, juicy, not-too-salty results, cherish it and don't ask questions.

While we're in a saline mood, let's talk about salt's ability to "draw the moisture out" of food, a historic method of drying and preserving meat and fish by covering it with rock salt. Isn't that contrary to what I've just said about salt water's *increasing* the moisture in brined meats? Not at all. (Watch me squirm out of this.)

Salt water and dry salt don't have the same effect on food. Osmosis works because of a *difference* in the amount of available water between the two sides of the cells' membranes. In brining, there are more water molecules available outside the cell than inside, so osmotic pressure forces some of the water inside. But when you cover a piece of high-water-content food (and that includes just about all food) with solid salt, some of the salt dissolves in the surface moisture to produce a film of extremely concentrated salt solution, with an extremely low proportion of water—lower than that inside the cells. Thus, there are more available water molecules inside the cells than outside, and moisture is extracted.

Rock Cornish Brined Hens

Bob's Mahogany Game Hens

Cornish game hens are flavorful and juicy, especially when brined before roasting. In this recipe we give them an Asian flair by basting with a soy-garlic-ginger sauce to produce beautiful mahogany-brown skins.

How much brine to use? Put the hens into the bowl, crock, or resealable plastic bag that you intend to brine them in and add water to cover them completely. Then remove the birds and measure the amount of water.

How strong should a brine be? As a rule of thumb, use 1 cup Morton's kosher salt or 1½ cups Diamond Crystal kosher salt for every 4 quarts of water. Sugar and other ingredients may be added to balance the flavors.

---

2 **Cornish game hens**

4 **quarts water**

1 **cup Morton's kosher salt**

1 **cup dark brown sugar, lightly packed**

⅓ **cup soy sauce, preferably Kikkoman**

2 **tablespoons peanut oil**

4 **cloves garlic**

3 **nickel-size slices of ginger**

---

1. Remove the hens from their wrappings, clean out the cavities, and rinse well. Pour the water into a large bowl or stockpot. Add the salt and sugar and stir until dissolved. Put the birds in the liquid, breast side down. Weight with a plate to keep the birds fully submerged. Allow to sit in a cool place or refrigerator for 1 hour. Remove the birds from the brine, and rinse and dry with paper towels. If not using them right away, refrigerate.

2. Preheat the oven to 400°F. Tie the legs loosely together with string, just so they do not splay.

3. Pour the soy sauce into a 1-cup glass measuring cup, and add the oil. Put the garlic cloves through a garlic press and add to the soy and oil. Mince the ginger, put in garlic press, and squeeze its juice and any bits that may come

through into the soy mixture. Whisk the mixture to blend as much as possible (the oil won't blend completely, of course), and paint the birds all over with the mixture. Place the birds breast side down on a rack over a roasting pan.

4. Roast the birds for 30 minutes, basting with the soy mixture after 10 and 20 minutes. Stir or whisk the sauce well each time to suspend the garlic and ginger fragments so that the basting brush picks some fragments up and deposits them on the skin. If the pan drippings begin to smoke, add ½ cup water to the pan. Turn the birds breast side up and continue to roast for another 30 to 40 minutes, basting every 10 minutes. Make sure to get some of the solids onto the skins, especially on the final basting.

The birds will be tender, juicy, and mahogany brown all over.

SERVES 2 GENEROUSLY

There's No Excuse for Losing Juice

> ### *Salt-Seared Burgers*

Hamburgers cooked on a gas or charcoal grill lose a lot of juice by dripping into the fire. But when they are cooked in a skillet, the evaporating juices leave behind flavorful "brown bits," or *fond* on the pan. That would be wonderful if the pan were to be deglazed with wine or another liquid to make a sauce. But when skillet-cooking plain, unsauced hamburgers, all those brown bits are lost.

The solution: Cook the burgers on a thin layer of salt in the skillet. The salt draws out juices and quickly congeals them, forming a crust on the meat that keeps it from sticking to the pan and leaving its brown goodies behind. The resulting burger is crunchy on the outside, and deliciously salty.

¾ to 1 **pound ground beef chuck**
½ to ¾ **teaspoon kosher salt**

---

1. Using your hands, pat and shape the meat gently into 2 fat ovals. Do not compress the meat more than is necessary to hold it together.
2. Sprinkle kosher salt evenly onto the surface of an 8-inch cast-iron skillet. It should not quite cover the bottom in a single layer. Heat the salted skillet for 5 minutes on medium high.
3. Place the burgers directly on the salt and cook without turning for 3 minutes on one side, then flip and cook for 3 minutes on the other side for rare or until done to your liking.

MAKES 2 BURGERS

GOOD NIGHT, SWEET RINSE

Recipes are always telling me to marinate
overnight, soak overnight, let stand overnight, etc.
How long is "overnight"?

. . . .

I'm with you. Why overnight? Are we to believe that daylight some-how interferes with the marinating process? What if it's only two o'clock in the afternoon when we arrive at the critical point in the recipe? How early can "overnight" begin? If we do leave it overnight, must we proceed with the recipe the moment the cock crows? What if we have to go to work in the morning? How do you stop something from standing, for heaven's sake?

Generally, "overnight" is intended to mean eight to ten hours, and in most cases even twelve probably wouldn't hurt. But a carefully writ-ten recipe should let us set our own schedules. Just tell us how many hours, thank you; we're old enough to choose our own bedtimes.

SKIM THAT SCUM!

When I make chicken soup, shortly after the water
starts to boil around the bird, a foamy, white
scum appears. I can skim most of it off, but the
rest soon disappears. What is this stuff, and am I
correct in removing it?

. . . .

The stuff is coagulated protein, held together by fat. While it won't hurt you, it won't taste good and it's best to remove it on purely aes-thetic grounds.

When protein is heated, it coagulates. That is, its long, convo luted molecules unfold and then clump together in new ways. What happened was that some of your chicken's protein had dissolved in the water where, as the temperature went up, it began to coagulate. Meanwhile, some of the bird's fat had melted into oil which, as oil is wont to do, began making its way up to the water's surface, because it is less dense than water. Wherever the two met, the oil coated the coagulated protein and acted as a life preserver, keeping it afloat as an oily scum. All edible stuff, but not a pretty sight.

As the temperature rises all the way to a simmer, the oil thins out and flows away, leaving the protein to continue clumping. It eventually forms those small brown particles that you can see in the finished soup—that is, if you haven't removed the scum in its early stages. The scum hasn't disappeared; it has just tightened up into those little brown specks, many of which will stick to the sides of the pot at the waterline, forming a kind of (excuse the metaphor) bathtub ring.

So skim away early and diligently and you'll be rewarded with a nice, clear soup.

The widely recommended slotted spoon for skimming scum from soups and stews isn't really the best tool, because its holes are too big and it will miss a lot. The best tool for skimming is called (surprise!) a skimmer. It has a round, flat business end covered with a screenlike mesh. It's available in kitchenware shops.

LOOKY, LOOKY, LOOKY. AIN'T THAT OOKY?

*After I roast a chicken, there are all these
ooky drippings in the pan. Can I use them
for anything?*

. . . .

No. If you have to ask, you don't deserve them. Pour off the fat, scrape the rest of the "ook" into a jar, and ship it to me by overnight express.

Seriously, this stuff is composed of marvelously flavorful juices and gels, and it would be a crime to feed it to your dishwashing machine. I have often thought that if I were a king or an emperor, I would order my cooks to roast a hundred chickens, throw them to the peasants, and serve the combined drippings to me on a silver platter along with several loaves of crusty French bread.

Or else I would soon have a barrel of the best gravy ever made, because all those wonderful fats, chicken juices, protien gels, and browned bits are the flavor foundations of great gravies.

JACK SPRAT WOULDN'T TOUCH IT

*Why does my gravy turn out to be either
lumpy or greasy?*

. . . .

It doesn't have to be either lumpy or greasy. We all know people who can make it both lumpy and greasy at the same time, don't we?

Lumps and grease arise from the same basic phenomenon: Oil and water won't mix. In your gravy, you want some of each, but you have to trick them into blending.

First, let's get some terminology straight. Oil, fat, and grease are the same stuff. It's called a fat when it's solid and an oil when it's liquid. Any solid fat can be melted to a liquid, and any liquid oil can be solidified by cooling.

In their natural forms, solid fats are generally found in animals and liquid oils are found in the seeds of plants. But food professionals call them all fats anyway, because they play the same role in nutrition.

Grease is an intermediate consistency between solid fat and liquid oil. The word has an unsavory connotation (a crummy restaurant is called a greasy spoon), and it is never heard at the dinner table except in the most dire of circumstances. In what follows, I'll use the words *fat*, *oil*, and *grease* as necessary to get my point across. Or frankly, I'll use whichever one I feel like using.

A bit more about nomenclature: Originally, *gravy* meant the juice that drips from meat while it is cooking. When a roast is served with that relatively unmodified liquid, it is said to be served *au jus* (o-ZHOO), which is French for "with juice." (Menus that say "with *au jus*" were written by bilingual stutterers.) Unfortunately, most restaurant *jus* is just a powdered commercial "base" made of salt, flavorings, and caramel coloring, dissolved in hot water.

When you add other ingredients to the pan drippings and cook them together, you're making gravy. And what, then, is a sauce? It's made in a separate pan, usually by incorporating some of the same drippings, but augmented by any number of seasonings, flavorings and other ingredients.

Let's talk about the most common kind of gravy: pan gravy made from the drippings of roast meat or fowl.

No one likes watery gravy, so a thickening agent must be used. That's where flour comes in. Flour contains both starch and protein. Thickening a sauce with cornstarch or arrowroot, which are nonprotein-containing starches, is a totally different ball game, so don't try to substitute them for flour in what follows.

When your turkey is done, remove it from the roaster and examine the godawful-looking mess in the pan. You'll notice that there are two kinds of liquids: an oil-based liquid consisting of melted turkey fat and a water-based liquid, which is the juices from the meat and vegetables plus any broth or water that you may have added. The trick is to incorporate both of these incompatible liquids into your gravy, because each contains a unique set of flavors. That is, certain flavors are fat-soluble and others are water-soluble. Your goal is to get the fat-based flavors and the water-based flavors to mix into a smooth, homogeneous sauce.

It's all in how you handle the flour, because flour is not only a thickening agent; it also does the job of blending the oil and water together.

Flour is a very fine powder containing certain proteins (glutenin and gliadin) that combine form a sticky substance, gluten, when they absorb water. Now if you were just to dump some flour into the roasting pan and stir, the proteins and the water would get together and form a sticky glop. And since the glop is water-based, the oil wouldn't be able to penetrate it. You'd wind up with lumps of glop wallowing in a pool of grease. This may be standard fare in some households, but most experts agree that gravy should not be the chewiest part of a Thanksgiving dinner.

What should you do instead? It's as simple as one-two-three (plus two): (1) You separate the watery and oily liquids from each other in one of those clever gravy separators that pour from the bottom. (The fat is the top layer, if you must ask.) (2) You mix the flour into some of the fat. This blend of flour and fat is called a roux (pronounced *roo*). (3) You cook the roux a bit to brown it and to get rid of any raw floury taste. (4) Only then do you slowly stir in the watery liquids. The flour, oil, and water will blend magically into a smooth sauce just as if they weren't natural enemies. (5) Finally, you simmer the sauce to break down the flour grains and release their thickening starches.

Here's how it works.

By mixing the flour with fat first, you ensure that each microscopic grain of flour becomes coated with oil, so that the watery juices can't get through to gum up the flour's protein. Then, when you stir the juices into the roux, the flour grains become widely dispersed, taking their coatings of fat along with them. And that's exactly what you want: fat and flour uniformly dispersed throughout the liquid to make a smooth, homogeneous mixture. In short, you've persuaded the oil and water to fraternize by using the flour as a carrier of oil throughout the water. Then, when you simmer the sauce to let the flour do its thickening job, it does it uniformly throughout. No thick spots or thin spots. No lumps.

If you make your roux with too much fat, though, it won't all be picked up by the flour, and the excess fat will just hang around in greasy little pools, ruining your reputation. On the other hand, if you use too much flour, it won't all be coated by the available fat, and the extra flour will turn into lumpy library paste as soon as you add the watery liquid. So it's essential to keep the amounts of flour and fat just about equal.

How much flour, fat, and watery liquid? To one part flour and one part fat, use eight or more parts of liquid juices and/or stock, depending on how thin you like it. Your gravy will be legendary.

Are you concerned about cleaning your chickens and other poultry before cooking them? Do you have trouble getting all the gutsy gook out of the cavity? I use a hair brush with stiff plastic bristles for my "gut brush." Rotating it inside the cavity gets all the fragments of liver, lung, and god-knows-what out from between the ribs. I then rinse the brush under hot water and put it in the dishwasher.

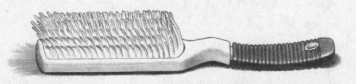

A "gut brush" for cleaning out the cavities in raw poultry.

Good Gravy!

Perfect Chicken or Turkey Gravy Every Time

There are three important things to remember when making gravy:

1. Combine and cook equal parts fat and all-purpose flour.
2. Whisk in the right amount of broth to the consistency you like.
3. Simmer gravy for a total of 7 minutes.

The standard proportion for gravy is 1 part fat, 1 part flour, 8 or 12 parts liquid. For example: ½ cup fat drippings, ½ cup flour, 4 or 6 cups broth. Another: 4 tablespoons fat, 4 tablespoons flour, 2 or 3 cups broth. Use the same proportions when making beef gravy.

Here's how to do it: The turkey or chicken has been removed from the oven and set to rest. Now look into the roasting pan. It should be a glorious mess of fat, brothy juices, and browned vegetables. The essence of gravyness comes from these drippings, along with the broth that you make from the giblets.

Yes, you can make the gravy right in the roasting pan, but there is a downside. It's hard to measure the amount of fat, and that alone can skew the proportions. It's hard to straddle two burners on the stove with that gigantic roasting pan, and it makes for one big cleanup job after dinner.

Better to make the gravy like this: Pour the contents of the roasting pan, both fat and juices, but leaving the roasted vegetables behind, into a large measuring cup. The fat and drippings will separate with the fat on top and be easier to measure.

Basic Turkey or Chicken Gravy

Turkey or chicken

½ cup each of chopped onion, celery, carrots

¼ cup fat from the roasting pan

¼ cup all-purpose flour

Pan juices

About 2 cups turkey or chicken broth

Salt and freshly ground pepper

---

1. Prepare the turkey or chicken for roasting. Before placing it in the oven, add the chopped onion, celery, and carrots to the roasting pan.
2. Roast the bird according to your recipe.
3. Make the giblet broth while the bird roasts.
4. When the bird is done, remove it to a platter to rest while you make the gravy.
5. Pour off all the juices into a glass measuring cup.
6. Measure ¼ cup fat and return it to the roasting pan.
7. Measure and reserve the brown liquid drippings. (Discard the remaining fat or set it aside to make additional gravy for leftovers.)
8. Scrape the bottom of the pan to loosen the vegetables and baked-on bits.
9. Add the flour to the roasting pan.
10. Blend the fat and flour with a wooden spoon, making a thick, smooth mixture.
11. Over low heat, let the pan's contents bubble and cook for 2 minutes. This eliminates the flavor of raw flour.
12. Slowly whisk in the reserved brown drippings and enough broth to bring the gravy to the consistency you like, about 2 cups of liquid in all.
13. Simmer for barely 5 minutes longer, until the gravy is thick and smooth. Season with salt and pepper.
14. Strain into a gravy boat.

MAKES ABOUT 2 CUPS

IN THE SEA

THE *REAL* WHITE MEAT

*Why does fish cook so much faster than
other meats?*

. . . .

Meats, like wines, can be either red or white. Beef is red; fish and shellfish are generally white. Salmon are pink—rosé, if you like—because they eat pink-shelled crustaceans. Flamingos, if you care, are pink for a similar reason.

In the kitchen, we soon learn that white fish flesh cooks much more quickly than red meat. It's more than just color, of course; fish flesh is inherently different in structure from the flesh of most running, slithering, and flying creatures.

First of all, cruising through the water doesn't exactly qualify as body-building exercise, at least when compared with galloping across the plain or jetting through the air. Therefore, fish muscles don't get to be as Schwarzeneggish as those of other animals. The more active fish, such as tuna, have more red muscle, containing more red myoglobin (see page 126) and therefore a darker flesh.

More important is the fact that fish have a fundamentally different kind of muscle tissue from that of most land animals. To dart away from their enemies, fish need quick, high-powered bursts of speed, as opposed to the long-haul endurance that other animals need for running—or that they needed at one time, before we domesticated some of them into indolence.

Muscles are generally made up of bundles of fibers, and fish muscles consist predominantly of so-called fast-contracting fibers. These are shorter and thinner than the big, slow muscle fibers of most land animals, and are therefore easier to tear apart, such as by chewing, or to break down chemically, such as by the heat of cooking. That's why fish is tender enough to eat raw in sushi, whereas steak has to be chopped for steak tartare to render it vulnerable to our molars.

Another big reason that fish flesh is more tender than that of other animals is that fish live in an essentially weightless environment, so they have little need for connective tissue—the cartilage, tendons, ligaments, and such that other creatures need for supporting their body parts against gravity and fastening them to the skeletal tree. So fish are made mostly of muscle, with very little gristly, chewy stuff, and little more than a simple spine suffices in the bone department. Fish's relative lack of connective tissue means a relative lack of collagen, the protein that changes into nice, juicy gelatin when heated. That's one reason why fish cooks up drier than many other kinds of flesh. Another reason is that, being cold-blooded, fish don't need a lot of insulating fat, which would contribute to juiciness.

For all these reasons, the main problem with fish is to keep from cooking it too much. It should be cooked only until the protein loses its translucent quality and becomes opaque, pretty much the same as what happens to the protein in the white of an egg. Fish will get tough and dry if you cook it too long because the muscle fibers contract, shrinking and toughening the flesh; at the same time, too much water is lost, drying out the tissue. The usual rule of thumb is eight to ten minutes of cooking per inch of thickness.

Fish Cooked Just Right

Fish in a Package

Fish cooks so easily that it can even be steamed, a method that also prevents it from drying out. One classic method is *en papillote*, or wrapping the fish in parchment paper and heating the package in the oven. These days, we can use aluminum foil.

Almost any fish fillet will work: black sea bass, coho salmon, grouper, red snapper, or perch. The fish cooks perfectly (and unwatched) every time. The juices of the steamed fish mingle with the flavors of the vegetables and seasonings.

---

2 15-inch lengths of aluminum foil

2 teaspoons olive oil

2 fish fillets

   Salt and pepper

2 scallions, both white and green parts, cut in half crosswise

2 sprigs of parsley

2 small slices of onion

8 ripe cherry tomatoes

2 tablespoons dry white wine or lemon juice

2 teaspoons capers, drained, optional

---

1. Preheat the oven to 425°F. Rinse the fillets under cold water and dry on paper towels. Tear off two pieces of aluminum foil. Drizzle olive oil onto half of each piece of foil.

2. Pick up one of the fillets by one end and slide it around in the olive oil to coat. Repeat with the other side. Repeat this procedure with the other fillet on its own piece of aluminum foil. Season each with salt and pepper. Drape with scallions and parsley and top with onion slices. Add the cherry tomatoes, wine, and capers, if desired.

3. Fold each foil sheet over the fish and vegetables. Fold and crimp the edges to seal them and make tight packets. Place the packets on a cookie sheet with sides and bake for 10 to 12 minutes.

4. Remove from the oven. Place each foil packet in a wide soup or pasta dish, open by slitting the uncrimped side with a knife or scissors, and gently slide the contents, with its liquid, into the dish.

SERVES 2

SOMETHING'S FISHY

Does fish have to smell fishy?

. . . .

Not at all. People put up with fishy-smelling fish because they're probably thinking, Well, what else should it smell like? Odd as it may seem, though, fish needn't smell like fish at all.

When they're perfectly fresh, only a few hours removed from carousing around in the water, fish and shellfish have virtually no odor. A fresh "scent of the sea," perhaps, but certainly nothing the least bit smelly. It's only when seafood starts to decompose that it takes on that fishy aroma. And fish starts to decompose much faster than other kinds of meat.

Fish flesh—fish muscle—is made up of different kinds of protein from, say, beef or chicken. It is not only tenderized more quickly by cooking but it is also more quickly decomposed by enzymes and bacteria; in other words, it spoils faster. That fishy smell comes from decomposition products, notably ammonia, sulfur compounds, and chemicals called amines that come from the breakdown of the amino acids in proteins.

The odors of these chemicals are noticeable long before the food gets downright unpleasant to eat, so a slight fishy smell indicates only that you've got a good nose and the fish isn't quite as fresh as it might be, not necessarily that it's bad. Amines and ammonia are counteracted (Techspeak: neutralized) by acids; that's why lemon wedges are often served with fish. If you have scallops that smell a trifle ripe, rinse them quickly in lemon juice or vinegar before cooking.

There's another reason why fish spoils quickly. Most fish have the unfriendly habit of swallowing other fish whole, and they are therefore equipped with enzymes that digest fish. If any of these enzymes should escape from the guts by rough handling after a fish is caught, they'll quickly go to work on its own flesh. That's why fish should be gutted as soon as possible after being caught.

The decomposition bacteria in and on fish are also more efficient than those in land animals, because they're designed to operate in the cold, cold seas and streams. To stop them from doing their dirty work, we have to cool them down a lot faster and a lot more than we do to preserve warm-blooded meat. That's why ice, which never gets above 32°F, is the fisherman's best friend. Your home refrigerator is at about 40°F.

A third reason that fish flesh spoils faster than land meat is that it contains more unsaturated fats. Unsaturated fats turn rancid (oxidize) much more readily than the saturated fats in beef, for example. The oxidation of fats turns them into bad-smelling fatty acids, which contribute further to the fishy odor.

HAKE MAKES FAKE

I bought some artificial crab sticks the other day,
and they really weren't bad. The label said they
were made of surimi. What is that, and
how do they make it?

. . . .

Surimi is fish flesh that has been minced and fabricated into crab- and shrimp-like shapes. Developed in Japan to utilize the waste scraps from filleting and to exploit some of the less desirable fish species caught in the nets, it has gained a foothold in the United States as a low-cost alternative to the real things.

The fish scraps, most often of pollack and hake, are minced, washed thoroughly to eliminate fat, pigments, and flavors, rinsed, strained, and partially dried to reduce the moisture content to about 82 percent, after which they are frozen until needed. That's surimi.

To fabricate a given product, the surimi may then be shredded into fibers, after which ingredients such as egg white and starch and a little oil are added to give it a texture similar to that of real crab, shrimp, or lobster. The mixture is then extruded as a sheet and heated briefly to stabilize it into a gel. The sheets are then rolled, folded and/or molded into sticks or other shapes, flavored, and colored to mimic the real things, and frozen for shipping to the market.

WOULD YOU LIKE FRIES OR CAVIAR WITH THAT?

In a catalog I saw various kinds of caviar
spoons ranging in price from $12 to $50.
Why does caviar have to be served with
a special, fancy spoon?

. . . .

One can imagine several reasons. (1) Merchants assume that anyone who eats caviar regularly is an easy sell. (2) Caviar *deserves* it. (3, and least romantically) There is a chemical reason for it.

Caviar is the roe of the sturgeon, a huge, dinosaur-era fish with armored plates instead of scales. The sturgeon lives primarily in the Caspian and Black Seas although there is a growing supply of good American caviars from farm-raised sturgeon and other fish. The Caspian coastline used to be monopolized by Iran and the Soviet Union but is now shared by Iran, Russia, Kazakhstan, Turkmenistan, and a smidgen of Azerbaijan.

Of three main species of Caspian sturgeon, the beluga is largest (up to 1,700 pounds) and has the largest eggs, ranging in color from light to dark gray to black. Next largest is osetra, which can grow to

500 pounds and has grayish, gray-green, or brown eggs. The smallest is sevruga (up to 250 pounds), with small, greenish black eggs.

Because caviar can contain anywhere from 8 to 25 percent fat (and lots of cholesterol), it is perishable and must be preserved with salt. The highest quality caviars contain no more than 5 percent by weight of added salt. They are called *malassol*, which is Russian for lightly salted.

Therein lies the problem: salt is corrosive. It can react with silver and steel spoons to produce traces of compounds that reputedly impart a metallic taste to the caviar.

Spoons made of inert materials have therefore always been used for caviar. Gold, which is impervious to corrosion by salt, is often used, though the time-honored material has been mother-of-pearl, the hard, white, lustrous substance called *nacre* of which pearls and the inner surfaces of mollusk shells are made.

But this is the twenty-first century. We now have an extremely inexpensive material that is every bit as nonreactive, noncorroding, and flavorless as mother-of-pearl. We call it plastic. Luckily, a variety of plastic spoons are available just for the asking at fast-food restaurants, although I need not to point out that they were not intended for caviar.

As a public service, I have researched the caviar suitability of spoons from Wendy's, McDonald's, KFC, and Dairy Queen. (Taco Bell doesn't provide spoons. They provide *sporks*: utensils shaped like spoons with tinesat the ends. Remember the Owl and the Pussy-cat's runcible spoon? It was a kind of spork.) Alas, all of these spoons were too big. Eventually I found the tasting spoons at Baskin Robbins to be the ideal size—and a pretty pink color to boot. (It's only polite to order some ice cream when you go to acquire your free spoon.)

If you think it sacrilegious to serve caviar from plastic, yet you don't want to spend $600 for a gold-plated Fabergé caviar spoon, try the so-called body shot. Make a fist of one hand, with thumb pointing downward, and place a dollop of caviar onto the web of skin between the thumb and forefinger. Then eat it off your hand and wash it down with a shot of ice-cold Russian or Polish vodka from a narrow tequila glass.

Na zdorovye! Here's to your health!

IT'S A CRUEL, CRUEL WORLD

Are clams and oysters on the half shell still
alive when we eat them?

. . . .

You're on vacation at the shore, right? Seafood restaurants abound. Many have raw bars, at which hordes of heedless hedonists are slurping hundreds of luckless mollusks that have been forcibly demoted from bivalve to univalve status. It's only natural to be squeamish about chomping on a creature so recently relieved of its shielding shells and, gentle soul that you are, you can't help but wonder if they're still alive.

To settle this question once and for all, let me make this definitive statement: Freshly shucked clams and oysters are indeed sort of, kind of, more or less alive, one might say, in a manner of speaking. So if you're one of those people who believe that plants feel pain when you prune them, you may want to skip the rest of this answer.

Consider the lowly clam. He spends his days buried in sand or mud, huddling within his shells, sucking in water through one of his two tubes (siphons), filtering out the yummies (plankton and algae), and spurting the waste water out through the other tube. And, of course, on occasion he reproduces. (Yes, there are boy clams and girl clams.)

But that's just about all he ever does. And by the time he reaches a restaurant, shells tightly clamped against the indignity of being yanked into the atmosphere, he isn't even doing that much. He has no organs of sight or hearing and unquestionably feels neither pleasure nor pain, especially when numbed by being kept on ice. You call that living?

So much for biology. Now for the physics: How do you get the damn things open without killing *yourself*?

AW, SHUCKS!

I bought live clams at the fish market, but had the devil of a time getting them open. Is there any easy way?

. . . .

Almost as much human resourcefulness has been expended on shucking clams as on opening childproof medicine bottles, but with far more injuries. People have seriously recommended everything from hammers, files, and hacksaws to execution in the microwave chamber. But brute force is entirely unnecessary, and microwave heat can seriously compromise their flavor.

To open clams the easy way, put them in the freezer for 20 to 30 minutes, depending on their size; you want to get them very cold but not frozen. In this anesthetized condition, they can't hold on to their shells very tightly. Then, nestling the clam in a towel-protected hand, you press a flat, rounded clam knife—*not* a pointed oyster knife—between the shells at the slight indentation near the more pointed of the two ends. (That's where the clam sticks out its siphons.) Sliding the knife against the inner surface of one shell, you cut the two shell-holding muscles (Techspeak: the adductor muscles), twist the shell off at the hinge and discard it. Then you detach the muscles in the same way from the remaining shell, leaving the clam in it. Add a dollop of half-and-half horseradish and chili sauce and maybe a dash of Tabasco or a spritz of lemon, and slide it into your mouth.

A clam knife. The flat blade is inserted between the shells, whereas an oyster knife is more pointed for "popping" the hinge.

COME CLEAN!

Once on vacation at the shore, I found a few live clams. I took them back to the hotel and asked the kitchen to prepare them for me. I wanted to eat them raw. After eating them, I asked the chef how he had prepared them. He said, "I opened them." Why doesn't this live creature, plucked straight out of its natural habitat, need to be cleaned or something before being eaten whole?

. . . .

They should be, but they really don't have to be. That step is often skipped.

As they arrive from the ocean or the fish market, live clams generally need to be purged. When they were snatched from their snug little beds in the sand, they pulled in their siphons and clamped their shells together tightly, possibly trapping some sand and whatever other jetsam happened to be in the vicinity. Moreover, the clam has an alimentary canal akin to the vein in a shrimp. Although it won't hurt you, it may be a bit gritty and isn't the prettiest thing to eat. Best to clean it out.

So after scrubbing the outsides of their shells, treat your clams to a restful soak in mock seawater—a third of a cup of table salt per gallon of water—with a tablespoon or so of cornmeal stirred in, and leave them alone for about an hour. If you watch quietly (they spook at vibration, not actual sound), you'll see them feeding on the cornmeal and cleaning themselves out. After a while, you'll be surprised at how much ejected debris there will be at the bottom of the container. Leaving them there too long won't do any good, though, because they'll use up the oxygen in the water, slam their gates, and stop purging.

So many cookbooks and magazine articles tell us to purge live clams by soaking them in tap water, either with or without the cornmeal, but a moment's reflection shows how useless that is. Although there are such things as freshwater clams, the ones we're talking about live in salt water. If you were a saltwater clam plunged into fresh water, you'd clam up immediately, not daring to open your shells so much as a crack, hoping that the environment would eventually become more hospitably salty. So soaking clams in unsalted water accomplishes nothing. A soak in salt water of the right salinity, on the other hand, fools the clams into thinking they're back home, whereupon they will stick out their siphons, feed, and purge themselves of debris.

Some restaurants skip the purging step, and their clams can be gritty. That's less important if the clams are to be cooked, but sand in the bottom of the chowder bowl is a tip-off to this kitchen shortcut. At least you'll know that the chowder was made from real live, rather than canned or frozen, clams.

Soft-shell clams, or steamer clams, have big siphons ("necks") and can't close their shells completely. They will therefore always have some sand in them. That's why you swish them in clam broth before dipping them in melted butter and eating them.

BETWEEN A ROCK AND A CARAPACE

*Clam and oyster shells are hard as a rock, but
shrimp and crab shells look like thin plastic.
Why the difference?*

. . . .

We call them all shells because they are worn on the outside, but when we talk about "shellfish," we're including two totally different classes of animals: crustaceans and mollusks.

Among the crustaceans are crabs, lobsters, shrimps, and prawns. Their shells are horny, flexible plates of hinged "armor." The top covering of a crab or lobster is called its carapace. (I had to throw that in to justify the pun in the heading.)

Crustaceans make their thin shells out of mostly organic matter—chitin (KITE-in), a complex carbohydrate that they manufacture from the foods they eat. You won't enjoy knowing this, but shrimps, crabs, and lobsters are closely related to insects and scorpions, which also make their outer crusts of chitin. (If that grosses you out, be aware that many biologists now prefer to believe that crustaceans and insects evolved independently. Biologists like seafood, too, you know.)

On the other hand, bivalve mollusks—clams, oysters, mussels, scallops, and other critters that live between pairs of hard shells—make their shells out of mostly inorganic minerals that they take out of the ocean, primarily calcium carbonate, the same versatile substance that limestone, marble, and eggshells are made of. The next time you have a whole clam or mussel on your plate, notice the curved growth lines or ridges that are parallel to the outer edges. These represent the successive additions of new shell material, deposited by the animal whenever it grew enough to need more room, usually during the warm seasons.

The Shell Game

Mussels in White Wine

Mussels are nature's fast-food gifts from the sea. They are beautiful to behold in their ebony shells, decorated with concentric growth lines. They cook almost instantly (they're done when their shells pop open) and are very low in fat and high in protein. Their texture is meaty, and they taste of the sea, a little briny and slightly sweet.

Farm-raised mussels (*Mytilus edulus*) from Maine are available in two-pound bags at many fish markets and better supermarkets. But if you can find them, the biggest, plumpest, juiciest, and most flavorful mussels we have ever eaten are the Mediterranean mussels (*Mytilus galloprovincialis*), raised in the state of Washington by Taylor Shellfish Farms.

In either case, cultivated mussels are grit-free and barnacle-free, and need only a light brushing before cooking. Most of the dark, steel-wooly beards have been removed. A light tug removes any that may remain protruding between the shells.

Use the same wine for cooking and drinking.

---

2   **pounds mussels, cleaned and debearded**
1   **cup dry white wine, such as sauvignon blanc, sancerre, or muscadet**
¼   **cup minced shallots**
2   **cloves garlic, minced**
½   **cup parsley, chopped**
2   **tablespoons salted butter**

---

1. Rinse the mussels in tap water, pulling off any protruding beards by tugging away from the hinge. Discard any mussels whose shells are parted and don't close up promptly when struck with another mussel. They are either dead or moribund, and will spoil very quickly.

2. To a large, deep pot with a tight-fitting cover, such as a large stockpot, add the wine, shallots, garlic, and parsley. The pot must be large enough to

accommodate the mussels after their shells open, plus some shaking room; allow at least twice their precooked volume. Bring the wine to a boil, then reduce the heat to low and simmer for about 3 minutes. Increase the heat to high. Add the mussels; cover tightly and cook, shaking the pan several times until the mussels open, 4 to 8 minutes, depending on the pot and mussel size.

3. Remove the mussels from the liquid with a slotted spoon or skimmer and divide between 2 large soup bowls. Quickly swirl the butter into the pan liquid to make a slightly emulsified sauce.

4. Pour the broth over the mussels and serve immediately with crusty bread and the chilled white wine.

SERVES 2

The two different kinds of shells in crustaceans and mollusks mean that the creatures have to devise two different strategies for growth. Mollusks, which grow by adding more material to the outer edges of their shells, in effect let out their pants, while crustaceans manufacture whole new suits.

When a crab or lobster gets too big for its breeches, it molts: It splits the seams of its shell, crawls out, and makes a new one in a larger size. If we catch one just after the act of disrobing, we may be treated to the Epicurean delight of a soft-shell crab or lobster. The "soft shells" are the new shells in the earliest stages of construction.

The Atlantic blue crab, for example, needs twenty-four to seventy-two hours to complete this construction job, which gives salivating predators like us just enough time to catch them—which isn't easy, because being shorn of their armor, they hide in the eel grass and have to be scraped out. But if we're lucky, we can catch them out in the open just before they molt. Skilled watermen can tell at a glance when a crab is getting close to shedding its shell, and when such "peelers" are found, they're kept in a special pen until the deed is done.

And then what do we do with them? Why, we cook them as soon as possible and eat the whole things. Why spend time picking the meat out of a shell when we can find crabs without shells? All we have to do is three little cleanup steps, which are best done while the crabs are still alive.

Okay, if you're squeamish get your fishmonger to do it for you. But here's what needs to be done. (1) Tear off and discard the abdominal apron (see below). (2) Cut off and discard the eyes and mouth parts, which are on the long side between the two big claws. (3) Lift up the pointed tips to find and remove the feathery gills or, as exuberant folklorists like to call them, the devil's fingers. They call them that because gills are effective filters for any toxic impurities that might be in the water, and eating them can be risky. Besides, they don't taste very good. And what about "all that yellow-green stuff" inside the crabs? Don't ask. Just eat it. It's delicious.

Male blue crabs are generally bigger than females, and are used mostly for steamin' and pickin', while the females are used more for canning. How do you tell a male crab from a female, you ask? Look at the underside, and you'll see an "apron," a thin flap of shell that covers most of the abdomen. If the apron is shaped exactly like the Capitol dome in Washington, D.C. (honest!), it's a mature female, or sook. If the apron is shaped like the Eiffel Tower in Paris, it's a male, or jimmie. But if it's a young, immature female, the apron looks like a Capitol dome with a bit of Eiffel Tower at the top. During the last molting before maturity, she discards the tower part.

Oh, and have you ever wondered why those drab, blackish green crab and lobster shells turn red when cooked? The red color, a chemical called astaxanthin, is present but not visible in the uncooked shells because it is tied up (Techspeak: complexed) with certain proteins to form blue and yellow compounds that together look green. When heated, the astaxanthin-protein complex breaks up, releasing free astaxanthin.

She Sells Soft-Shells by the Seashore

Sautéed Soft-Shell Crabs

Some chefs like to show off by gussying up their crabs with batter, bread crumbs, cracker meal, flour dustings, or spices. None of that is necessary. In fact, they smother the delicate flavor of a really fresh crab. Save the seasonings for the table. All you need are fresh, live crabs, bubbling butter, and a little respect. Allow 2 large or 3 small crabs per serving.

If the crabs haven't been cleaned by your fishmonger, tear off and discard the abdominal apron, cut off and discard the eyes and mouth parts, which are on the long side between the two big claws, and lift up the pointed tips to find and remove the feathery gills.

Heat a skillet over medium-high heat.

Add a lump or two of unsalted butter and when it foams and sizzles, slide in the crabs. Don't crowd the pan.

Sauté until golden brown, about 2 minutes. Season with salt and pepper. Turn with tongs, season, and cook the other side for about 2 minutes longer, until nicely colored and crisp. Serve at once.

IT'S MAINE-LY A MATTER OF OPINION

Some people say the best way to cook a live lobster is to boil it. Others insist that steaming is better. Which method should I use?

. . . .

To find an authoritative answer, I went to Maine and interviewed several leading chefs and lobstermen. I found two distinct camps: the staunch steamers and the passionate plungers.

"I plunge," defiantly declared the chef at a well-known French restaurant. He plunges his lobsters into boiling water laced with white wine and lots of peeled garlic.

But according to the chef at another eminent restaurant, "Boiling extracts too much flavor from the lobsters. You can even see the water turn green from the tomalley [liver] that leaks out. We steam our lobsters over fish stock or vegetable broth."

The chef at a renowned inn at first pledged allegiance to the "boiling-draws-out-flavor" school of thought and said he steams his lobsters over salted water. "They wind up with less water inside," he said. But when pressed, he said that for flavor "both boiling and steaming are good. Arguing over it is splitting hairs."

The latter sentiment was echoed by the owner of a venerable lobster pound, who has been fishing, selling and cooking lobsters for forty years. "I used to steam them for about twenty minutes," he said. "I have customers who insist that they absolutely must be steamed over salted water. Everybody has an opinion. Now I boil them in seawater for about fifteen minutes." A believer in the philosophy that the customer is always right, he refused to list either to port or starboard and recommend one method over another.

My conclusion? *Double, double, toil and trouble; lobster steam or lobster bubble.* It's a draw.

The one thing that everybody seemed to agree upon, though, is that steaming takes longer. Why, I wondered? Theoretically, when water boils, the steam should be the same temperature as the water. But are they, really? To answer this question I repaired to my kitchen "laboratory."

I put a few inches of water into a three-gallon lobster pot, brought it to a boil, covered the pot as tightly as one must when steaming foods, and then measured the temperature of the steam at several distances above the water's surface with an accurate laboratory thermometer. (How I managed to rig the thermometer bulb inside the covered pot while I read the temperatures from outside will be explained upon receipt of a self-addressed, stamped envelope and a check or money order for $19.95 to help defray my medical expenses.)

Results? With the burner set high enough to maintain the water at a rolling boil, the temperatures at all distances above the water were exactly the same as that of the boiling water: 210°F. (No, not 212. My kitchen, along with the rest of my house, is one thousand feet above sea level, and water boils at lower temperatures at higher altitudes.)

But when I turned the burner down to a slow boil, the steam temperature dropped substantially. My explanation is that some of the steam's heat is always being lost through the side of the pot (which in this case was rather thin), and the water has to be boiling fast enough to keep replenishing that heat with fresh, hot steam.

Conclusion: Steam your lobsters on a rack over vigorously boiling water in a tightly covered, heavy pot and they will be exposed to exactly the same temperature as if they were being boiled.

The mystery, then, is why all the cooks tell me they steam lobsters for a somewhat longer time than when they boil them. In his comprehensive book *Lobster at Home* (Scribner, 1998), for example, Jasper White recommends boiling a 1½ -pound lobster for 11 to 12 minutes or steaming it for 14 minutes. (These times are shorter than the Maine chefs reported because they cook several lobsters in a batch and it's a simple case of more meat, more heat.)

The answer, I believe, lies in the fact that liquid water can hold more heat (Techspeak: it has a higher heat capacity) than steam does at the same temperature, so it has more heat to donate to the lobsters. Moreover, liquid water is a much better conductor of heat than steam is, so it can deliver those calories more efficiently into the lobsters and they will cook in a shorter time.

Now, I'm not a chef. But on the other hand, chefs are not scientists. So the chefs I interviewed can be excused for making some scientifically erroneous statements. Here are a few of them and why they're wrong.

"Steaming makes a higher cooking temperature than boiling." As my experiments showed, the temperatures are the same.

"Salted water makes higher-temperature steam." Well, perhaps a trifle, because the boiling temperature is higher, but by a few hundredths of a degree at most.

"Sea salt in the steaming water gives a better flavor to the steam."
Salt does not leave the water and enter the steam, so the type of salt—
or no salt at all can have no effect. I even doubt that the essences of
wine or stock in the steaming water could penetrate the lobster's
shell enough to have any effect on the flavor of the meat. Lobsters are
well-armored beasts.

Here's how Chip Gray, a native Down-Easter, told me he cooks
lobsters at the shore: First, procure a 4- to 6-foot length of stovepipe
at a hardware store. At the shore, build a campfire. Now plug one end
of the pipe with seaweed and throw in a couple of lobsters and a
handful of clams. Stuff in a second plug of seaweed and top it with
more lobsters and clams. Continue alternating seaweed and shellfish
until you run out of either lobsters or stovepipe. Top it all off with a
final plug of seaweed and lay the pipe across the campfire. As the food
cooks, baste it continually with a cup or two of seawater poured into
the higher end of the pipe; it'll turn to steam as it rolls down to the
bottom. After about 20 minutes, dump the contents of the stovepipe
out onto a sheet on the ground.

"It's wicked good," says Chip.

How to Cook a Lobster

Boiled Live Lobster

At the fish market, select one lively, tail-flipping, claw-raising lobster per person. (You pick up a lobster by grasping its back, behind the head.) If it droops when picked up, forget it and come back another day; it's not fresh.

Take the lobsters home in a container that allows lots of breathing space and keeps them cool. Even though they're aquatic, they can live in the air for several hours if kept cool and moist.

Select a covered, deep stockpot big enough to contain the lobsters completely immersed in water. (Use 3 quarts of water per 1½ to 2 pounds of lobster, taking into account that the pot should be filled no more than three-quarters full.)

As the moment of truth draws near, add ⅓ cup kosher salt for each gallon of water (to create mock seawater) and bring it to a rolling boil.

Pick up the lobsters one at a time and plunge them in head first. Cover, return to the boil, then reduce the heat and simmer. A 1¼-pound lobster will take about 11 minutes; 1 pound, about 8 minutes; 2 pounds, about 15 minutes. Do not overcook, or the delicate meat will toughen.

With tongs, remove the lobster from the water, being careful not to let it slip back into the water and splash. Place on a paper- or cloth-covered counter.

Drain the excess water from the lobster by punching a small hole between the eyes with the tip of a small knife. Prop each lobster in a pot or in the sink with its head down so that the liquids drain from the carcass. This makes less of a mess when the lobster is opened.

Whisk to the table and serve with melted butter and lemon wedges.

Chapter Six

Fire and Ice

....

Look around the kitchen at all your modern conveniences: your toaster, your blender, your food processor, your coffee grinder, your mixer, your coffeemaker—all devices that you use only now and then for specialized purposes.

Now look at the only two appliances in your kitchen that you use daily and couldn't do without: one that makes heat and one that makes cold. Compared with your food processor, you might not think of your stove and refrigerator as modern appliances, but they are surprisingly recent additions to the human arsenal of cooking and food-preserving equipment.

The first kitchen range, an enclosure containing a burning fuel (initially, coal) that heats a flat surface for cooking, was patented less than 375 years ago, heralding the end of more than a million years of cooking over open fires. And the electric refrigerator replaced ice for cooling only within the memories of some of the readers of this book.

When you bring fresh food home from the market, you may put it in the refrigerator, whose low temperatures will keep it from spoiling. Then you may use the stove's high temperatures to convert some of that food into a form that is more palatable and digestible. After you've cooked and served the food, you may put some of the leftovers back into the refrigerator or freezer to keep. And some time later, you may take them out of the refrigerator and heat them up again. The manipulation of foods in our kitchens seems to involve a continual round of heating and cooling, of using figurative fire and ice. Only today, we do those jobs with gas and electricity.

What do heat and cold do to our foods? How can we control them to produce the best results? We can burn our food with too much heat, but on the other hand the freezer can "burn" it with . . . well, what *is* freezer burn, anyway? And just what is going on when we perform that most elementary of all cooking operations, the boiling of water? There's more to it than you may think.

HOT STUFF

C IS FOR CALORIE

*I know that a calorie is a unit of heat, but why
does eating heat make me fat? What if I ate
only cold foods?*

. . . .

A calorie is a much broader concept than just heat; it's an amount of any kind of energy. We could measure the energy of a speeding Mack truck in calories, if we wanted to.

Energy is whatever makes things happen; call it "oomph" if you wish. It comes in many forms: physical motion (think Mack truck), chemical energy (think dynamite), nuclear energy (think reactor), electrical energy (think battery), gravitational energy (think waterfall), and yes, the most common form of all, heat.

It's not heat that's your enemy; it's energy—the amount of energy-for-living that your body gets by metabolizing food. And if metabolizing that cheesecake produces more energy than you use up in walking from the refrigerator to the TV, your body will store the excess energy as fat. Fat is a concentrated storehouse of energy, because it has the potential of giving off lots of heat when burned. But don't jump to any conclusions. When an advertisement promises to "burn off fat," it's only a metaphor; a blowtorch is not a feasible weight-loss device.

How much energy is a calorie, and why do different foods "contain" (that is, produce) various numbers of calories when metabolized?

Since heat is the most common and familiar form of energy, the calorie is defined in terms of heat—how much heat it takes to raise the temperature of water by a certain amount. Specifically, as the term is used in nutrition, a calorie is the amount of heat it takes to raise the temperature of one kilogram of water by 1 degree Celsius.

(Chemists, as opposed to nutritionists and dieticians, use a much smaller "calorie," only one-thousandth as big. In their world, the nutritional calorie is called a *kilocalorie*. But in this book I use the word *calorie* to mean the common one that food books, food labels, and diets talk about.)

Here's an idea of how much heat a calorie is: A nutritional calorie is the amount of heat it would take to raise the temperature of a pint of water by 3.8°F.

Different foods, as everyone knows, provide us with different amounts of food energy. Originally, the calorie contents of foods were measured by actually burning them in an oxygen-filled container immersed in water and measuring how much the water's temperature went up. (The apparatus is called a calorimeter.) You could do the same thing with a serving of apple pie to find out how many calories it releases.

But is the amount of energy released when a slice of pie is burned in oxygen the same as the amount of energy released when it is metabolized in the body? Remarkably, it is, even though the mechanisms are quite different. Metabolism releases its energy much more slowly than combustion does, and mercifully without flames. (Heart-burn doesn't count.) The overall chemical reaction is exactly the same, however: Food plus oxygen produces energy plus various reaction products. And it's a basic principle of chemistry that if the initial and final substances are the same, then the amount of energy given off is the same, regardless of how the reaction took place. The only practical difference is that foods aren't digested or "burned" completely in the body, so we actually get out of them somewhat less than the total amount of energy they would release by being burned in oxygen.

On the average, we wind up getting about 9 calories of energy from each gram of fat and 4 calories from each gram of protein or carbohydrate. So instead of running into the lab and setting fire to every food in sight, nutritionists these days just add up the numbers of grams of fat, protein and carbohydrate in a serving and multiply by either 9 or 4.

Your normal basal metabolism rate—the minimum amount of energy you use up just by breathing, pumping your blood around, digesting your food, repairing your tissues, keeping your body temperature normal, and keeping your liver and kidneys, etc., doing their jobs—is about 1 calorie per hour for every kilogram (2.2 pounds) that you weigh. That's about 1,600 calories per day for a 150-pound male. But that can vary quite a bit depending on sex (women require about 10 percent less), age, health, body size, shape, and so on.

Among other things, weight gain depends on how much your intake of food energy above and beyond your basal metabolism rate exceeds your expenditure of energy by exercise, not counting fork-lifting. For an average healthy adult the National Academy of Sciences recommends a daily intake of 2,700 calories for men and 2,000 for women—more for jocks and fewer for couch potatoes.

The hopeful theory about eating cold, calorie-deprived food has been bandied about in various forms for some time, but unfortunately, it won't work. One variation that I've heard is that drinking ice water will help you lose weight because you must expend calories in warming the water up to your body temperature. That's true in principle, but trivial. Warming an 8-ounce glass of ice water up to body temperature uses less then 9 calories, the equivalent of a single gram (one 454th of a pound) of fat. If dieting were that simple, "fat-farm" spas would have ice-water swimming pools. (Shivering also uses up energy.) And unfortunately, while most substances shrink when their temperatures are lowered, people don't. Not for long, anyway.

THE EFFECTS OF FUDGE ON DIETING

If there are nine calories in a gram of fat, that means that there are more than 4,000 calories in a pound (454 grams) of fat. But I've read that in order to lose a pound of fat I must cut my intake by only 3,500 calories. Why the discrepancy?

. . . .

Not being a nutritionist, I asked Marion Nestle, professor and chair of the Department of Nutrition and Food Studies at New York University.

"Fudge factors," she said.

First of all, the actual energy content of a gram of fat is closer to 9.5 calories. But that would only make the discrepancy bigger. The fact is that the number of calories of energy we get from eating a gram of fat is quite a bit less than that because of incomplete digestion, absorption, and metabolism. That's one fudge factor.

"Another fudge factor," Nestle continued, "is applied to the number of calories in a pound of body fat. The idea is that body fat is only about 85 percent actual fat." The rest consists of connective tissue, blood vessels, and other stuff that you'd probably rather not know about.

Thus, in order to lose a pound of real-life blubber, your bottom line, so to speak, is that you must deprive yourself of only about 3,500 calories.

And stay away from the fudge.

REALLY HAUTE CUISINE

> *My husband, daughter, and I will be returning to La Paz, Bolivia, to adopt another baby. Because of the high altitude, boiling water can take hours to cook things. Is there any rule of thumb about how long it takes to cook something at various altitudes? And will boiling bottles at this altitude kill germs?*

. . . .

The elevation at La Paz runs from 10,650 to 13,250 feet above sea level, depending on which part of town you're in. And as you are aware, water boils at lower temperatures at higher elevations. That's because in order to escape from the liquid and boil off into the air, water molecules have to fight against the downward pressure of the atmosphere. When the atmospheric pressure is lower, as it is at higher altitudes, the water molecules can boil off without having to get as hot.

The boiling temperature of water decreases about 1.9°F for every 1,000 feet above sea level. So at 13,000 feet, water will boil at 187°F. Temperatures above 165°F are generally thought to be high enough to kill most germs, so you should be okay on that score.

It's hard to generalize about cooking times, because different foods behave differently. I'd suggest asking the locals how long they cook their rice, beans, and the like. Of course, you can always schlep a pressure cooker onto the airplane and manufacture your own high-pressure atmosphere at will.

Baking is a whole different ball game. For one thing, water evaporates more readily at high altitudes, so you will need to add more water to doughs and batters. And because there is less pressure to hold down the carbon dioxide gas released by baking powder, the gas can rise clear out the top of your cake, leaving it flat. So you must use less baking powder. All this can be very tricky. My advice is to leave the baking to the local *pastelerías*.

PROJECT HEAD-START

*My husband claims that warm water takes longer
to boil than cold water, because it is in the
process of cooling as you place it on the stove.
I think that's ridiculous. But he took physics in
college and I didn't.*

. . . .

What grade did he get in physics? Apparently, your intuition is paying off better than his tuition, because you're right and he's wrong.

I can guess what he's thinking, though. Something about momentum, I'll bet, because if an object is already falling—in temperature, presumably—it should require extra time and effort to turn it around and make it rise. You first have to kill its downward momentum.

That's all very well and true for physical objects, but temperature isn't a physical object. When the weather report says that the temperature is falling, we hardly expect to hear a crash.

Temperature is just our artificial human way of expressing the average speed of the molecules in a substance, because their speed is what makes a substance hot; the faster its molecules are moving, the hotter it is. We can't get in there and clock the speed of every single molecule, so we invented the concept of temperature. It's really little more than a handy number.

In a pot of warm water, the zillions of molecules are flitting about at a higher average speed than in a pot of cold water. Our job in heating the pot is to give more energy to those molecules and make them move even faster—eventually fast enough to boil off. Obviously, then, warm molecules will require less added energy than cold ones, because they're already partway to the finish line: the boiling point. So the warm water will boil first.

And you can tell him I said so.

Using hot tap water for cooking may be unwise for another reason. Older houses may have copper water pipes that are joined with lead-containing solder. Hot water can leach out tiny amounts of lead, which is a cumulative poison. So it's a good idea always to use cold water to cook with. Yes, it'll take longer to boil, but since you may live longer you can spare the time.

PUT A LID ON IT!

My wife and I disagree on whether a pot of water will boil sooner if you keep the lid on. She says it will, because without the lid a lot of heat would be lost. I say that it will take longer to boil, because the lid increases the pressure and raises the point at which water will boil, as in a pressure cooker. Who's right?

. . . .

Your wife wins, although you do have a point.

As a pot of water is heated and its temperature goes up, more and more water vapor is produced above the surface. That's because more and more of the surface molecules gain enough energy to leap off into the air. The increasing amount of water vapor carries off an increasing amount of energy that could otherwise go into raising the water's temperature. Moreover, the closer the water gets to its boiling temperature, the more energy each water vapor molecule carries off, so the more important it becomes not to lose them. A pot lid partially blocks the loss of all those molecules. The tighter the lid, the more hot molecules are retained in the pot and the sooner the water will boil.

Your point, that a lid increases the pressure inside the pot as in a pressure cooker, thereby raising the boiling point and delaying the actual boiling, is correct in theory but insignificant in reality. Even a tightly fitting, hefty one-pound lid on a ten-inch pot would raise the pressure inside by less than a tenth of a percent, which would in turn raise the boiling point by only four hundredths of a degree Fahrenheit. You could probably delay the boiling longer by watching the pot.

REDUCING ISN'T EASY

The other day I was making a glaze by reducing veal stock down to a small fraction of its volume. But it seemed to take forever! Why is it so hard to reduce a stock?

. . . .

Evaporating water sounds like the simplest thing in the world. Why, just leave a puddle of water standing around and it evaporates all by itself. But that takes time, because the necessary calories won't flow into the water very fast from the room's relatively cool air. Even on the stove, where you're feeding lots of calories into a stockpot from a hot burner, you might have to simmer for an hour or more to accomplish that maddeningly simple-sounding recipe instruction to "reduce by half."

Reducing an excess amount of water can be every bit as frustrating as reducing an excess amount of body fat, in that it is much harder to get rid of than you'd expect. To boil off even a small amount of water requires a surprising amount of heat energy.

Here's why.

Water molecules stick very tightly to one another. It therefore requires a lot of work, that is, the expenditure of a lot of energy, to separate them from the bulk of the liquid and send them flying off into the air as vapor. For example, in order to boil off a pint of water, that is, to convert it from liquid to vapor after it is already at the boiling point, your range burner must pump more than 250 calories of heat energy into it. That's the amount of energy a 125-pound woman would use up in climbing stairs nonstop for 18 minutes. Just to boil off one pint of water.

You can, of course, turn up the burner to add heat more rapidly. The temperature of the liquid will never rise above its boiling point, but it will bubble more vigorously and more bubbles will carry off more steam. It's unwise to do that to a stock, however, unless you have already strained and defatted it. Until then, boiling, as opposed to gentle simmering, will break up solids into tiny pieces and fat into tiny, suspended globules, both of which will muddy up the liquid. A better way to speed things up is to transfer the liquid to a wider, shallower pan. The more surface area the liquid has, the more of it is exposed to the air and the faster it can vaporize.

WHY YOU CAN'T COOK OVER A CANDLE

I'm shopping for a new range, and all the literature keeps talking about "Btu's." I know they have to do with how hot the burners will get, but exactly what should those Btu numbers mean to me?

. . . .

A Btu is an amount of energy, just as a calorie is an amount of energy. Both are most commonly used to measure amounts of heat.

The Btu, which stands for British thermal unit, was invented by engineers, so while it makes sense to the guys who design the stoves, it doesn't mean much to us in the kitchen. But by sheer luck it turns out to be almost exactly one quarter of a nutritional calorie. So, for example, the 250 calories that it takes to boil off a pint of water is equal to 1,000 Btu.

Another example: The total amount of heat given off by the burning of an average candle is about 5,000 Btu. That's the amount of chemical energy the wax inherently contained, and the combustion process converts that chemical energy into heat energy. But a candle releases its heat slowly over a period of several hours, so it's no good for cooking. In case you've been wondering, that's why you can't sauté a hamburger over a candle.

For cooking, we need a lot of heat delivered in a short period of time. Range burners are therefore rated according to how fast they can pump out heat, expressed as *Btu per hour* at their top settings. The confusion comes when people neglect to say "Btu per hour" and just say "Btu." But the burners' Btu ratings are not *amounts* of heat; they are the maximum *rates* at which they can pump out heat.

Most home gas or electric range burners produce from 9,000 to 12,000 Btu per hour. The gas burners in restaurant kitchens are capable of putting out heat twice as fast, because for one thing their gas-supply pipes are bigger and can feed in more gas per minute. Also, restaurant ranges generally have several concentric burner rings instead of just one. Chinese restaurants that need to do high-temperature wok cooking have broad gas burners that spew out heat like a dragon with a mouthful of habanero peppers.

Remember that to boil off a pint of water from a stock requires 1,000 Btu of heat? Well, using your 12,000-Btu-per-hour burner, that should take one-twelfth of an hour or five minutes. But you know that it takes a lot longer than that. The reason is that most of the heat emitted by the burner is wasted. Rather than going directly into the liquid in the pan, most of it goes into heating up the pan itself and the surrounding air. Put two different pots of food on two identical burners set at identical levels and they will heat and cook quite differently depending on their shapes and sizes, what materials they're made of, how much and what kinds of foods they contain, and so on. That's why you have to keep your eye on the pot and continually adjust the burner for every specific situation.

> When shopping for a range, look for one that has at least one burner rated at 12,000 or preferably 15,000 Btu per hour. With that much heat output you'll be able to boil water in no time, sear meats quickly, and stir-fry in your wok or stir-fryer like a Chinese chef.

WINE, OR WINE NOT?

When I cook with wine or beer, does all the alcohol
burn off, or does some remain, which could be a
problem for a strict teetotaler, such as a
recovering alcoholic?

. . . .

Does the vino lose its power in the Crock-Pot overnight?
In a flambé baked Alaska, does the brandy lose its bite?
Does the alcohol all burn off, as the cookbooks say it does?
Or can you eat a plate of coq au vin and get a little buzz?
Well, <u>when</u> you cook with wine or cook with brandy,
    here's the scoop:
There will always be some alcohol remaining in the soup.

Many cookbooks assert that all or virtually all of the alcohol "burns off" during cooking (what they mean is that it evaporates; it won't burn unless you light it). The standard "explanation," when there is one, is that alcohol boils at 173°F, while water doesn't boil until 212°F, and therefore the alcohol will boil off before the water does.

Well, that's just not the way it works.

It's true that pure alcohol boils at 173°F and pure water boils at 212°F. But that doesn't mean that they behave independently when mixed; each affects the boiling temperature of the other. A mixture of alcohol and water will boil at a temperature that's somewhere between 173 and 212 degrees—closer to 212 if it's mostly water, closer to 173 if it's mostly alcohol, which I certainly hope is not the case in your cooking.

When a mixture of water and alcohol simmers or boils, the vapors are a mixture of water vapor and alcohol vapor; they evaporate together. But because alcohol evaporates more readily than water, the proportion of alcohol in the vapors is somewhat higher than it was in the liquid. The vapors are still very far from pure alcohol, however, and as they waft away from the pan, they're not carrying off very much of the alcohol. The alcohol-loss process is much less efficient than people think.

Exactly how much alcohol will remain in your pan depends on so many factors that a general answer for all recipes is impossible. But the results of some tests may surprise you.

In 1992 a group of nutritionists at the University of Idaho, Washington State University, and the USDA measured the amounts of alcohol before and after cooking two Burgundy-laden dishes similar to *boeuf bourguignon* and *coq au vin*, plus a casserole of scalloped oysters made with sherry. They found that anywhere from 4 to 49 percent of the original alcohol remained in the finished dishes, depending on the type of food and the cooking method.

Higher temperatures, longer cooking times, uncovered pans, wider pans, top-of-the-stove rather than closed-oven cooking—all conditions that increase the general amount of evaporation of both water and alcohol—were found, not surprisingly, to increase the loss of alcohol.

Do you think you're burning off all the alcohol as you march triumphantly into your darkened dining room bearing a tray of blazing cherries jubilee or *crêpes suzette*? Well, think again. According to the

1992 test results, you may be burning off only about 20 percent of the alcohol before the flame goes out. That's because in order to sustain a flame, the percentage of alcohol in the vapor must be above a certain level. Remember that you had to use a high-proof brandy and warm it to make more alcohol vapor before it would even ignite. (You can't light wine, for example.) When the alcohol burns down to a certain, still-substantial level in the dish, the fumes are no longer flammable and your fire goes out. That's show biz.

How much weight should you give these test results when trying to accommodate your guests?

One thing you should consider is the dilution factor. If your recipe for six servings of *coq au vin* calls for 3 cups of wine, and if about half of the alcohol cooks off during a 30-minute simmer (as the researchers found), each serving will wind up with the amount of alcohol in two ounces of wine. On the other hand, those same 3 cups of wine in a six-serving *boeuf bourguignon* that simmers for three hours and loses 95 percent of its alcohol (according to the test results) will wind up giving each diner the alcohol equivalent of only two-tenths of an ounce of wine.

Still, *some* alcohol is still alcohol. Use your judgment.

HOT ENOUGH FOR YA?

Does it ever really get hot enough to fry an egg on the sidewalk?

. . . .

It's unlikely. But scientific opinion has never been known to discourage people from trying to prove an age-old urban legend.

When I was a kid in The Big City in the days before air conditioning, at least one newspaper would cook up an egg-on-the-sidewalk story sometime during the "silly season"—the dog days of summer, when even bank robbers were too lazy to make news and reporters had little to do. But to my recollection no one ever claimed to have actually pulled off the egg trick.

That hasn't stopped the 150 citizens of the old Mojave Desert mining town of Oatman, Arizona, from holding an annual solar egg-frying contest every Fourth of July by the side of the fabled Route 66. According to Oatman's exalted Egg Fry Coordinator, Fred Eck (get it?), the contestant who comes closest to cooking an egg in 15 minutes by sun power alone wins.

An occasional egg has indeed been cooked in Oatman, but the rules allow such gimmicks as magnifying glasses, mirrors, aluminum reflectors, and the like. No fair, I say. We're talking here about breaking an egg directly onto the ground and leaving it alone.

A couple of years ago, finding myself in Austin, Texas, during a heat wave, I determined to find out whether it was possible to fry an egg on a sidewalk without any optical or mechanical aids. In order to draw meaningful conclusions, I had to measure the sidewalks' temperatures. Fortunately, I had with me a wonderful little gadget called a non-contact thermometer. It's a little gun that you point at a surface and when you pull its trigger, it instantly reads out the temperature of that surface, anywhere from 0°F to 500°F. The so-called MiniTemp, manufactured by Raytek in Santa Cruz, California, works by analyzing the amount of infrared radiation being emitted and/or reflected from the surface; hotter molecules emit more infrared radiation. My MiniTemp was an ideal tool for the sidewalk cooking experiment, because I already knew how hot it has to be to cook an egg, and if you keep on reading, so will you.

On a particularly scorching day I went around measuring the mid-afternoon temperatures of a wide variety of sidewalks, driveways, and parking lots, trying not to upset any Texans by looking as if I were pointing a real gun.

The ground temperatures varied quite a bit depending, not unexpectedly, on the darkness of the surface. Blacktop paving was much hotter than concrete, because dark objects absorb more light and therefore more energy. So there goes one cherished notion about outdoor egg-fries; you'd have a better chance in the middle of a blacktop street than on the sidewalk.

Although the air temperatures hovered around 100°F, I never found a surface hotter than about 125°F on concrete or 145° on blacktop (remember that number). In either case, the temperatures plunged almost immediately when the sun went behind a cloud (okay, a cloud went in front of the sun), because much of the infrared radiation coming from the surfaces is simply solar radiation that is being reflected back. Bright, shiny metal surfaces, in fact, reflect so much solar radiation that the MiniTemp won't give accurate readings of their temperatures.

Now it was time for the crucial experiment. I had previously taken an egg from the refrigerator and warmed it to room temperature. I cracked it directly onto the 145°F surface of an asphalt-paved parking lot at high noon. I didn't use cooking oil, which might have cooled the surface too much. Then, I waited.

And waited.

If you don't count the odd glances I received from passersby, nothing whatsoever happened. Well, maybe the egg white became slightly thicker at the edges, but there wasn't anything remotely resembling cooking. The surface just wasn't hot enough to cook an egg. But why not, I wondered?

First of all, only the white of the egg, or albumen, was in contact with the hot surface—the yolk floats on the white—so it's a matter of what temperature might be required to cook the albumen. And what do we mean by "cook," anyway? Egg white is a mixture of several kinds of protein, each of which is affected differently by heat and coagulates at a different temperature. (You expected a simple answer?)

But in an eggshell, it all boils down to this: Egg white begins to thicken at about 144°F, it ceases to flow at 149°F, and it becomes fairly firm at 158°F. Meanwhile, a yolk will begin to thicken at 149°F and lose its fluidity at 158°F. So to cook an entire egg to a non-runny, sunny-side-up condition, you'd want both the white and the yolk to reach 158°F and to stay there long enough for the rather slow coagulation reactions to take place.

Unfortunately, that's quite a bit hotter than any reasonably attainable ground temperatures. But more important, when you break a 70°F egg onto the 145°F ground it cools the surface down considerably, and there is no continual replenishment of heat from below, as there would be in a frying pan over a fire. Also, pavement is a very poor conductor of heat, so none can flow in from the surroundings. Thus, even though a parking lot's black surface might get close to the coagulation temperature of 158°F on a really, really hot day, I'm afraid that actually cooking an egg on a sidewalk must forever remain but a midsummer night's dream.

But wait! The roof of one sun-baked, dark blue, 1994 Ford Taurus station wagon measured 178°F, more than hot enough to coagulate both white and yolk. And because steel is a good conductor of heat, that temperature could be maintained by heat feeding into the egg from other parts of the roof. Maybe cars, rather than streets and sidewalks, were the way to go.

Indeed, after I wrote about my experiments in my newspaper column, a reader wrote to tell me that in a World War II German newsreel he saw two Afrika Korps soldiers fry an egg on the fender of a tank. (Austin's streets were mercifully free of tanks, although some SUV's came close.) "They cleaned off a spot," he wrote, "poured on a little oil, spread it around and then broke two eggs onto the surface. The whites turned opaque just as quickly as they do in my frying pan."

I checked the Almanac and found that the highest weather temperature ever recorded was 136°F on September 13, 1922, in El Azizia, Libya, not far from that German tank.

Another reader reported that she and some friends once cooked an egg on a sidewalk in Tempe, Arizona, when the air temperature was 122°F, although she didn't measure the temperature of the sidewalk.

"The egg came straight out of the refrigerator," she wrote. "We cracked it directly on the sidewalk and immediately the white started cooking. In less than 10 minutes the yolk broke . . . and spread out and the whole egg cooked. We thought maybe it was a fluke that the yolk broke, so we tried another one and the yolk broke on that one, too, in about the same amount of time."

Now, of course, I had to figure out why the yolks broke and spoiled the possibility of preparing sunny-side-up street food. I could only guess, but my reader gave me a clue.

"We went back inside the house," she continued, "and a little while later my friend told us we'd better go clean up the eggs before her husband got home, so we went back outside. The eggs were completely dehydrated and broken into little pieces and there were a bunch of ants carrying off the pieces; we had nothing to clean up."

Aha! That's the answer: *dehydration*. In Arizona, the humidity can be so low as to be almost nonexistent, so liquids evaporate and dry up in a flash. What must have happened is that the surface of the egg yolk quickly dried out, became brittle, and cracked open, spilling its still-liquid contents. Eventually, the whole egg schmear dried out and cracked into small platelets, like mud does in a dry lake. The platelets were just the right size for the happy ants to cart off to wherever it is that ants take their afternoon tea.

The wonderful thing about science is that it can even explain things that nobody needs to know.

PLAYING WITH FIRE

What's the best kind of fire for grilling: charcoal or gas?

. . . .

The answer to that question is an unequivocal "It depends." You can make burned-on-the-outside, raw-on-the-inside chicken equally well over charcoal or a gas flame.

As in all cooking, what matters is how much heat the food ultimately absorbs; that's what determines its done-ness. Grilling infuses the necessary amount of heat by subjecting the food to a very high temperature for a short period of time, so a small difference in cooking time can make all the difference between succulence and cinders.

But the main reason that grilling is so tricky is that the temperature is hard to control. It's easy to adjust a gas flame, but with charcoal you have to adjust the temperature continually by such antics as moving the food sideways to a hotter or cooler location, raising or lowering the grilling rack, and bunching up the charcoal to make it hotter or spreading it out to make it cooler. And the rules of the game differ, depending on whether you're using a covered grill or cooking topless.

The ingredients of any fire are two: fuel and oxygen. If there isn't enough oxygen available, the combustion process will be incomplete and some unburned fuel will show up as smoke and yellow flame. The yellow color comes from unburned carbon particles that are heated to incandescence. Because combustion is never 100 percent complete, there will also be some poisonous carbon monoxide, instead of carbon dioxide, produced. That's why you should never barbecue or grill indoors, no matter how cute your hibachi.

For cooking, we want complete combustion, so it's essential that the fuel receive enough air. (Smoked foods are made by deliberately starving the heated wood of oxygen.) In a well-adjusted gas grill, the gas is automatically mixed with the right amount of air on its way to the burner; in charcoal grills, you have to manipulate the vent openings.

When the cave persons discovered fire and grilled their first mastodonburgers, wood was undoubtedly the fuel. But wood contains resinous and sappy substances that don't burn completely and therefore produce dirty flames. Hardwoods contain less of these substances, and hardwood is still preferred for grilling by purists who believe that there's no fuel like an old fuel and who value the unique, smoky flavor that a wood fire imparts.

The fuelish question that most people ask is whether to burn charcoal or gas—and, of course, which equipment to burn it in. These days, the equipment can range anywhere from a fire-escape hibachi to a suburban behemoth equipped with everything but tail fins and radar.

Charcoal is wood that has been heated at a high temperature, but in the absence of air so it can't actually burn. All the sap and resins are decomposed or driven off, leaving almost pure carbon that will burn slowly, quietly, and cleanly. Natural hardwood charcoal, still wearing the shapes of the chunks of wood it was made from, contains no additives and imparts no off-flavors to the food. Charcoal briquettes, on the other hand, are manufactured from sawdust, wood scraps, and coal dust, held together with a binder. Coal is far from pure carbon, however; it contains an assortment of petroleumlike chemicals whose smoke can affect the flavor of food.

The cleanest-burning fuel of all is gas, either the propane sold in tanks or so-called natural gas (methane) that's piped into our houses. Gas grills are made for both kinds. The gases contain no impurities to speak of, and they burn to produce essentially nothing but carbon dioxide and water.

But what about that "charcoal flavor" that everyone values so highly? Can you really get it by cooking over a gas flame?

That wonderful grilled flavor comes not from the charcoal but from the intense browning that takes place on the seared surface of the food because of the very high temperature. It also comes from melted fat, which drips down onto a hot surface—a glowing briquette or a gas grill's lava stones or porcelain bars—is vaporized, and sends its smoke back up to condense on the surface of the food.

But if too much fat drips you'll have flare-ups, which are undesirable because fat, although a great fuel, doesn't have the time or oxygen to burn completely, and it therefore produces a sooty, yellow flame that licks at your food, charring it and depositing horrible chemicals and unpleasant flavors. To avoid burning at the steak, trim off most of the fat beforehand and if a flare-up nevertheless occurs, move the meat off to the side until the flames subside.

Then there's the problem of getting a charcoal fire started. No fuel will start burning until it gets hot enough for some of it to vaporize. Only then can its molecules mix with oxygen molecules in the air and react with them in the heat-producing reaction called combustion. Once the combustion reaction gets going, the heat it releases keeps vaporizing more fuel and the whole process becomes self-sustaining.

Gas, of course, is already vaporized, so all you need is a spark or a match to get it going. But the bugaboo of charcoal grilling is getting the stuff hot enough to accomplish that all-important initial vaporization. Enter starter fluid, the fuel that kindles fuel. Starter fluid is a petroleum-derived liquid that lies somewhere between gasoline and fuel oil. If you wait about a minute for it to soak into the charcoal before lighting it, most of its fumes will be absorbed. But in my opinion charcoal is the world's champion odor retainer (it's used in water purifiers and gas masks), and the starter smell never really burns off

A chimney-type charcoal starter. Crumpled newspapers are
ignited through the holes at the bottom.

completely. Electric loop starters work slowly but well, if you have electricity handy. But in my opinion the best way of starting a charcoal fire is the newspaper-fueled chimney, which is both fast and odorless. You just stuff some newspaper into it, load it with charcoal, light the paper, and in 15 or 20 minutes the charcoal will be well ignited and ready to be dumped into the grill.

The most burning question of all, however, is which fuel, gas or charcoal, is better? Well, which political party is better? There are staunch partisans of each. I personally prefer charcoal for two reasons. One, there are too many puny gas grills on the market that don't produce much more heat than a Zippo lighter. And two, while burning charcoal produces only carbon dioxide, burning gas produces carbon dioxide and water vapor. Although I haven't done any experiments, I believe that the water vapor might prevent the food from getting as hot as a charcoal fire would make it, and high, dry heat is the absolute essence of successful grilling.

Oven-"Grilled" Vegetables

Roasting the Garden

Outdoor grilling is great for meats and fish, but grilling most vegetables can be a problem. Put them on the grate and they tend to fall through into the fire; put them on skewers and some parts will burn while others steam.

Roasting vegetables in a hot oven is a lot easier. It results in nicely browned, tender vegetables with a flavor much like grilled, but sweeter. You can roast an assortment of brilliantly colored vegetables and serve them in the same dish in which they were roasted, a wide, shallow, ovenproof baking dish or casserole. Or you can roast them on a baking sheet and transfer them to a serving dish. The various vegetables will all cook in the same amount of time, because they are approximately the same size.

---

2 large Vidalia or sweet onions, peeled and scored across the top

1 whole red pepper, halved, cored, ribs and seeds removed

1 whole yellow pepper, halved, cored, ribs and seeds removed

1 whole medium green zucchini, stem removed

1 whole medium yellow squash, stem removed

4 ripe plum tomatoes, halved and seeded

3 large whole carrots, peeled

6 thick asparagus spears

1 head of garlic, top sliced off

Extra-virgin olive oil

Coarse salt

Thyme sprigs and basil leaves for garnish

---

1. Preheat the oven to 400°F. Wash all the vegetables and arrange attractively in a shallow, wide ovenproof dish that is pretty enough for the table. Or arrange them in a single layer on a baking sheet with sides. Drizzle all over with olive oil.

2. Roast on a low shelf in the oven for about 50 minutes to an hour, until the edges of the vegetables are somewhat browned. Remove the baking dish or tray and allow the vegetables to cool.

3. If you used a baking sheet, transfer the vegetables to a serving platter. To arrange for serving, cut the onions into quarters. Rub off the skins of the peppers with your fingers, and cut the flesh into large segments. Slice the zucchini, squash, tomatoes, and carrots into chunks or strips. Leave the asparagus and garlic head whole. Be sure to save all the accumulated juices and spoon them back over the vegetables.

4. Drizzle the vegetables with extra-virgin olive oil and sprinkle with coarse salt. Garnish with the herbs. Serve at room temperature or warm, with toast made from a hearty bread. Butter the bread with the soft, roasted garlic cloves.

MAKES ABOUT 4 SERVINGS

REAL COOL STUFF

UNFREEZING YOUR ASSETS

*What's the best and fastest way to defrost
frozen foods?*

. . . .

I know what you mean. You come home after a hard day's work. You don't feel like cooking, and you can't face the hassle of going to a restaurant. Where do you turn?

To the freezer, of course. And like a crowd of football fans, a little voice in your head begins to chant, "DEE-frost! DEE-frost!"

Scanning your frozen assets, you're wondering not so much about what is in there ("Why didn't I label those packages?"), but about what would defrost in a minimum amount of time.

Your options are (a) leaving it out on the kitchen counter while you go through the mail, (b) soaking it in a sink full of water or (c) the best and fastest method of all, which I shall divulge in due time and which, I promise, will astound you.

For commercially packaged frozen foods, just follow the directions. You wouldn't believe the armies of home economists and technicians who slaved away to determine the best methods of defrosting their company's products in the home kitchen. Trust them.

While the defrosting directions on commercial packages often involve a microwave oven, that usually doesn't work for thawing home-frozen foods, because it's hard to keep the outer regions of the food from beginning to cook.

"Frozen food" is something of a misnomer. Technically speaking, freezing means converting a substance from its liquid form into its solid form by cooling it below its freezing point. But meats and vegetables are already solid when they are put into the freezer. It's their water content that freezes into tiny ice crystals, and those ice crystals are what make the whole food hard. The job of defrosting, then, is to melt those tiny ice crystals back to their liquid form.

How do you melt ice? Why, you heat it, of course. Your first problem, then, is to find a source of low-temperature heat. If that phrase sounds paradoxical, please realize that heat and temperature are two very different things.

Heat is energy, the energy that moving molecules have. All molecules are moving to some extent, so heat is everywhere, in everything. Even an ice cube contains heat. Not as much as a hot potato, but some.

On the other hand, temperature, as I have pointed out earlier, is just a convenient number by which we humans express how fast the molecules are moving. If the molecules of one substance are moving faster, on the average, than those of another, we say that the first substance has a higher temperature, or is hotter, than the other.

Heat energy will travel automatically from a warmer substance into an adjecent, cooler one, because the faster molecules in the warmer one can bang against the molecules of the cooler one, making *them* move faster. Obviously, then, we could warm our frozen food most quickly by putting it in contact with a hot substance, such as the air in a hot oven. But that would cook the outer parts of the food before much heat could penetrate into the inner parts.

The air in your kitchen is at a very moderate temperature compared with the air in a hot oven, but it still contains a lot of heat that can be tapped to defrost frozen food. So should we just leave the food out in the air? No. It would take too long for the air to transfer its heat, because air is just about the worst conductor of heat that you can imagine. Its molecules are just too far apart to do much banging against other molecules. Besides, slow air-thawing is dangerous because bacteria can grow rapidly on the outside portions that are first to thaw.

How about soaking in water? Water is a much better heat conductor than air is, because its molecules are much closer together. If the food package is waterproof (and if you're not sure, seal it in a zipper-top bag after pressing out most of the air), then by all means soak it in a bowl—or in the case of a whole chicken or turkey, a sink or bathtub—full of cold water. Since the frozen bird will make the water even colder, change the water every half hour or so and the whole process will go even faster.

The quickest method of all, I now reveal, is to place the unwrapped frozen food on an unheated, heavy skillet or frying pan. Yes, unheated. Metals are the champion heat conductors of all substances, because they have zillions of loose electrons that can transmit energy even better than clashing molecules can. The metal pan will conduct the room's heat very efficiently into the frozen food, thawing it in record time. The heavier the pan the better, because thicker metal can conduct more heat per minute. Flat foods like steaks and chops will thaw fastest, because they make the best contact with the pan, so keep this in mind when making up your packages for the freezer. (Round, bulky roasts and whole chickens or turkeys won't thaw much faster on the pan than on the counter; however, neither method is recommended because of the danger of bacterial growth. Thaw them either in cold water or in the refrigerator.) Non-stick pans won't work, incidentally, because the coatings are poor heat conductors, nor will a cast-iron pan because it is porous.

I discovered the frying-pan gimmick while experimenting with one of those "miracle" defrosting trays sold in catalogs and cookware stores. They are reputedly made of an "advanced, space-age super-conductive alloy" that "takes heat right out of the air." Well, the space-age alloy turns out to be ordinary aluminum (I analyzed it), and it "takes heat out of the air" exactly the way an aluminum frying pan does, and for exactly the same reasons.

So save the water method for the bulky stuff and just put that frozen steak or fillet on a heavy frying pan. It'll be thawed before you can say, "Where did I put those frozen peas?" Well, not quite, but a lot sooner than you'd think.

HOW TO MAKE A COOL BUNCH OF DOUGH

Why do cookbooks recommend rolling out pastry dough on a marble surface?

. . . .

Pastry dough must be kept cool during rolling so that the shortening—most often a solid fat such as butter, lard, or Crisco—doesn't melt and soak into the flour. If it does, your piecrust will have the texture of a shipping carton. Flaky pastry is produced when many thin layers of dough are kept separated from one another by layers of fat. In the oven the separated dough layers begin to set, and by the time the fat melts, steam from the dough will have forced the layers permanently apart.

Marble is recommended for the rolling surface because, according to the books, it is "cool." But that's playing fast and loose with the concept of temperature, because the marble isn't one bit cooler than anything else in the room.

But, you protest, the marble *feels* cold. Yes, it does. And so does the "cold steel" of your chef's knife and every one of your pots, pans, and dishes. In fact, run into your kitchen right now (I'll wait), pick up anything at all except the cat and hold it against your forehead. By George, everything feels cold! What's going on here?

What's going on is that the temperature of your skin is about 95°F, while the temperature of your kitchen and everything in it is around 70°F. Is it any surprise, then, that things should feel cold if they actually are 25 degrees colder than your skin? When you touch such an object, heat flows from your skin into the object, because heat always flows from a higher temperature to a lower one. Your heat-deprived skin then sends the message "I feel unusually cool" to your brain.

So it's not that the object is cold; it's that your skin is hot. As Einstein never said, "Everything is relative."

But all things won't feel equally cold, even though they are all at the same 70°F room temperature. Go back to the kitchen, please. Notice that the steel blade of your chef's knife feels colder than, say, the wooden cutting board. Is it actually colder? No, because the two objects have been in the same environment long enough to have come to the same temperature.

The steel knife blade feels colder on your forehead than the wooden cutting board does because steel, like all metals, is a much better conductor of heat than wood is. When in contact with your skin, it conducts heat away into the room much faster than the wood can, thereby cooling your skin faster.

Marble isn't as good a heat conductor as metal, but it's ten to twenty times better than a wood or plastic-laminate countertop. Just as marble feels cold to your skin because it steals away heat, the marble feels cold also to the pastry dough because it removes the rolling-generated heat rapidly. Thus, the dough doesn't warm up enough to melt the shortening.

Okay, okay, so I'm splitting hairs. If something feels cold, acts cold, and does everything but quack like a cold duck, why the heck can't we just say that it's cold? So be my guest. Say that marble is cold. But take secret pleasure in the knowledge that it isn't strictly correct.

Cold-Rolled Pastry

Easy Empanadas

In Spanish, *empanada* means "breaded," derived from *pan*, meaning bread. But that's a bit misleading, because in Latin America today an empanada is a filled pastry—almost any kind of pastry made from flour or cornmeal and filled with almost anything imaginable, but usually with meats or seafoods of some kind. We might call them turnovers or individual meat pies, and they can be either baked or deep-fried. Every Latin American country has its own versions. They go together quickly if you organize your work area like an assembly line.

In this variation, a traditional filling is wrapped in store-bought puff pastry instead of homemade pastry crust. This avoids the effort of making dough. But with puff pastry it's particularly important to do the rolling on a "cool" surface such as marble. If marble is not available, roll it out as quickly as possible on a wooden board.

You will find frozen puff pastry sheets in the freezer section of your supermarket. Ground turkey or chicken can be substituted for the beef.

One 17-ounce package frozen puff-pastry sheets

1 tablespoon olive oil

½ cup finely chopped onion

½ cup finely chopped red bell pepper

1 clove garlic, finely minced

1 pound lean ground beef

2 teaspoons all-purpose flour

1 tablespoon chili powder

1 teaspoon salt

½ teaspoon hot pepper flakes

½ teaspoon dried oregano

½ teaspoon ground cumin

¼ teaspoon ground cloves

Freshly ground pepper to taste

3 tablespoons ketchup

1 large egg yolk mixed with 1 tablespoon water

1. Thaw the puff pastry for 8–12 hours in the refrigerator.

2. Heat the oil in a large skillet over medium-high heat and cook the onion and pepper until soft, 5 minutes. Add the garlic and cook 1 minute longer. Add the ground meat and cook until it is browned and crumbles, about 5 minutes. Pour off the accumulated fat. Remove from the heat.

3. In a small bowl, stir together the flour, spices, and seasonings. Add to the meat mixture and mix well. Add the ketchup and mix again. Check the seasonings. It should be spicy.

4. Transfer the mixture to a 10- by 15-inch cookie tray, and spread it out in a thin layer to cool. The empanadas are quickly made if you take an assembly line approach. Divide the filling into 18 small portions of 2 tablespoons each. Here is one way: Using a metal spatula, push the filling into 3 long rows, then divide each row into 6 sections so that the filling is now in 18 small portions. Set aside until needed.

5. Preheat the oven to 400°F.

6. Remove one thawed puff pastry sheet from the refrigerator. Place it on a well-floured work surface. The sheet will be rather stiff. As soon as it is just warm enough to be unfolded without cracking, open it out flat. Dust both sides with a little flour.

7. With a sharp knife, cut the pastry sheet into three long strips along the fold lines. Cut each strip into three 3-inch squares. Using a rolling pin, roll each square into a 5- by 5-inch square. Flour the squares lightly and stack them to one side. Repeat with the second sheet of pastry. You will have 18 squares.

8. Make the empanadas: Place one square of pastry on the floured surface. Using a small, soft brush, paint a ½-inch strip of egg wash on the left and bottom edges of the square. Place one portion of the meat mixture onto the square slightly toward the brushed corner. Fold over the other half of the pastry to make a triangular turnover. Press the cut edges together. With the tines of a fork, pinch the edges together to seal. With a sharp knife, cut off the ragged

edges, if necessary. Transfer the turnover to a baking sheet. Repeat until all of the pastry and filling are used.

9. Lightly brush the empanadas with the remaining egg wash. With the tip of a small knife, poke two holes in the top of each so that steam can escape. Bake for 18 to 20 minutes until puffed and browned. Wrap individually and freeze.

MAKES 18 EMPANADAS

HOT WATER FREEZES FASTER!

My guests were due to arrive for a party in three hours and I needed to make some ice in a hurry. I've heard that hot water freezes faster than cold water. Should I have put hot water in my ice-cube trays?

. . . .

The hot-water-freezes-faster paradox has been debated since at least the 17th century when Sir Francis Bacon wrote about it. Even today, Canadians claim that a bucket of hot water left outdoors in cold weather will freeze faster than a bucket of cold water. Scientists, however, have been unable to explain why Canadians leave buckets of water outdoors in cold weather.

But believe it or not, hot water really may freeze faster than cold water. Sometimes. Under certain conditions. It depends on a lot of things.

Intuitively, it seems impossible because the hot water simply has further to go in its downhill race toward 32°F. In order to chill down by each four degrees, a pint of water has to lose about one calorie of heat. So the more degrees the water has to fall, the more heat must be taken out of it, and that means a longer cooling time, all other things being equal.

But according to Wolke's Law of Pervasive Perversity, all other things are never equal. As we'll see, hot and cold water are different in more ways than their temperatures.

When cornered and pressed for an explanation of how hot water could possibly freeze first, chemists are likely to mumble something about cold water containing more dissolved air, and dissolved substances lower the freezing temperature of water. True, but trivial. The amount of dissolved air in cold tap water would lower its freezing temperature by less than a thousandth of a degree Fahrenheit, and no hot-cold race can be controlled that precisely. The dissolved-air explanation just doesn't hold water.

A real difference between hot and cold water is that the hotter a substance is, the faster it radiates its heat away into the surroundings. That is, warmer water cools off at a faster rate—more degrees per minute—than cooler water does. The difference is especially great if the containers are shallow, exposing large surfaces of water. But that still doesn't mean that the hot water will reach the finish line first, because no matter how fast it cools off at first, the most it can do is catch up with the cold water. After that, they're neck and neck.

A more significant difference between hot and cold water is that hot water evaporates faster than cold water. So if we start by trying to freeze equal amounts of hot and cold water, there will be less water remaining in the hot-water container when it gets down to rug-cuttin' time at 32°F. Less water, naturally, will freeze in less time.

Can that really make a significant difference? Well, water is a very unusual liquid in many ways. One of those ways is that an unusually large amount of heat must be removed from water before its temperature will go down very much. (Techspeak: Water has a high heat capacity.) So even if the hot container has lost only slightly more water by evaporation than the cold container has, it may require a lot less cooling time to freeze.

Now don't go running into the kitchen to try it with ice-cube trays, because there are simply too many other factors operating. According to Wolke's Law, the two trays can never be identical. They are not in exactly the same place at exactly the same temperature, and they are not necessarily being cooled at the same rate. (Is one closer to the cooling coils in the freezer?) Moreover, how are you going to tell exactly when the water freezes? At the first skin of ice on top? That doesn't mean that the whole tray full has yet reached 32°F. And you can't peek too often, because opening the freezer door can cause unpredictable air currents that will affect the evaporation rates.

Most frustrating of all, undisturbed water has the perverse habit of getting colder than 32°F before it freezes. (Techspeak: It supercools.) It may refuse to freeze until some largely unpredictable outside influence perturbs it, such as a vibration, a speck of dust, or a scratch on the inside surface of its container. In short, you're running a race with a very fuzzy finish line. Science isn't easy.

But I know that won't stop you. So go ahead and measure out equal amounts of hot and cold water, put them in identical (ha!) freezer trays, and don't bet too much on the outcome.

HUMPTY DUMPTY NEVER HAD IT SO BAD

Can raw, whole eggs be frozen? I have almost two
dozen eggs that I won't be able to use up before I go
on a trip and I'd hate to have them go to waste.

. . . .

I hate to see food go to waste too, but in this case freezing the eggs might cause more trouble than they're worth. For one thing, the shells will probably crack because, as you might expect, the whites expand when they freeze, just as water does when it turns to ice. There's nothing you can do about that. There may also be some deterioration of flavor, depending on how long you keep them in the freezer.

More troublesome is the fact that the yolks will be thick and gummy when you thaw them out. That's called gelation—the formation of a gel. It happens because as the eggs freeze, some of the proteins' molecules bind themselves into a network that traps large amounts of water, and they can't unbind themselves when thawed. The thickened egg yolks won't be very good for making custards or sauces, where smoothness of texture is important. Using thick-yolked eggs in other recipes can be risky, and if a recipe bombs, you'll be wasting a lot more than a few eggs.

Next time, leave them in the fridge if your trip isn't going to last more than a couple of weeks, or hard-cook them all before you leave.

Manufacturers of prepared foods use tons of frozen eggs in making baked goods, mayonnaise, and other products. The gumminess is prevented by adding 10 parts of salt or sugar to every hundred parts of shelled, beaten eggs before they are frozen. I suppose you could do that too if you wanted to take the trouble, but the salt or sugar would sure limit your use of the eggs.

BURN, BABY, FREEZE!

What actually happened to food that is freezer-burned?

. . . .

"**F**reezer burn" has to be one of the more ridiculous oxymorons going. But take a good look at that emergency pork chop that's been in your freezer much longer than you ever intended. Doesn't its parched and shriveled surface look as if it had been seared?

The dictionary tells us that *seared* doesn't necessarily refer to heat; it means withered or dried out, no matter what did the drying. Notice that the patches of "burn" on your forlorn pork chop are indeed dry and rough, as if all the water had been sucked out.

Can the cold alone make frozen foods dry out, especially when the water is in the form of ice? Yes indeed. While your hapless chop was languishing in the freezer, something was stealing water molecules from its icy surface.

Here's how water molecules, even when firmly anchored in solid ice, can be spirited off to another location.

A water molecule will spontaneously migrate to any place that offers it a more hospitable climate. And to water molecules, that means a place that's as cold as possible, because that's where they will have the least amount of heat energy, and "all other things being equal" (see Wolke's Law of Pervasive Perversity on page 209), Nature always favors the lowest energy. So if the food's wrapping isn't absolutely molecule-tight, water will migrate through it, from the ice crystals in the food to any other location that happens to be the tiniest bit colder, such as the walls of the freezer. (That's why nonfrost-free freezers have to be defrosted.) The net result is that water molecules have left the food, and the food's surface is left parched, wrinkled, and discolored. Burned-looking.

This doesn't happen overnight, of course; it's a slow process that takes place molecule by molecule. But it can be slowed to practically zero by using a food-wrapping material that blocks wandering water molecules. Some plastic wraps are better at this than others.

Moral No. 1: For the long-range keeping of frozen foods, use a wrapping material specifically designed for freezing because of its impermeability to migrant water molecules. Best of all are vacuum-sealed, thick plastic packages like Cryovac, which are quite impermeable to water vapor. Freezer paper is obviously good; it has a moisture-proof plastic coating. But ordinary plastic food wraps are made of various materials, some better than others. Polyvinylidine chloride (Saran Wrap) is the best, and polyvinyl chloride (PVC) is also good. Read the fine print on the plastic wrap package to learn what it is made of. Thin polyethylene food wraps and ordinary polyethylene food-storage bags aren't very good, but polyethylene "freezer bags" are okay because they're unusually thick.

Moral No. 2: Wrap the food tightly, leaving no air pockets. Any air space inside a package will allow water molecules to float through it to the inner wall of the wrapping where it is colder, and settle there as ice.

Moral No. 3: When buying already-frozen foods, feel for ice crystals or "snow" in the space inside the package. Where do you think that water (to make the ice) came from? Right: the food. So either it's become dehydrated from being kept too long in a loose package or it's been thawed, which releases juices from the food, and then re-frozen. In either case, it's been abused and, while still safe to eat, will have an off flavor and poor texture.

BLOWING HOT AND COLD

Why does blowing on hot food cool it?

. . . .

As we have all learned from experience when the etiquette police were looking the other way, the cooling of hot food by blowing on it works best with liquids, or at least with wet foods. You won't substantially diminish the heat of a hot dog by blowing on it, but hot tea, coffee, and soup are notorious for inspiring such gauche table manners. In fact, it works so well that there must be something more going on than the mere fact that the blown air is cooler than the food.

What's going on is evaporation. When you blow, you're speeding up the evaporation of the liquid, just as blowing on nail polish dries it faster. Now everyone knows that evaporation is a cooling process, but almost no one seems to know why.

Here's why.

The molecules in water are moving around at various speeds. The average speed is reflected in what we call the temperature. But that's only an average. In reality, there is a wide range of speeds, some molecules just poking along while others may be zipping around like a Taipei taxi. Now guess which ones are most likely to fly off into the air if they happen to find themselves at the surface. Right. The zippy, high-energy ones. The hotter ones. So as evaporation proceeds, more hot molecules are leaving than cool ones, and the remaining water becomes cooler than it was.

But why blow? Blowing on the surface speeds up evaporation by whisking away the newly evaporated molecules and making room for more. Faster evaporation makes faster cooling.

Miss Manners just doesn't appreciate some of the applications of science to gastronomy.

Chapter Seven

Liquid Refreshment

. . . .

I N CHEMISTRY 101 we all learned that matter comes in three physical forms (Techspeak: states of matter): solid, liquid, and gas. And so do our foods, although most of our foods aren't purely one or the other.

Stable combinations of solid and gas are called foams and sponges, porous solid structures filled with bubbles of air or carbon dioxide and usually made by beating and whipping. Think of breads, cakes, meringues, marshmallows, soufflés, and mousses. If it can soak up large quantities of water without dissolving, as breads and cakes do, it's a sponge, whereas if it breaks down and dissolves in water as a meringue does, it's a foam.

Stable combinations of two liquids that don't ordinarily mix, such as oil and water, are called emulsions. In an emulsion, one of the liquids is dispersed through the other one in such tiny globules that they stay suspended and don't settle out. The prime example is mayonnaise, a flavored mixture of vegetable oil, egg or egg yolks (which are half water), and vinegar or lemon juice. It is made by adding the oil gradually and beating it vigorously into the watery egg and vinegar mixture. The oil breaks down into tiny droplets that will not separate from the egg and vinegar.

Beverages are foods in the liquid state. They are invariably water-based, but may contain various amounts of another liquid: ethyl alcohol, also known as grain alcohol because it is most easily and economically produced by fermentation of the starches in grains such as corn, wheat, and barley. Fermentation, from the Latin *fervere*, meaning to boil or bubble, is the chemical breakdown of an organic substance by enzymes released by bacteria and yeasts while feeding on it. Various types of fermentation produce various products, but the word is most often used for the conversion of starches and sugars into ethyl alcohol and bubbles of carbon dioxide gas.

Alcohol fermentation has been used for making beer from starches and wines from fruit sugars for at least ten thousand years. Our earliest ancestors quickly discovered that all they had to do was leave some crushed grapes or other fruits around in a warm place and the juices would ferment, developing an intriguing intoxicating quality.

In this chapter we will look at three main types of beverages: hot water extracts of plant materials; beverages containing carbon dioxide gas, whether naturally present from fermentation or deliberately added because we get a kick out of its fizziness; and beverages containing alcohol, whether directly from fermentation or deliberately enhanced by distillation to provide a bigger kick of a different sort.

On, then, to our coffees, teas, sodas, Champagnes, beers, wines, and spirits. *Skoal!*

HAVE A CUPPA'

DON'T BLAME THE COFFEE

Can you tell me how to find the lowest-acid coffee?
I'm looking for something that isn't bitter and
won't tear my stomach apart.

. . . .

Acidity often gets a bum rap. Maybe it's because of all the television commercials for drugs designed to control heartburn and acid reflux. But the acid in our stomachs (hydrochloric acid) is thousands of times stronger than any acid you'll find in coffee. It's only when the acid gets out of the stomach, splashing up into the esophagus, that it burns. In some people, coffee makes that happen, but it's not the coffee's acid that's burning; it's the stomach's.

Several of the weak acids in coffee are the same as those found in apples and grapes, and are not at all stomach-upsetting. But if you're still not convinced, most of these acids are volatile and are released upon roasting, so it may surprise you to know that the darkest roasts may have the lowest acid content.

The citric, malic, acetic, and other acids in coffee add liveliness to the flavor, not bitterness. Acids in general are not bitter; they're sour. Caffeine is bitter, but it contributes only about 10 percent of the bitterness in coffee. And don't turn your nose up at bitterness; it's an important flavor component of coffee, just as it is in the other two essential food groups, beer and chocolate.

So forget about acid, and just find a coffee you like. If all coffees "tear your stomach apart," I don't have to tell you what to do. Just say "No."

JANGLED BELLE

*When my wife has a cup of espresso, she's high
for hours. Does espresso contain more caffeine
than regular coffee?*

. . . .

It depends. (You knew I was going to say that, didn't you?)

A direct comparison is complicated by the fact that there is no such thing as "regular coffee." We have all had everything from vending-machine dishwater to truck-stop battery acid. Even at home, there are so many ways of brewing coffee that no generalizations can be made.

And let's face it: In our current Starbucks-struck society, what goes by the name of espresso in every neighborhood joint that can scrape up the price of a machine and a minimum-wage teenager to run it would make a professional Italian *barista* (espresso maker) cry in his *grappa*. So there's not much consistency there, either.

Any espresso is, of course, a lot smaller in volume than a standard cup of American coffee. But does the espresso's high concentration more than make up for its small volume?

Each drop of liquid in a typical one-ounce shot of espresso certainly contains more caffeine—and more of everything else, for that matter—than a drop of liquid from a six-ounce cup of regular coffee. But in many instances, the entire cup of well-brewed American coffee will contain more total caffeine than the cup of espresso. (Notice that I said "well-brewed." I'm not talking about that brown water they call coffee at your office, which may contain not only a tiny amount of caffeine but a tiny amount of coffee.)

What do the experts say? The consensus of Francesco and Riccardo Illy in their beautifully illustrated coffee-table book *From Coffee to Espresso* (Arnoldo Mondadori Editore, 1989) and of Sergio Michel in his book *The Art and Science of Espresso* (CBC srl Trieste, undated) is that a typical cup of good espresso can contain from 90 to 200 milligrams of caffeine, while a cup of good American coffee will contain from 150 to 300 milligrams. As you can see, there may be some overlap, but on the average, espressos contain less caffeine.

The amount of caffeine in any cup of coffee depends first of all on the type of coffee bean it was made from. Arabica beans contain an average of 1.2 percent caffeine, while Robusta beans contain an average of 2.2 percent and as high as 4.5 percent. But unless you're a connoisseur, you may not know the types of beans in your brew, either at the local espresso bar or in your home blend. The odds are that both are primarily Arabica beans, because Arabica constitutes three-quarters of the world's coffee production, although there is currently a shift toward more Robusta for economic reasons.

What's important, of course, is how much of the caffeine dissolves out of the beans and into the water during brewing. That depends on several factors: how much ground coffee is being used, how finely it is ground, how much water is being used, and how long the water is in contact with the coffee. More coffee, finer grounds, more water, and longer contact time will all extract more caffeine. That's where the differences between espresso and other brewing methods come in.

Espresso coffee is ground finer than the drip grind you may be using at home. But on the other hand, for approximately the same amount of grounds per cup, only about one ounce of water contacts the grounds during espresso-making, compared with about six ounces of water per regular cup. Moreover, the water is in contact with the grounds for only about thirty seconds in the espresso process, rather than a couple of minutes in most other brewing methods.

The result is that in your local coffee establishment you will probably imbibe less caffeine in your single shot of espresso or in your Tall Latte or Tall Cappuccino than in your Americano. On the other hand, all bets are off with the Grande and Venti Lattes and Cappuccinos, which are made with two shots of espresso.

Now about your wife: Why is she so high-strung after a cup of espresso? For one thing, it may be her metabolism, that human variable that no simple chemical analysis for 1,3,7-trimethylxanthine, aka caffeine, can explain. There are great variations in the rates of caffeine metabolism among individuals, and according to the Illy book, women tend to metabolize it faster. But that would apply, of course, to any coffee.

I'm not a physician or nutritionist, but I suppose it's possible that in some people the caffeine is metabolized faster when it is concentrated in a small amount of liquid than when it is dispersed throughout a larger volume. On the other hand, a friend tells me that she gets more sleeplessness and more of a "jangly" feeling from her regular coffee than from an espresso.

In the absence of a series of controlled physiological studies on the effects of many kinds of espresso compared with many kinds of other coffee, all consumed both with and without food at various times of day, no one can generalize that espresso causes more caffeine excitability than American coffee. In fact, on the average, it's probably the other way around.

Tell that to your wife when she comes down off the ceiling.

A Double Hit of Caffeine

Mocha Soy Pudding

That vague, raspy noise you hear is the sound of hordes of health-conscious people wringing their hands, baffled about how they might add soy to their daily meals. Even though they'd like to, most people don't have a clue about how to eat more soy. They're not even sure what it is. Try this easy fix, an almost instant, no-cook pudding that partners soy in the form of tofu with the double caffeine whammy of chocolate and espresso. You can substitute Kahlúa for the coffee if you like.

---

1   **cup or 6 ounces semisweet chocolate chips**

1   **(12-ounce) package firm tofu, drained**

¼   **cup soy milk or whole milk**

2   **tablespoons leftover strong coffee or espresso**

1   **teaspoon vanilla**

   Pinch of salt

---

1. Melt the chocolate in the top of a double boiler, heavy saucepan, or microwave-safe bowl in the microwave oven.

2. To the container of a blender, add the tofu, milk, coffee, vanilla, and salt. Blend for 30 seconds.

3. With the motor running, add the melted chocolate and blend until smooth and creamy, about 1 minute. Chill for 1 hour or until ready to serve.

MAKES 1 VERY LARGE OR 4 NORMAL SERVINGS

THE DECAF CHRONICLES

*Are the chemicals used in decaffeinating coffee
really safe? A chemist told me that they're related
to cleaning fluid.*

. . . .

Related, yes, but different. Like my Uncle Leon. In chemical families, as in human families, there are both similarities and idiosyncrasies.

Caffeine itself, for example, is a member of the alkaloid family of powerful plant chemicals that includes such bad actors as nicotine, cocaine, morphine, and strychnine. But then again, tigers and pussycats belong to the same family. The methylene chloride that's used in some decaffeinating processes is related to, but quite different from, the toxic perchlorethylene used in dry cleaning. But it's still no pussycat.

Chemists have identified from eight hundred to fifteen hundred different chemicals in coffee, depending on whom you ask. As you can imagine, removing the 1 or 2 percent of caffeine without ruining the flavor balance of all the others is no small trick. Caffeine dissolves easily in many organic solvents such as benzene and chloroform, but those are obviously out because they're toxic. (No, chloroform wouldn't cancel the caffeine's effects by putting you to sleep.)

Since 1903, when a German chemist named Ludwig Roselius lost sleep over how to remove the caffeine from coffee and finally settled on methylene chloride, that has been the solvent of choice. It dissolves other components minimally and vaporizes easily, so that its remaining traces can be driven off by heat. Herr Roselius marketed his coffee under the name Sanka, a word he invented from the French *sans caffeine*. Sanka was introduced into the United States in 1923 and became a brand name of General Foods in 1932.

But in the 1980s methylene chloride came under fire as a carcinogen. It is still used for decaffeinating, but the FDA limits its amount in the finished product to ten parts per million. Industry sources point out that the actual amount is less than a hundredth of that.

Caffeine is removed from the green coffee beans before they are roasted. First they are steamed, which brings most of the caffeine up to the surface, and then the caffeine is dissolved out by the solvent. To be called decaffeinated, a coffee must have more than 97 percent of its caffeine removed.

An indirect method, sometimes called the water method, is often used: The caffeine—together with many desirable flavor and aroma components—is first extracted into hot water. (Caffeine dissolves in water, of course, or we wouldn't be worrying about its presence in our cups.) The caffeine is then removed from the water by an organic solvent, and the now caffeine-free water, with all of its original flavor components, is returned to the beans and dried onto them. The solvent never actually touches the beans.

An interesting new wrinkle is the use of the organic solvent ethyl acetate instead of methylene chloride. Because this chemical is found in fruits and, indeed, in coffee itself, it can be said to be "natural." The label of an ethyl acetate—treated coffee may therefore claim that it is "naturally decaffeinated." But don't be impressed. A similar claim could be made for using cyanide, because it occurs "naturally" in peach pits.

Much decaffeinated coffee today is made by a recently developed process that extracts the caffeine into familiar, harmless old carbon dioxide, but it's in a peculiar form that chemists call supercritical; it's neither gas, liquid, or solid.

Finally, there's the ingenious "Swiss water process," which washes the beans with hot water that is already fully loaded with all possible coffee chemicals except caffeine, so there's no room for anything but caffeine to dissolve into it from the beans.

How does all this percolate down to your supermarket's coffee aisle?

First of all, you may see the words *naturally decaffeinated* on the can. It may refer to the ethyl acetate method or it may mean nothing at all. Doesn't everything come from Nature? What else should we expect? *Supernaturally* decaffeinated coffee?

Nor do the words *water process* mean much, because water is used in several methods, not just in the Swiss water process.

The best advice is to forget about the technology—they're all safe methods—and choose your decaf on the basis of objective intellectual criteria, such as whether you're more partial to Juan Valdez or Mrs. Olson.

TO TEA OR NOT TO TEA?

In a restaurant, I asked for hot tea and was presented with a box from which to choose any one of a dozen fancy kinds, including lapsang souchong, Darjeeling, jasmine, chamomile, and so on. How many kinds of tea are there, anyway?

. . . .

One. That is, there is only one plant—*Camellia sinensis* and a couple of hybrids thereof—whose leaves can be steeped in hot water to make real tea. They may have different names, depending, among other things, on where they were grown.

Some of those "tea" bags you were offered, such as chamomile, for example, do not contain tea. They contain various other leaves, herbs, flowers, and flavorings that can be steeped in hot water to make an infusion that is properly called a tisane, but that is also unfortunately known as an "herbal tea." When you hear the words *herbal tea*, you're supposed to think, Wow! Herbs. Natural. Healthy. Good. But you could make a tisane out of poison ivy leaves if you wanted to.

Real tea comes in three types, depending on how the leaves were processed: unfermented (green), semi-fermented (oolong), and fermented (black) by the action of enzymes, which oxidize tannin compounds in the leaves. Among the blacks, which are by far in the majority, you'll find Assam, Ceylon, Darjeeling, Earl Grey, English Breakfast, Keemun, and Souchong. Any other names and you're on your own; they may be real teas or they may be whatever someone thinks should taste good when soaked in hot water. The latter probably won't kill you, but only real tea has withstood the test of time without any apparent ill effects except a British accent.

Hot "Tea" That's Not Tea

Fresh Mint Tisane

Do you have an old Chemex coffeepot or one of those postwar (and that would be World War II) upstairs-downstairs glass percolator coffeepots? Either one is perfect for making a mint tisane, often called mint tea, because the herb turns it a brilliant green and you will want to see it. The aroma is at once soothing and refreshing.

---

1 to 2 **handfuls of freshly picked mint**
Boiling water
Sugar to taste

---

1. Wash a handful or two of freshly picked mint and put it into a warm glass coffeepot. Add boiling water to slightly more than cover. Allow to steep for 5 minutes.
2. Pour into tea glasses, sweeten to taste, and inhale deeply before sipping.

A (NOT-SO-) NICE CUP OF TEA

When I make tea with microwave-heated water, why doesn't it taste as good as when I make it with teakettle water?

. . . .

Microwave-heated water isn't as hot as kettle-heated water, even though it may look as if it's boiling.

Water for tea must be boiling hot in order to extract all the color and flavor. Caffeine, for example, won't dissolve in water that's much cooler than 175°F. That's why the teapot—or if you're a bag-at-a-time brewer, the cup—should be preheated, to prevent the water from cooling too much during brewing.

When you've got a full, vigorous boil going in a teakettle you know that all of the water is boiling hot—around 212°F. That's because the heated water at the bottom of the kettle rises, to be replaced by cooler water, which then becomes heated and rises, and so on. So the entire kettleful reaches boiling temperature at pretty much the same time. The bubbling further mixes it, to a uniform temperature.

But microwaves heat only the outer inch or so of the water all around the cup, because that's as far as they can penetrate. The water in the middle of the cup gets hot more slowly, through contact with the outer portions. When the outer portions of the water have reached boiling temperature and start to bubble, you can be tricked into thinking that all the water in the cup is that hot. But the average temperature may be much lower, and your tea will be short-changed of good flavor.

Another reason that kettle-heated water is better is that heating a cup of water to boiling in a microwave oven can be tricky, if not to say risky (see p. 262).

WELL, TAN MY TONGUE!

*What is the brown sludge that forms in my cup
when I make microwaved tea?*

. . . .

*P*atient: *Doc, it hurts when I bend my arm this way.*

Doctor: So don't bend your arm that way.

My answer to your question is similar: Don't make microwaved tea.

The water isn't as hot as if you had used fully boiling water from a kettle. Thus, some of the caffeine and tannins (polyphenols) in the tea don't stay dissolved; they precipitate out as a brown scum. Tannins are a broadly defined category of chemicals that give tea, red

wine, and walnuts that puckering, astringent sensation in the mouth.
They're called tannins because they have historically been used to tan
skins into leather. And that's what they do, in a small way, to the
"skins" of your tongue and mouth.

THE FIZZICS OF CARBONATION

A PHOSPHORIC FUSS

*I just read about a medical study indicating that
teenage girls who drink a lot of soda have weaker
bones than girls who don't drink soda. According
to the article, the researchers speculate that it
might be an effect of "the phosphorus in carbonated
drinks." What is there about carbonation that
involves phosphorus?*

. . . .

Nothing whatsoever. The article shouldn't have generalized to that
extent.

It's a mistaken notion that all carbonated soft drinks are rich in
the chemical element phosphorus (which almost everyone, it seems,
wants to misspell as "phosphorous"). The only thing that all carbonated soft drinks have in common is carbonated water: carbon dioxide
dissolved in water. Beyond that, they contain a wide variety of flavorings and other ingredients.

A few of them, including Coca-Cola, Pepsi-Cola, and some other
colas (sodas containing the caffeine-rich extract of tropical kola
nuts) do contain phosphoric acid. It's a weak acid of phosphorus, just
as the carbonated water itself is a weak acid of carbon: carbonic acid.
All acids taste sour, and the phosphoric acid is there to increase the
acidity and provide a bit more of a tang to set off the sweetness. Phos-

phoric acid is also used to acidify and flavor baked goods, candies, and processed cheeses.

About the bone-weakening effect: Maybe the study was limited to phosphorus-containing colas. Even so, just as one rose does not a summer make, neither does one study prove a cause-and-effect relationship between Cokes and bones.

THE BIG TANG THEORY

*I have read that using powdered Tang in an
empty dishwasher cycle will clean out all the soap
scum and stains. I've also read that Coca-Cola
will remove rust from a tennis net crank.
What on Earth have we been drinking?*

. . . .

I don't know what *you've* been drinking, but there are plenty of riskier beverages out there than Tang and Coke. I'd be concerned about this particular duo only if my stomach were made of soap scum or rust. Just because a chemical does something to one substance doesn't mean it'll do the same thing to another substance. That's what keeps chemists so busy.

It is undoubtedly the citric acid in Tang, Gatorade, and other fruit drinks that dissolves the calcium salts in dishwasher grunge. But it's also citric acid that gives us that nice, tart . . . well, tang. Citric acid is, of course, a perfectly natural and harmless component of citrus fruits. You could probably clean your dishwasher as well by running it on lemonade.

The phosphoric acid in Coca-Cola can dissolve iron oxide (rust). There's nothing special about tennis net cranks, however, except that their rust films are likely to be rather thin because of frequent use. I wouldn't try to rejuvenate a rusty old lawn mower by throwing it into a vat of Coca-Cola.

A BURP IN THE BUCKET

Does belching contribute to global warming?
. . . .

Don't laugh. That's a good question. So good, in fact, that I thought of it myself when I learned that 15.2 billion gallons of carbonated soft drinks and 6.2 billion gallons of beer were consumed in 1999 in the United States. And what do you suppose happened to all the carbon dioxide in those beverages? It was ultimately released into the atmosphere by respiration and eructation—breathing and belching, to be plain-spoken about it.

On the traditional back of an envelope (scientists collect old envelopes for this purpose), I quickly calculated that 21.4 billion gallons of American beer and soda would contain about 800,000 tons of carbon dioxide. Wow! I thought, that's one helluva collective burp. And that's not even considering the chorus of harmonizing eructations from around the globe.

Why worry about carbon dioxide? It's one of the so-called greenhouse gases that are acknowledged to be raising Earth's average temperature. Granted, it hasn't been easy to take the temperature of a planet. But modern scientific analyses are infinitely more sophisticated than stationing people on street corners with thermometers. Today, there is very little doubt that carbon dioxide and other gases produced by human activities have indeed been inching up the global thermostat.

Here's how the greenhouse effect works:

There is a natural balance of energy between the radiations that shine upon Earth from the sun and those that are reradiated back out to space. When sunlight hits Earth's surface, about two-thirds of it is absorbed by the clouds, the land, the sea, and George Hamilton. Much of this absorbed energy is converted—degraded in energy—to infrared radiation, often called heat waves. Normally, a significant fraction of these heat waves bounce back out through the atmosphere and return to space. But if there happens to be an unnatural amount of infrared-absorbing gas in the atmosphere—and carbon dioxide is a prodigious absorber of infrared waves—then some of the waves will never get out; they'll be trapped near Earth's surface and warm things up.

So should we all stop drinking soda and beer for fear of belching more carbon dioxide into the atmosphere? Luckily, no.

According to the Department of Energy's figures for 1999, the last figures available at this writing, 800,000 tons of beverage-inspired carbon dioxide emissions amounts to 0.04 percent of the amount of carbon dioxide that was belched into the American atmosphere by gasoline- and diesel-burning vehicles. Our guzzling of carbonated beverages, then, is a mere burp in the bucket compared with our guzzling of gasoline.

So by all means keep on drinking. But don't drive.

SLOW LEAK

My frugal sister-in-law buys her soda pop in large quantities at a discount warehouse club, and she claims that it's often flat when she opens it. Can a bottle of soda go flat if it's never been opened?

. . . .

My first reaction was no, not if there isn't a slow leak somewhere in the bottle's seal. But after extensive research, which consisted of dialing the 800 Consumer Information number on a Coca-Cola label, I find that it is not only possible, it's quite common.

After prompting the nice woman who answered the phone to enter the appropriate words into her computer, I eventually learned that plastic pop bottles (they're made of polyethylene terephthalate or PET) are slightly permeable to carbon dioxide gas and that over time, enough gas can diffuse out through the walls to diminish the effervescence. That's partly why—again to my surprise—many plastic soda bottles bear "drink by" dates on their caps. Glass bottles, of course, aren't porous at all.

Classic Coke in plastic bottles, the woman said, has a recommended shelf life of nine months for optimum flavor and quality, whereas Diet Coke's recommended shelf life is only three months. Why? "Try plugging 'aspartame' into your computer," I suggested, whereupon after a few blind alleys we both discovered that the artificial sweetener aspartame is somewhat unstable and loses its sweetness over time.

By now we were having lots of fun with her computer, so I probed some more about what might affect the beverage's quality. Freezing, the computer informed us, can lower the fizziness. That one was a challenge for me to figure out, but this is what I think may happen: When the bottle freezes, the expanding ice can bulge out the bottle, and when it thaws the bottle may retain its expanded shape. That makes more gas space into which more carbon dioxide can escape from the liquid, lowering its effervescence level.

The moral of the story is always to check the "drink by" dates on your plastic pop bottles. A visit to my supermarket showed that Coke and Pepsi products are dated, but many other brands aren't, except in the form of unintelligible codes. Store them all in a cool place—heat deteriorates the flavor—and chill thoroughly before opening.

And, yes, if your sister-in-law's purveyors aren't careful about how they handle the soda during distribution, or if it has been on their shelves, or hers, for years, it's quite possible that when opened it will be as flat as her budget.

HOW TO FIX A FLAT

What's the best way to keep soda pop
from going flat?

. . . .

If you can't finish the whole bottle and you want to keep the leftovers gassy and sassy until the next pizza, just stopper it tightly and keep it cold. You knew that. But why?

The objective is to keep all of the remaining carbon dioxide in the bottle, because it's the carbon dioxide, bursting its tiny bubbles on our tongues, that gives us that nice tingly sensation. Also, carbon dioxide dissolved in water makes a sour acid: carbonic acid, which provides tartness. A tight stopper, obviously, keeps the gas from escaping. But the necessity of keeping the soda cold may not be so obvious.

For reasons that are better covered in Chemistry 101 than in Food 101, the colder a liquid is, the more carbon dioxide (or any other gas) it can absorb and hold. Your soda, for example, can hold about twice as much carbon dioxide at refrigerator temperature as at room temperature. That's why there's a big blast of escaping gas when you open a can of warm soda or beer: There's a lot more gas in there than can stay dissolved in the warm liquid.

Now how about those pump-up fizz retainers that are sold in supermarkets and discount stores? You know, the ones that work like a miniature bicycle pump. You screw the thing onto your partially depleted two-liter soda bottle, pump the piston a few times, and put it away in the fridge. The next time you open the bottle, you're treated to the biggest, most satisfying whoosh! you ever heard, and you're supposed to think, Hallelujah! My soda is born again!

But guess what? There isn't one bit more carbon dioxide in there than if you had simply screwed the cap on tight. What you've pumped into the bottle is air, not carbon dioxide, and air molecules are totally irrelevant to the behavior of carbon dioxide molecules. (Techspeak: It is solely the partial pressure of CO_2 that determines its solubility.)

That pump-up gizmo is nothing but a fancy stopper. Save your money.

TO YOUR HEALTH!

SHOWER POWER

When I open a bottle of Champagne, it often foams up all over the place, and I hate to waste that expensive stuff. What makes it behave that way?

. . . .

The bottle had undoubtedly been treated roughly some time earlier, without having been given enough time to recover. It must rest quietly on ice or in the refrigerator for at least an hour before being gently removed and opened.

In contemporary American society, Champagne is not meant to be drunk anyway. It is meant to be sprayed at Super Bowl winners in locker rooms.

The proper technique for these ebullient shenanigans, which I record here purely for its scientific and educational value (DO NOT TRY THIS AT HOME!), is first to pour out a little of the liquid to get more shaking space, then place a thumb over the bottle's opening, shake the bottle vigorously, and quickly slide the thumb slightly backward—not sideways!—in order to aim a concentrated stream of frothing liquid precisely in the forward direction.

The scientific and educational point I want to make is this: The reason the liquid squirts out is not—repeat, not—because of any increased gas pressure within the bottle. You could fool any number of chemists and physicists on this point, but it's true. The gas pressure does go up temporarily inside a shaken, sealed bottle, but that's not what propels the liquid, because as soon as you pop the bottle open or slide back your thumb the pressure drops down to that of the air in the room. And anyway, how could gas pressure in the space *above* a liquid shoot the liquid out of the bottle? The powder charge in a bullet has to be *behind* the slug, doesn't it?

Then why does the liquid shoot out with so much force when you release it immediately after shaking? The answer lies in the extremely rapid release of carbon dioxide gas from the liquid; that's what provides the shower power. It's like an air gun that gets its power from the sudden release of trapped air. There is something about shaking the bottle that makes the gas want to escape almost instantly from the liquid. And in the mad rush to escape it carries a lot of liquid along with it.

Here's why.

Carbon dioxide dissolves very easily in water, but once it's there it is extremely reluctant to leave. For example, you can leave an open bottle of soda, beer, or Champagne on the table for several hours before it will go totally flat. One reason for this is that gas bubbles can't just form spontaneously. The gas molecules need something to grab onto, some kind of an attractive gathering place where they can congregate in one spot until there are enough to form a bubble. The gathering spots, called nucleation sites, might be microscopic specks of dust in the liquid or tiny imperfections in the container's wall. If there are very few such nucleation sites available, the gas won't form bubbles and will stay dissolved in the liquid. Beverage bottlers use highly filtered water for that reason.

But if many nucleation sites happen to be available, gas molecules will quickly gather around them and form baby bubbles. As more and more gas molecules gather, the bubbles grow, eventually becoming big enough to rise through the liquid and escape at the surface.

Shaking the bottle puts millions of tiny bubbles into the liquid from the gas space—the "head space"—above the liquid. These baby bubbles are extremely effective, ready-made nucleation sites upon which zillions of other gas molecules can quickly gather to form bigger and bigger bubbles. And the bigger the bubbles become, the more surface they offer for their fellow gas molecules to gather upon and the faster they grow. Thus, shaking the container immensely speeds up the release of gas, which occurs with such explosive force that a lot of liquid is swept along with it. Result: a very effective weapon for drench warfare.

Fluid fusillades aside, there are a couple of peacetime implications of these principles.

First, you don't have to be afraid that jostling or shaking an unopened bottle or can of carbonated beverage will make it explode. Shaking it will indeed sweep out some gas from the liquid into the head space, but there just isn't enough head space in the bottle to hold much pressure. Besides, not long after a can or bottle has been shaken, all the baby-bubble nucleation sites will have risen back into the head space, where they can no longer do their dirty deed of, if you'll pardon the expression, releasing gas. Just don't open a container right after it has been shaken, while the nucleation bubbles are still distributed throughout the liquid. Let it rest first, to return to what chemists call "a state of equilibrium."

The trick with Champagne and other sparkling beverages is to let them rest quietly for a couple of hours before opening them. What is so effective about fizzical combat is that you release the bottles' contents immediately after shaking, while the bubbles are still down inside the liquid making their bubble trouble. But remember: Even though the Champagne is well rested, the Geneva Convention strictly forbids aiming a Champagne cork at anyone, civilian or combatant; it can do serious damage.

One last point: Because heat expels some of the gas from the liquid into the head space, a warm beverage will spritz more upon opening than a cold one will. That's the other trick with Champagne; it must be cold. In fact, heat can cause so much gas pressure in the head space of a beverage container that an occasional can or bottle has burst in the trunk of a car parked in the hot sun.

SAVOIR FAIRE

What's the best way to open a bottle of
Champagne without looking like a bumbling
idiot or hitting the ceiling with the cork?

. . . .

The most important thing in opening a bottle of Champagne is to accomplish the task with such aplomb that it will appear to your guests as if you do it every day. This is very difficult to pull off while wincing at the expectation of imminent disaster. So conquer your fears by practicing a couple of times alone with some cheap sparkling wine as follows.

First, remove the foil wrap covering the wire muzzle and the cork. To help you do that neatly without tearing all the foil away from the neck of the bottle, there is often a small tab to pull. (In my experience, either I can't find it or it tears off when I pull it.)

With one hand, grasp the bottle firmly around its neck while pressing your thumb down on the top of the cork as insurance against the embarrassment of a premature evacuation. With your other hand, untwist the wire loop at the base of the muzzle and remove the wire. Now move your bottle-holding hand down to the bottle's widest part and tilt it away from you at a 45° angle. (More about that later.) With your free hand, grip the cork firmly and twist the bottle—not the cork—until the cork begins to loosen, and then continue more slowly until the cork eases out. If you are faced with a recalcitrant cork that refuses to move, rock the cork with a forward-backward motion to loosen the stickiness between the glass and the cork.

Now, why did I say that you should twist the bottle, not the cork?

Both Newton and Einstein agree that it shouldn't matter at all which one you twist, because the motion is strictly relative. You could slice a loaf of bread by rubbing the loaf against the knife, couldn't you? But think about it: In twisting out a cork, you must reposition your fingers several times, temporarily relinquishing your grip on it. During one of those times, it could pop out uncontrollably, depositing wine on the floor and egg on your face.

About tilting the bottle: You don't want it to be vertical, of course, because you'd be in danger of shooting yourself in the face if the cork popped out. On the other hand, if the bottle is too close to horizontal the neck gets filled with liquid and the "head-space" gas floats up to form a bubble in the bottle's shoulder. Then, when you release the pressure by removing the cork, the bubble expands suddenly, expelling the liquid in the neck. A 45° tilt will usually ensure that the head-space gas stays up in the neck, where it belongs.

Champagne for Dessert

Champagne Jelly

Champagne can be eaten, not just drunk. The flavor and even some of the bubbles can be captured in this spectacular dessert. Created by California pastry chef Lindsey Shere, the sparkling and tender jelly literally melts in your mouth. Use an inexpensive Champagne or Prosecco, a sparkling Italian wine. Layer the jelly with berries or grapes for a parfait effect. (Eat your heart out, Jell-O.)

3¼ teaspoons unflavored gelatin (1 envelope plus part of a second)

1 cup cold water

¾ cup plus 3 tablespoons sugar

1 bottle dry Champagne (750 ml)

1 pint raspberries

1. Sprinkle the gelatin over the cold water in a medium saucepan and let soften, about 5 minutes.
2. Put the saucepan over low heat and stir with a spatula just until the gelatin has dissolved; do not overcook.
3. Reserve 1 tablespoon sugar. Stir in the remaining sugar and remove from the heat. Stir until the sugar has thoroughly dissolved, then stir in the Champagne. Pour the gelatin into a shallow container, cover, and refrigerate until set, 8 or 10 hours.
4. At serving time, toss the raspberries with the remaining 1 tablespoon of sugar. With a fork, jumble the gelatin into small chunks.
5. Spoon a few tablespoons of Champagne Jelly into each of six parfait or stemmed glasses. Add a few berries and repeat layering until all of the jelly and berries are used, ending with berries. Refrigerate until ready to serve.

MAKES 6 SERVINGS

A REAL CORKER OF A PROBLEM

Some of the wines I buy have "corks" made of
plastic. Is there a world cork shortage, or are there
technical reasons for this?

. . . .

I asked the same question on a trip to Portugal and western Spain, where more than half of the world's cork is grown, but I was unable to get a satisfactory answer. It was like asking a silkworm about polyester.

Back home, I learned why many wineries are switching to plastic stoppers. Yes, they're more economical than top-grade natural corks, but it's as much about technology as economics.

We all learned in school that cork grows on trees called cork oaks. After picturing thousands of tree-ripened corks hanging from the branches, we were disappointed to learn that corks are actually cut from the bark of the tree.

Cork oaks are the very model of a renewable resource, because once the trees have reached maturity, which takes twenty-five years, the bark grows back time and again after being stripped. This is done by scoring circles around the trunk and large branches, slitting the bark lengthwise, and peeling it off in sheets, which are then boiled in water, stacked, and flattened. In the miles upon miles of cork oak groves that I saw in Portugal, each tree was marked in white paint with a big number, indicating the year in which its bark had last been stripped. It would be stripped again nine years from that date.

Looking at some freshly stripped bark, I was pleased to learn one thing that I had always wondered about: Is the bark really thick enough for the length of a wine cork? Yes, after nine years it is. The corks are punched out perpendicularly through the flattened sheets of bark like cutting tall, narrow cookies.

Throughout the hundreds of years that cork has been used to stopper wine bottles, there has been a nagging problem. Known as cork taint or wine taint, it is a musty smell from a mold that afflicts a small percentage of corks and affects the taste of the wine. Quality control in modern wineries, especially in the large ones, has lowered the chances that your bottle will be "corked" or "corky" to somewhere between 2 and 8 percent. Nevertheless, replacing the cork with a synthetic plastic is an attractive alternative, because mold won't grow on plastic.

Here's how the taint arises.

During the stripping, sorting, storage, and processing of the bark, there are many opportunities for molds to grow on it. The finished corks are usually treated with a chlorine solution to disinfect and bleach them. The chlorine doesn't succeed in killing all the mold, however, and it has the side effect of producing chemicals called chlorophenols from natural phenolics in the cork. The surviving molds, plus others that join them during long ocean voyages from Portugal to California, for example, are able to convert some of these chlorophenols into a powerfully odoriferous chemical called 2,4,6-trichloroanisole, mercifully nicknamed TCA. It's the TCA that makes wines taste and smell corky. It can be detected in concentrations of a few parts per trillion.

Plastic "corks" (synthetic closures, in the trade lingo) are now used to varying degrees by more than two hundred wineries worldwide. Companies such as Neocork and Nomacorc are turning out extruded polyethylene stoppers by the millions, while SupremeCorq makes its plastic stoppers by a molding process and takes the prize for creative spelling.

How do the synthetics compare with real corks? They seem to pass the tests for leakage, exclusion of oxygen, and printability—a requirement because many wineries use printing on the cork to carry marketing messages. But because the synthetic closures haven't been around long enough for long-term aging studies, most wineries are using them for wines that are meant to be drunk young—within, say, six months of bottling, although Neocork says that its closures will hold up for as long as eighteen months.

But when connoisseurs pay more than a hundred dollars for a bottle of top-quality wine, they generally don't want to see any new-fangled gimmicks. In an attempt to defuse any snobbishness, some wineries have been introducing plastic stoppers and even—would you believe?—screw-top closures on some of their top-of-the-line products. After all, an aluminum cap is probably the ideal closure; it's airtight, never gets moldy, and can be removed without any tools.

What next? Mouton-Rothschild in a box?

Some wine bottles these days have synthetic "corks," which may be made of a rather tough plastic that gives you and your corkscrew a hard time. Check the point on your corkscrew to see if it's really sharp. If not, sharpen it up with a file and it will penetrate even the toughest of "corks" with ease.

THE NOSE KNOWS

In a restaurant, when the waiter opens the wine and places the cork on the table, what am I supposed to do with it?

. . . .

You're not expected to sniff it for evidence of moldiness. That's rare in this day and age. Moreover, when a small amount of the wine is poured for monsieur or madame's approval, a couple of swirls and sniffs will tell all that one needs to know. If the wine smells and tastes fine, who cares what the cork smells like?

If you have an unquenchable urge to sniff something, sniff the glass before the wine is poured. If it smells like disinfectant or soap or anything else, for that matter—clean glass has no odor—ask for another glass, that is, unless you've ordered a bottle of plonk, in which case a little soap might be an improvement.

You might, however, glance casually at the cork to see if it is wet (and stained, if it's a red wine) partway up. That means that the bottle has been properly stored on its side, with the cork being constantly wet for a tight seal.

Historically, a restaurateur's presentation of the cork to the patron was for an entirely different reason than sniffing for taint. It's a practice that began in the nineteenth century when unscrupulous merchants developed the habit of passing off cheap wines as expensive ones. Wine producers began to combat this practice by printing their names on the corks to prove authenticity. And, of course, the bottle was and still is always opened in the patron's presence.

Today, rather than risk insulting a good restaurant by either sniffing the cork or putting on your reading glasses to scrutinize it, the best advice is just to ignore it. I like to fiddle with it during the breaks between courses, when in olden times I used to light a cigarette.

SAY WHEN!

I keep reading that moderate alcohol consumption can be a benefit to heart health. But what, exactly, is "moderate consumption"?

. . . .

The usual evasive answer to this question is "one or two drinks a day." But what is "a drink," anyway? A bottle of beer? A glass of wine? A brimful, six-ounce martini? There are tall drinks and short drinks, stiff drinks and weak drinks. One man's drink may look to the next guy like a thimbleful or a bucketful.

At home, if you're in the habit of splashing scotch into your glass without measuring, the splash tends to grow bigger and bigger as the years go by. In a restaurant, how much alcohol is that bartender really giving you when he's being either generous or stingy? In short, how much actual alcohol is there in "a drink?"

That's the question that has been on everybody's mind—well, mine, anyway—ever since the USDA came out with its latest "Dietary Guidelines for Americans" (fifth edition, 2000; it is revised every five years). I intend to answer that burning question right here and now.

But first, as they say on the radio, this message.

After warning that excessive drinking can lead to accidents, violence, suicide, high blood pressure, stroke, cancer, malnutrition, birth defects, and damage to the liver, pancreas, brain, and heart (whew!), the USDA guidelines state plainly that "drinking in moderation may lower risk for coronary heart disease, mainly among men over age forty-five and women over age fifty-five."

(But hey, you college kids: It also states that "moderate consumption provides little, if any, health benefit for younger people." In fact, it adds, "Risk of alcohol abuse increases when drinking starts at an early age.")

At virtually the same time, a Harvard University epidemiological study published in the July 6, 2000, *New England Journal of Medicine* reported that after following 84,129 women from 1980 to 1994, those who drank moderately were found to have a 40 percent lower risk of cardiovascular disease than those who didn't drink at all. For more than ten years now, similar research findings have been making headlines. The conclusion seems clear that, as the authors of the Harvard study put it, "moderate alcohol consumption is associated with a lower risk of coronary heart disease" in both men and women.

Moderate alcohol consumption? Excessive drinking? What do these terms mean?

In an attempt to be helpful to the man and woman in the street—or in the bar—the USDA report boils "moderate consumption" down to "no more than one drink per day for women and no more than two drinks per day for men." The difference has nothing to do with machismo, but is due to sex differences in weight and metabolism.

But that still doesn't help if "a drink" can mean anything you want it to mean. The medical researchers, good scientists that they are, invariably speak not in terms of "drinks" but in terms of the number of grams of alcohol, which of course is the only thing that counts. Various research studies have defined moderate consumption—that single drink per day for women—as anywhere from 12 to 15 grams of alcohol. (It's fun to note that a "standard drink" in other countries varies from 8 grams of alcohol in Britain to 20 grams in Japan.) Twelve to 15 grams is roughly the amount of alcohol in 12 ounces of beer, 5 ounces of wine, or 1.5 ounces of 80-proof distilled spirits. But just try asking bartenders for a drink that contains 15 grams of alcohol. They'll think you've had too many grams already.

The million-dollar question, then, is this: How can you know how many grams of alcohol you're getting in your "one or two drinks"?

It's really simple. To find the number of grams of alcohol in your drink, all you have to do is multiply the number of fluid ounces of alcoholic beverage by its percentage of alcohol by volume (which in distilled spirits is one-half the "proof"), then multiply by the number of milliliters in a fluid ounce and by the density of ethyl alcohol in grams per milliliter, and divide the result by 100.

Okay, okay, I've done the arithmetic for you. Here's the formula: *To find the number of grams of alcohol in a drink, multiply the number of ounces by the percentage of alcohol, and then multiply the result by 0.23.*

Example: 1.5 ounces of 80-proof (40 percent alcohol) gin, vodka, or whiskey contains $1.5 \times 40 \times 0.23 = 14$ grams of alcohol.

For wine drinkers: Five ounces of a 13 percent wine contains $5 \times 13 \times 0.23 = 15$ grams of alcohol.

Beer hounds: A 12-ounce bottle of 4 percent beer contains $12 \times 4 \times 0.23 = 11$ grams of alcohol.

But you can't count on those "typical" percentages of alcohol. Although most distilled spirits are standardized at 80 proof or 40 percent alcohol by volume, there are several 90 to 100 proof liquors out there. Wines can vary anywhere from 7 to 24 percent (for fortified wines) and beers can vary from around 3 to 9 or 10 percent (for so-called malt liquors). At home, read the labels and measure your drinks accordingly. At a restaurant or bar, the bartender should always be able to tell you the size of the pour and the percentage of alcohol in the beverage. Complicated mixed drinks can be anyone's guess.

Putting it all together: If you are in good health and choose to drink, calculate your daily intake of alcohol and limit it to about 15 grams if you're a woman and 30 grams if you're a man.

A good bartender will always chill the glass before mixing and pouring a martini. But in my experience, they all do it wrong. They fill the glass with ice, add a little water, intending to improve thermal contact between the ice and the glass, and let it stand for a minute or two. But adding the water is a mistake. Ice from the freezer is colder than 32°F; it *has* to be, or it wouldn't be ice. But the added water can never get colder than 32°F, so it diminishes the ice's cooling power. For your at-home martinis, put some cold ice in the glass (cracked if you wish), but hold the water. Straight from the freezer, your ice will be as cold as 8 or 9° below zero. Don't worry about making good thermal contact; a tiny amount of ice will melt wherever it touches the glass.

It's Margarita Time!

Bob's Best Margarita

After three days of exhaustive research to test as many margaritas as possible in San Antonio, Texas, I returned home to concoct my own recipe incorporating what I thought were the best qualities. Many recipes specify top-shelf orange liqueurs such as Cointreau and Grand Marnier, but their orange-rind oils and brandy overpower the flavor of the tequila, which is what margaritas are really all about. I've found that an unassuming triple sec such as Hiram Walker works best. These margaritas go down easy because of their sweetness, but they contain 16 grams of alcohol apiece and should be "nursed."

Salt on the rim of a margarita glass should be on the outside of the rim only, so it doesn't fall into the drink. I coat the rims by dipping a finger in the lime juice and wetting only the outer surface of the rims with it.

---

1 ounce freshly squeezed lime juice
   Kosher salt
3 ounces Jose Cuervo Especial tequila
1 ounce Hiram Walker triple sec
   Small ice cubes or cracked (not crushed) ice

---

1. Dip a finger in the lime juice and use it to wet the outsides of the rims of 2 martini glasses. Roll the rims in salt, leaving a deposit on the outside edges. Place the glasses in the freezer until ready to mix the drinks.

2. Using a one-ounce jigger or a shot glass marked in ounces, measure the liquid ingredients into a cocktail shaker. Add the ice and shake vigorously for 15 seconds. Strain into the chilled glasses.

MAKES 2 MARGARITAS, EACH CONTAINING 16 GRAMS OF ALCOHOL

DON'T ASK, DON'T TELL

Sometimes the label on a bottle of beer tells me the
percentage of alcohol in it and sometimes it
doesn't. Isn't there some law about that?

. . . .

It used to be that the federal government prohibited brewers from listing the percentage of alcohol on the labels of beers to discourage people from choosing their beverages based on alcohol content. But that's not true anymore.

In 1935, two years after the repeal of Prohibition, the Federal Alcohol Administration (FAA) Act prohibited the labeling of beers' alcohol potencies for fear of "strength wars" breaking out among competitive brewers. Ironically, some sixty years later when light beers and low-alcohol beers were becoming popular, brewers wanted the right to brag about how *little* alcohol their products contained, and they challenged the "no tell" law. In 1995 the U.S. Supreme Court decided that the labeling ban violated the First Amendment by interfering with the brewers' right to free speech.

I hereby quote from the April 1, 2000, revision of The U.S. Code of Federal Regulations, Title 27 (Alcohol, Tobacco Products and Firearms), Chapter 1 (Bureau of Alcohol, Tobacco and Firearms, Department of the Treasury), Part 7 (Labeling and Advertising of Malt Beverages), Subpart C (Labeling Requirements for Malt Beverages), Section 7.71 (Alcoholic content), Subsection (a): "Alcoholic content . . . may be stated on a label unless prohibited by State law."

Individual states are therefore explicitly allowed to trump federal law if they wish, which is not the case with wine or distilled spirits, over which federal law rules supreme. As you can imagine, state beer-labeling laws now vary all over the lot.

From The Beer Institute I obtained information published in the *Modern Brewery Age Blue Book*, which summarizes the crazy quilt of labeling laws in all fifty states, the District of Columbia, and Puerto Rico.

By my count, about twenty-seven states still prohibit the labeling of alcohol content, four states require the labeling of beers containing less than 3.2 percent alcohol, and the rest either don't seem to care or have laws that are so complex as to raise questions about the alcoholic content of the legislators. (Minnesota laws win the prize for complexity.) Alaska, as far as I can tell, both prohibits and requires strength labeling.

HOW MUCH IS NONE?

Is there any alcohol at all in a non-alcoholic beer?

. . . .

The U.S. Code of Federal Regulations, Title 27, Chapter 1, part 7, etc., etc., etc. says that "the terms 'low alcohol' or 'reduced alcohol' may be used only on malt beverages containing less than 2.5 percent alcohol by volume" and that nonalcoholic beer must contain less than 0.5 percent alcohol by volume.

By volume? Yes, by volume. That's another fairly recent change. Various brewers had been in the habit of expressing alcohol contents as percent by weight: how many grams of alcohol there are in 100 grams of brew. Others had been accustomed to expressing it as percent by volume: how many milliliters of alcohol there are in 100 milliliters of brew. But again, the U.S. Code of Federal Regulations, Title 27, etc. has stepped in: "Statement of alcoholic content shall be expressed in percent alcohol by volume, and not by percent by weight. . . ." That's good, because the alcoholic contents of wines and distilled beverages are also expressed as percent by volume, so now they're all consistent.

Chapter Eight

Those Mysterious Microwaves

....

WITH TONGUE FIRMLY PLANTED in cheek, the British essayist and critic Charles Lamb (1775–1834), in "A Dissertation on Roast Pig," tells how humans first discovered cooking or, more precisely, roasting, after "for the first seventy thousand ages" eating their meat raw by "clawing or biting it from the living animal."

The story, purportedly discovered in an ancient Chinese manuscript, tells of the young son of a swineherd, who accidentally set fire to their cottage, which burned to the ground, killing the nine pigs within. (Swineherds apparently lived that way.) Stooping down to touch one of the dead pigs, the son burned his fingers and instinctively put them to his mouth to cool them, whereupon he tasted a delicious flavor never before experienced by mankind.

Recognizing a good thing when they tasted it, the swineherd and his son thenceforth built a series of less and less substantial cottages, burning them down each time with pigs inside to produce the marvelously flavorful meat. Their secret got out, however, and before long everyone in the village was building and burning down flimsy houses with pigs inside. Eventually, "in the process of time a sage arose . . . who made a discovery, that the flesh of swine, or indeed of any other animal, might be cooked (burnt, as they called it) without the necessity of consuming a whole house to dress it."

Right up until the beginning of the twentieth century, we humans continued to build fires whenever we wanted to cook. By then we had learned to build the fires on kitchen hearths and later to confine them in enclosures called ovens. Still, every cook had to obtain fuel and set fire to it in order to roast a pig or even to boil water.

But it need not be so.

What if we could build a single, huge fire in a remote location and somehow capture its energy and deliver it, like fresh milk, directly to thousands of kitchens? Well, today we can, through the miracle of electricity.

Only a hundred years ago we discovered how to burn huge quantities of fuel in a central plant, use the fire's heat to boil water and make steam, use that steam to generate electricity, and then send the electrical energy surging through copper wires for hundreds of miles to thousands of kitchens, in which thousands of cooks could turn it back into heat for roasting, toasting, boiling, broiling, and baking. All from a single fire.

We first used this new form of transmissible fire to replace gas for lighting our streets and parlors (when we had parlors). Then in 1909 electricity moved into the kitchen when General Electric and Westinghouse marketed their first electric toasters. Electric ranges, ovens, and refrigerators followed. Today, we can hardly turn out a meal without our electric ovens, ranges, broilers, beaters, mixers, blenders, food processors, coffeemakers, rice cookers, bread machines, deep fryers, skillets, woks, grills, slow cookers, steamers, waffle irons, slicers, and knives. (I once invented an electric fork to go with the electric knife, but it never caught on.)

Is that the end of humankind's energy-for-cooking story? It was, until fifty years ago, when a totally new, fireless method of making heat for cooking was invented: the microwave oven. It worked on a

brand-new principle that few people understood, and many consequently feared it. Some still fear and mistrust their microwave ovens,
which in spite of their omnipresence, remain the most baffling of all
home appliances. Yes, it runs on electricity, but it heats food in a
never-before-dreamed-of way, without even having to be hot itself.
It is the first new way of cooking in more than a million years.

I HAVE PROBABLY RECEIVED more questions about microwave
ovens than about any other subject. What follows are some of the
most frequently asked questions. I hope the answers will provide
enough understanding of these appliances to enable you to answer
your own questions as they arise.

What is a microwave?

There is so much anxiety among home cooks about microwave ovens
that you'd think they were kitchen-sized nuclear reactors. The situation is not helped by some authors of food books, who seem not to
know the difference between microwaves and radioactivity. Yes, they
are both radiations, but so are the television radiations that bring us
vapid sitcoms. It's hard to say which are more to be avoided.

Microwaves are waves of electromagnetic radiation just like radio
waves, but of shorter wavelength and higher energy. (Wavelength and
energy are related; the shorter the wavelength the higher the energy.)
Electromagnetic radiation consists of waves of pure energy, traveling
through space at the speed of light. Light itself, in fact, consists of
electromagnetic waves of even shorter wavelength and higher energy
than microwaves. It's the specific wavelength and energy of a radiation that gives it its own, specific properties. Thus, you can't cook
food with light (but see page 304) and you can't read by microwaves.

Microwaves are generated by a kind of vacuum tube called a magnetron, which spews them out into your oven, a sealed metal box in
which the microwaves continually bounce around as long as the mag-

netron is operating. Magnetrons are rated by their microwave power output, which is usually from 600 to 900 watts. (Note that this is the number of watts of microwaves produced, not the number of watts of electricity that the appliance uses, which is higher.)

But that doesn't tell the whole story. The cooking power of a microwave oven, and hence how fast it will do its chores, depends on the number of watts of microwaves there are per cubic foot of space in the box. To compare ovens, divide the microwave wattage by the number of cubic feet. For example, an 800-watt, 0.8-cubic-foot oven has a relative cooking power of $800 \div 0.8 = 1000$, which is pretty typical. Because different ovens have different cooking powers, recipes can't be specific about how long any given microwaving operation should take.

How do microwaves make heat?

Don't try to find the answer to that question in food books. With only one exception, every book in my food library, including those devoted exclusively to microwave cooking, either evades the question entirely or gives the same misleading answer. Evading the issue only reinforces the less-than-helpful notion of a magic box. But promulgating a wrong answer is even worse.

The ubiquitous nonexplanation is that "microwaves make water molecules rub up against one another, and the resulting friction causes heat." This misinformation rubs *me* the wrong way, because friction isn't involved at all. The idea of water molecules rubbing up against one another to make heat is just plain silly. Just try to start a fire by rubbing two pieces of water together. Nevertheless, you'll find the friction fiction even in some of the instruction manuals that come with the ovens.

Here's what really happens.

Some of the molecules in food—particularly water molecules—behave like tiny electric magnets. (Techspeak: The molecules are electric dipoles or, in other words, they are polar.) They tend to line up with the direction of an electric field, just as the magnet in a compass tends to line up with Earth's magnetic field. The microwaves in your oven, which have a frequency of 2.45 gigaHertz or 2.45 billion cycles per second, are producing an electric field that reverses its direction 4.9 billion times a second. The poor little water molecules go absolutely nuts trying to keep up by flipping their orientations back and forth 4.9 billion times a second.

In their agitation, the frenetically flipping, microwave-energized molecules bang up against neighboring molecules and knock them around, sort of like the way in which an exploding kernel of popcorn scatters its neighbors. Once knocked, a formerly stationary molecule becomes a fast-moving molecule, and a fast molecule is by definition a hot molecule. Thus does the microwave-induced molecular flipping get transformed into widespread heat.

Please note that nowhere have I said anything about friction between molecules. Friction, if I may remind you, is the resistance that keeps two solid surfaces from sliding freely over one another. This resistance saps away some of the energy of movement, and that sapped energy has to show up somewhere else, because energy can't just disappear into nowhere. So it shows up as heat. That's fine for high-friction rubber tires and even low-friction hockey pucks, but a water molecule doesn't need to be rubbed by some kind of molecular masseuse to get hot in a microwave oven. All it has to do is get knocked around by a fast-flipping neighbor that has swallowed a microwave.

Oddly, microwave ovens aren't very good at melting ice. That's because the water molecules in ice are tied pretty tightly together into a rigid framework (Techspeak: a crystal lattice), so they can't flip back and forth under the influence of the microwaves' oscillation, much as they may feel the urge. When you defrost frozen food in your microwave oven, you're heating mostly the other, non-ice parts of the food, and the resulting heat then flows into the ice crystals and melts them.

If you use a synthetic sponge to wipe up the sink and counter, you may want to sterilize it now and then, especially after you've handled raw meat or poultry on the counter (which you shouldn't do anyway; do it on disposable waxed paper). You could boil it in water, but a quicker way is to put it, dripping wet, on a dish and zap it in the microwave oven for one minute on high. Be careful in removing it; it'll be too hot to touch. Some people put their sponges in the dishwasher, but many dishwashers will not reach sterilizing temperatures.

Why does microwaved food sometimes have to stand for a while after it's been heated?

Unlike their electromagnetic cousins the X rays, which are of much higher frequency and energy, microwaves can't penetrate food more than an inch or so; their energy is completely absorbed and turned into heat within that region. That's one reason for the "cover and wait" injunction of recipes and "smart" ovens: It takes time for the outer heat to work its way into the food's interior. In the absence of a bossy oven, a recipe will often tell you to stop and stir the food before continuing the heating. Same reason.

The heat distributes itself in two ways. First, the hottest molecules bounce against adjacent, less-hot molecules in the food, transferring some of their motion—their heat—to them, so that the heat gradually works its way deeper into the food.

Second, much of the water has actually been turned into steam, which then diffuses through the food, giving up its heat along the way. That's why most microwave heating is done in loosely covered containers; you want to keep that hot steam in, but you don't want it to build up pressure and pop the lid. Both of these heat-transfer processes are slow, so if the heat isn't given enough time to distribute itself uniformly, you'll wind up with hot and cold spots in the food.

Virtually all food contains water, so virtually all food can be heated by microwaves. (Don't try to cook dried mushrooms, for example.) But the molecules of certain foods other than water, notably fats and sugars, are also heated by microwaves. That's why bacon cooks so well in the microwave oven, and why the sweet raisins inside a microwave-heated raisin bran muffin can get dangerously, tongue-burning hot, even though the cake part is merely warm.

It therefore pays to be careful with fatty and sugary foods. Very hot water molecules can boil off as steam, but very hot fat and sugar molecules stay in place as unexpected hazards. That's another reason why it's always wise to wait a while for the steam to calm down and the hot spots to even out before removing and eating microwaved food.

Why does my microwave oven sound as if it's going on and off all the time?

Because it is. The magnetron cycles on and off to allow periods of time for the heat to distribute itself through the food. When you set the oven for a percentage of full "power," what you're adjusting isn't the magnetron's wattage; it can operate only at its full, rated power (but see below). What you're setting is the percentage of time it's turned on. "Fifty percent power" means that it's on half the time. The on-and-off whirring sound is the sound of the magnetron's cooling fan.

In some of the more sophisticated ovens, various sequences and lengths of on and off periods are programmed into the machine to optimize specific jobs, such as "reheat dinner plate," "cook baked potato," "defrost vegetable," and, most important of all, "popcorn."

A relatively new development in microwave ovens, however, is "inverter technology." Instead of cycling on and off, the oven can actually deliver continuous, lower levels of power for more even heating.

Why do microwave ovens cook so much faster than conventional ovens?

Before it can heat the food, a conventional gas or electric oven first has to heat some two to four cubic feet of air ("preheating the oven"), after which the hot air must transfer its heat energy into the food. These are very slow and very inefficient processes. A microwave oven, on the other hand, heats the food—and only the food—by depositing its energy directly into it with no intermediary such as air or water (as in boiling) involved.

The statement found in several microwave cookbooks to the effect that microwaves cook food so quickly "because they are so tiny, they travel quickly" is nonsense. All electromagnetic waves travel at the speed of light, no matter what their wavelength. And the "micro" in microwave doesn't mean "tiny." They were named "microwaves" because they are essentially ultra-short radio waves.

Why does the food have to be rotated while cooking?

It's hard to design a microwave oven in which the intensity of the microwaves is completely uniform throughout the entire volume of the box so that food in all locations will be subjected to the same heating power. Moreover, any food in the oven is sucking up microwaves and upsetting whatever uniformity there might otherwise be. You can buy an inexpensive microwave-sensitive gadget in a kitchenware store, put it in various parts of the oven, and see that it registers different intensities at different locations.

The solution is to keep the food moving, so that it averages out nonuniformities in microwave intensity. Most ovens these days have an automatic turntable, but if yours doesn't, many recipes and defrosting instructions on frozen foods will remind you to rotate the food halfway through the heating time.

Why mustn't one put metal into a microwave oven?

Light bounces off mirrors; microwaves bounce off metal. (Radar is a kind of microwave that bounces off your speeding car and cooks your goose.) If what you put in the oven reflects too many microwaves back instead of absorbing them, the magnetron tube can be damaged. There must always be something in the oven to absorb microwaves. That's why you shouldn't ever run it empty.

Metals in microwave ovens can behave unpredictably unless you have a degree in electrical engineering. Microwaves set up electrical currents in metals, and if the metal object is too thin it may not be able to support the current and will turn red hot and melt, as in the blowing of an overloaded fuse. And if it has sharp points, it may even act like a lightning rod and concentrate so much microwave energy at the points that it will send off lightning-like sparks. (Those paper-covered wire twist ties are notorious because they are both thin and pointed, so beware.)

On the other hand, the engineers who design microwave ovens can devise safe sizes and shapes of metal that won't cause trouble, and some ovens actually do contain metal trays or racks.

Because it's so hard to predict which sizes and shapes of metal are safe and which may cause fireworks, the best advice is never to put anything metallic in a microwave oven. And that goes for fancy dishes that have gold or other metallic trim.

Toasting with Microwaves

Microwaved Bread Crumbs

Certain specialized microwave accessories have thin coatings of metal that get quite hot in the microwave oven and will brown foods that are in contact with it. Usually, microwaves won't brown food because their energy is absorbed mostly in the interior of the food and doesn't get the surface hot enough for browning reactions to take place.

So don't expect to be able to make croutons or toast in the microwave oven. But it will make quick work of toasting fresh bread crumbs if they are mixed with oil. The oil absorbs microwaves, becomes hot, and "fries" the bread.

When the last few slices of rustic bread are too stale to eat but are too good to throw away, make these bread crumbs in the microwave oven. Use as a topping for pasta or vegetables.

---

2 to 3 thick slices stale rustic bread, crusts removed

About 2 teaspoons olive oil

Pinch of coarse salt

---

1. Break the bread into pieces and place in the food processor. Slowly add the olive oil through the feed tube while processing to the desired size. Add a pinch of salt and whirl to mix.

2. Spread the crumbs in a thin layer on a microwave-safe plate. Microwave, uncovered, on HIGH for 1 minute. Stir the crumbs and microwave for 1 minute more, or until toasted. If the crumbs are large and somewhat moist, microwave an additional 30 seconds. Watch carefully, because the smaller the crumbs are, the more likely they are to overtoast.

MAKES ABOUT 1 GENEROUS CUP

Can the microwaves leak out of the box and cook the cook?

An old, beat-up oven with a warped door may indeed let enough microwaves out through the cracks to be a hazard, but there is extremely little leakage from today's carefully designed ovens. Moreover, the instant the door is opened, the magnetron shuts off and the microwaves disappear like the light when you turn off a lamp.

What about the glass door itself? Microwaves can penetrate glass but not metal, so the glass door is covered with a perforated metal panel that lets light come through so you can see inside, but that the microwaves can't get through because their wavelength ($4\frac{3}{4}$ inches) is simply too big to fit through the holes in the metal panel. There is no basis for the belief that it is hazardous to stand closer than several feet from an operating microwave oven.

What makes a container "microwave safe"?

In principle, the answer is simple: Containers whose molecules aren't dipoles and will not absorb microwaves. Such molecules will not be jerked around by the microwaves and will not get hot. But in practice, the answer isn't quite so simple.

Surprisingly, in what many people perceive as our overregulated society, there appears to be no government, industry, or trade definition of the term "microwave safe." I have attempted to extract a definition from the FDA, the Federal Trade Commission, and the Consumer Product Safety Commission, all to no avail. Nor could I get any manufacturers of "microwave-safe" products to tell me why they make that claim. (Lawsuits! Lawsuits!)

So it appears that we're on our own. But here are some guiding principles.

Metals: I've already explained why metals are to be avoided in microwave ovens.

Glass and paper: Glass (that is, standard kitchen glass, not fancy crystal), paper and parchment are always safe; they don't absorb microwaves at all. So-called crystal, which is glass with a high lead content, does absorb microwaves to some extent and may therefore get warm. In a thick piece, the heat might set up stresses that may lead to cracking. Best not to take the chance with that expensive stuff.

Plastics: Plastics don't absorb microwaves either. But microwaved food can get pretty hot, and any container, no matter what it's made of, will then get hot from the food. Some wimpy plastics, such as thin plastic storage bags, margarine tubs, and styrene foam "doggie boxes" from restaurants, may even melt from the food's heat. Certain kinds of plastic refrigerator containers may get distorted out of shape. You just have to learn this from experience.

Ceramics: Ceramic cups and dishes are usually okay, but some may contain minerals that absorb microwave energy and get hot. If in doubt, test the suspect by heating it empty in the oven along with some water in a glass measuring cup. If the test object gets hot, it's not microwave safe. (The water is in there to absorb microwaves and avoid the empty-oven problem that I referred to earlier.)

To further complicate our lives, some earthenware mugs and cups, even though made of purely innocent, non-energy-absorbing clays, can crack in the microwave oven. If the glaze has become chipped or cracked with age, water can seep into pores or air holes in the clay beneath the glaze, perhaps during dishwashing. Then, when microwaved, the trapped water will boil and its steam pressure can crack the cup. While that's a rare occurrence, it's best not to use your chipped or crazed heirloom cups in the microwave oven.

Why do some "microwave safe" containers still get hot in the oven?

"Microwave safe" means only that the container won't get hot from the direct absorption of microwaves. But the food it contains does absorb microwave energy and therefore gets hot, and as I pointed out earlier, much of that heat is transmitted to its dish. How hot the dish gets depends on how efficiently it absorbs heat from the food, and different materials—even different "microwave-safe" materials—can vary quite a bit in that respect. Always use potholders when removing microwaved containers from the oven. And when opening the container, beware of pent-up steam, which can be very hot.

Is it dangerous to heat water in a microwave oven?

No and yes. No, it's unlikely that anything serious will happen, but yes, you should be careful. Microwave-heated water that hasn't yet come to a full, vigorous boil can indeed be a booby trap.

Because microwave energy is absorbed only by the outer inch or so of the water in a cup, the resulting heat must then diffuse into the interior portions before all the water can uniformly reach its boiling point. This diffusion of heat is a slow process, and some of the outer-portion water can get very hot indeed before the whole cup is observed to boil. Parts of the outer water can, in fact, get even hotter than the boiling point without boiling; it is then said to be super-heated. Water—indeed, any liquid—may not boil even though hot enough, because in order to boil the molecules need a convenient place to congregate until there are enough of them in one spot to make a bubble of vapor. (Techspeak: They need nucleation sites.) A nucleation site can be a speck of dust or an impurity in the water, a tiny air bubble, or even a microscopic imperfection on the wall of the cup.

Now suppose that you have some clean, pure water in a clean, smooth, and blemish-free cup, so that there are virtually no nucleation sites at all. You put it in the microwave oven and, because you are of course in a hurry, you turn it on full blast, which heats the exterior portions of the water intensely. Under these conditions it is possible that you will produce some pockets of superheated water that are just dying to boil furiously if only given the chance. Then, when you open the oven door and grab the cup, you give them that chance by jostling the water. Because of the jostling, some of the excess "super heat" finds its way into a slightly cooler, not-quite-boiling portion, making it boil suddenly. This disturbance in turn makes the superheated portions also boil suddenly. The result is an eruption of unexpected bubbling that can spatter out hot liquid.

The reason that this delayed bubbling never happens in stove-heated water is that the heat at the bottom of the kettle continually creates tiny bubbles of air and water vapor that serve as nucleation sites, so superheating never gets a chance to develop. Also, the bottom-heated water is continually rising and circulating, which prevents too much heat from piling up in any one place.

Play it safe by never removing the cup from the microwave oven as soon as you see some bubbling going on, because there could still be some not-quite-boiling portions that could start boiling unexpectedly. Watch the water through the oven's window and allow it to boil vigorously for several seconds before you turn off the oven and take it out. Then you'll know that all the water is well mixed to a uniform boiling temperature.

Even so, always be careful when removing any hot liquid from the oven; it may still bubble up unexpectedly and scald you with its splatter. I have developed the habit of plunging a fork into the cup to "set off" any superheated spots before removing it from the oven.

When you subsequently add your tea bag or (ugh!) instant coffee to microwave-heated water, you will see some fizzing, but it's not boiling and it's not violent; it's mostly air bubbles. The solids are providing new nucleation sites that didn't exist before, and these sites liberate air that was dissolved in the original cold water but that didn't have time to come out during the few minutes of heating.

Zap Your Soup

> ### *Jade Green Summer Soup*

Move over, vichyssoise and gazpacho. Jade Green Summer Soup is just as cool and refreshing.

Soups don't have to be simmered for hours. This one takes about 15 minutes, thanks to microwave magic. It might have been created by a farmer's wife with an eye to using the midsummer bounty of her kitchen garden.

This soup is prettiest when ladled into a white or brightly colored bowl and garnished with chopped, fresh herbs. It's so low in calories, why not add more? Try a swirl of extra-virgin olive oil or a wee dollop of sour cream to round out the flavors.

---

5 **cups chicken broth**

2 **cups chopped raw green beans**

2 **cups chopped raw romaine**

2 **cups chopped raw zucchini**

2 **cups raw peas or 1 box frozen peas**

1 **cup chopped celery**

½ **cup chopped scallions, both white and green parts**

¼ **cup chopped parsley**

Salt and freshly ground black pepper

Chopped fresh herbs

Olive oil or sour cream, optional

---

1. Add the chicken broth, beans, romaine, zucchini, peas, celery, scallions, and parsley to a large glass bowl. Cover with a paper plate and microwave on HIGH for 15 minutes, or until the vegetables are tender.

2. The mixture will be very hot. Remove carefully from the oven, let it cool somewhat, and then whirl it carefully in the blender, adding about 1 cup at a time, until smooth. Season generously with salt and pepper, because when the soup is served cold, its flavor will be blunted. Transfer the pureed soup

into several small refrigerator containers and let cool before putting in the refrigerator, to prevent overheating the other contents. Chill thoroughly before serving in chilled bowls.

3. Garnish each serving with the chopped fresh herbs. Add a drizzle of olive oil or a dollop of sour cream if you like.

Note: To cook the soup on top of the stove, combine the broth and vegetables in a large saucepan and simmer, partially covered, for 15 to 20 minutes. Continue with step 2, above.

MAKES 6 TO 8 SERVINGS

Do microwaves change the molecular structure of foods?

Yes, of course they do. The process is called "cooking." All cooking methods cause chemical and molecular changes in our foods. A cooked egg certainly has a different chemical composition from a raw one.

Do microwaves destroy the nutrients in food?

No method of cooking will destroy minerals. But heat will destroy vitamin C, for example, no matter how the food is cooked.

Because microwave heating is uneven, parts of the food may be subjected to much higher temperatures than in other methods, so there is the possibility of some vitamin destruction. But even if microwaves destroyed all of the vitamin X in your dish, there certainly wouldn't be any nutritional harm in eating an occasional dish that doesn't contain vitamin X. In a balanced diet, every dish doesn't have to contain every vitamin and mineral.

Why does microwave-cooked food cool off faster
than food cooked in a conventional oven?

This answer may strike you as disappointingly simple: The micro-waved food may not have been as hot to begin with.

Many factors, such as the type, quantity, and thickness of the food, affect how it will heat in a microwave oven. If, for example, the cho-sen on-and-off cycle of the magnetron isn't exactly right for the par-ticular food and container, or if the stirring and/or rotation aren't thorough, or if the container isn't covered to keep the steam in, then the heat may not be distributed uniformly throughout the food. The outer parts may be scalding hot, but the inner parts may still be rela-tively cool. Then the food's average overall temperature will be lower than you think, and it will cool to room temperature faster.

In a conventional oven, on the other hand, the food is sur-rounded by very hot air for a relatively long time, and the heat is given plenty of time to work its way into all parts of the food. Thus, the food's temperature will eventually be the same as the oven's air tem-perature (unless you're deliberately making a rare roast, for exam-ple), and it will take longer to cool off.

There's another reason. In a conventional oven, the cooking ves-sel gets as hot as the air in the oven and conducts its heat straight into the food. But "microwave-safe" containers are deliberately designed not to get hot. Thus, food from a microwave oven is in contact with a container that has remained cooler than the food, and that saps away some of its heat.

FINALLY, HERE ARE TWO strange microwave mysteries that I was asked to solve by anxious and bewildered home cooks.

When I cook fresh peas in the microwave, the
water boils up and spills out of the container, yet
when I heat canned peas in the same way, they
behave themselves. What's the difference?

Microwave energy is absorbed primarily by water in the food. The waterlogged canned peas and their surrounding liquid absorb microwaves at pretty much the same rate and will therefore get hot more or less equally. When the water begins to boil, the peas are at about the same temperature, whereupon you undoubtedly consider them to be done and stop the oven.

The much drier fresh peas, on the other hand, don't absorb microwaves as readily as the surrounding water does, so the water heats faster. But the relatively cool peas prevent the water from being heated uniformly. At the same time, the peas are acting as bubble instigators (Techspeak: nucleation sites), encouraging the water to erupt exuberantly wherever there are hot spots. All this happens before the peas are adequately cooked and you deem them ready to remove from the oven.

Try using a less-than-full-power setting, in which the oven zaps the food on an intermittent schedule, giving the water time to distribute its heat through the peas. That way, they'll be cooked before the water has a chance to boil over.

Better yet, buy frozen peas. The producer has tested the best way to cook them in a microwave oven and the directions are right there on the package.

> *When I microwaved some frozen mixed vegetables in a glass bowl, they suddenly started to spark as if they contained metal. I quickly turned off the oven and examined the vegetables, but I couldn't find any metal particles. The veggies were actually charred black from the sparks! I repeated this with a fresh package of the same brand and it happened again. I got different stories from the microwave repairman and the supermarket's risk management department, who turned my complaint over to its supplier, who turned it over to their insurance company. What was going on?*

A lot of buck passing. Oh, you mean in your oven?

Relax. Don't sue. There was no metal in your vegetables. I'll bet it was mainly the carrots that got charred, right? Here's what probably happened.

Frozen foods usually contain ice crystals. But as I pointed out earlier, solid ice doesn't absorb microwaves nearly as well as liquid water does. The defrost setting on microwave ovens therefore doesn't try to melt the ice directly, but operates in short, food-heating blasts, leaving time between blasts for the heat to distribute itself and melt the ice.

But you didn't use the "defrost" setting, did you? (Or maybe your oven doesn't have one.) You set the oven for a high, constant heating level, which raised localized portions of the food to extremely high temperatures without allowing enough time for the heat to dissipate throughout the bowl. So those localized spots got burned and charred.

Why the carrots and why the sparks? (You'll love this.) The peas, corn, beans, and whatever all have rounded shapes, but the carrots are usually cut into cubes or oblongs with sharp edges. These thin edges dried out and charred faster than the rest of the vegetables. Now a carbonized, sharp edge or point can act just like the tip of a lightning rod, which attracts electrical energy toward itself and thereby prevents it from striking anywhere else. (Techspeak: Electrically conducting sharp points develop highly concentrated electric field gradients around themselves.) The highly concentrated, carrot-attracted energy is what made the sparks.

I know this sounds a bit farfetched, but it's quite logical. It has happened before. Next time, use the oven's "defrost vegetables" or other low-power setting. Or else just add enough water to the bowl to cover the vegetables.

Honest, your oven isn't possessed by the devil.

Chapter Nine

Tools And Technology

....

Today's cooks, like other artists, have their own figurative palettes and paintbrushes in the form of an arsenal of equipment that makes old tasks easier and new tasks possible. Today's kitchens boast a variety of mechanical and electrical devices ranging from the simplest mortar and pestle to the most technologically sophisticated oven and range.

As a species we have progressed so far from wood fires, hot stones, and clay pottery (will future archaeologists unearth bread machine shards from the early twenty-first century?) that we may not even know how some of our tools work. We use them, and often misuse them, without fully understanding them.

Microwave ovens were just the beginning. Come with me now into a kitchen filled with such high-tech gadgets as magnetic induction coils, light ovens, thermistors, and computer "brains" that sometimes seem to know more than you do. Along the way, we'll learn how to use our familiar old frying pans, measuring cups, knives, and pastry brushes to best advantage.

In the end, we'll wind up alongside Alice in Wonderland, a fitting place to terminate our journey through the only places on Earth where miracles really do happen every day: our wild and wonderful kitchens.

UTENSILS AND TECHNIQUES

THE SOUND OF ONE PAN STICKING

Why doesn't anything stick to nonstick cookware? And if the nonstick coating won't stick to anything, how do they get it to stick to the pans?

. . . .

Sticking is a two-way street. In order for sticking to occur, there must be both a stick-er and a stick-ee. At least one partner must be tacky.

Quiz: Identify the sticky one in each of the following pairs: Glue and paper. Chewing gum and a shoe sole. A lollipop and a little boy.

Very good.

In every case, at least one of the pair must be made of molecules that enjoy latching onto others. Glue, chewing gum, and lollipops contain notoriously fickle molecules; almost anything can be the object of their affections. Adhesives are deliberately created by chemists to form strong, permanent attachments to as many substances as possible.

But way over on the other hand, there's PTFE, that black coating on the nonstick pan. Its molecules simply refuse to be either the sticker *or* the stickee, no matter what its potential partner may be. And that's extremely unusual in the chemical world of intermolecular attractions. Even Super Glue won't stick to PTFE.

What does PTFE have that other molecules don't have?

This sticky question arose in 1938, when a chemist named Roy Plunkett at the E. I. DuPont de Nemours Corp. concocted a brand-new chemical that chemists call polytetrafluoroethylene, but which was fortunately nicknamed PTFE and trademarked by DuPont as Teflon.

After appearing in a variety of industrial guises, such as slippery bearings that don't need oil, Teflon began to show up in the kitchen in the 1960s as a coating for frying pans that would clean up in a jiffy because they didn't get dirty in the first place.

Modern variations are known by a variety of trade names, but they're all essentially PTFE, coupled with various schemes to make it stick to the pan, which as you can imagine is no small trick. I'm getting to that.

But first, let's understand why an egg tends to stick to a non-nonstick pan in the first place.

Things may stick to one another (and be unstuck from one another) for reasons that are primarily either mechanical or chemical. Although there are weak attractions between protein molecules and metals, the sticking of an egg to a regular frying pan is largely mechanical; the congealing egg white grabs onto microscopic crags and crevices. Scratching your frying pans by the too vigorous use of metal spatulas makes things even worse. I use PTFE-coated spatulas, even on my metal-surfaced pans.

To minimize mechanical sticking we use cooking oil. It fills in the crevices and floats the egg above the crags on a thin layer of liquid. (Any liquid would do that, but water wouldn't last long enough in a hot pan to do much good unless you use lots of it, in which case you've got yourself a poached egg instead of a fried one.)

The surfaces of nonstick pan coatings, on the other hand, are extremely smooth on a microscopic scale. Because they have virtually no cracks, there's nothing there for food to grab on to. Of course, glass and many plastics share this virtue, but PTFE is resilient and stands up well to high temperatures.

But chemical sticking is also important. The world's strongest stickinesses, such as in adhesives, are largely due to those molecule-to-molecule attractions I mentioned, which then require chemical warfare to break down. For example, paint thinner (mineral spirits) will get the chewing-gum residue off your shoe after mechanical scraping has failed.

In the kitchen, the atoms or molecules of a frying pan surface can form weak chemical bonds to certain food molecules. But the molecules of PTFE are unique in that they won't form bonds to anything. Here's why.

PTFE is a polymer, made up of only two kinds of atoms, carbon and fluorine, in a ratio of four fluorine atoms to every two carbon atoms. Thousands of these six-atom molecules are bonded together into gigantically bigger molecules that look like long carbon backbones with fluorine atoms bristling out like the spikes on a woolly caterpillar.

Now of all types of atoms, fluorine is the one that least wants to react with anything else once it has comfortably bonded with a carbon atom. PTFE's bristling fluorine atoms therefore effectively constitute a suit of caterpillar armor, protecting the carbon atoms against bonding with any other molecules that may come along. That's why nothing sticks to PTFE, including the molecules in an egg, a pork chop, or a muffin. PTFE won't even let most liquids adhere to it strongly enough to wet it. Put a few drops of water or oil on a nonstick pan and you'll see.

Which brings us (finally) to the question of how they get the coating to stick to the frying pan in the first place. You can now guess that they use a variety of mechanical, rather than chemical, techniques to roughen up the pan's surface so that the sprayed-on PTFE coating can get a good foothold. Dramatic improvements in those techniques have made today's nonstick cookware vastly superior to the thin, flaky, scratchable coatings of yesteryear. Some manufacturers now even dare you to use metal implements on their pans.

There are quite a few kinds of nonstick coatings, and most of them are still based on PTFE. One example is the Whitford Corp.'s Excalibur, used on several brands of quality cookware. In this process, tiny droplets of white-hot, molten stainless steel are blasted at the surface of a stainless-steel pan. The droplets splatter and weld themselves onto the pan, leaving a jagged, toothy surface. Several layers of PTFE-based formulations are then sprayed on, building up a thick, strong coating that is held tightly by those microscopic steel teeth. The Excalibur process works only on stainless steel, but other processes, such as DuPont's Autograph, work on aluminum.

FEAR OF FRYING

(... with apologies to James Barber, Jill Churchill, Josh Freed, Ed Goldman, Barbara Kafka, Rosa A. Mo, John Martin Taylor, Virginia N. White, and all the other authors who couldn't resist using this pun)

I want to buy a high-quality, general-purpose frying pan, but there are so many kinds of metals and coatings that I can't figure out what's best. What should I be looking for?

... .

First, loosen up your wallet, because you said "high quality" and that doesn't come cheap.

The ideal frying pan will distribute the burner's heat uniformly over its surface, transfer it quickly to the food, and respond promptly to changes in heat settings. That boils down to two qualities: thickness and heat conductivity. Look for a thick pan made out of a metal that conducts heat as efficiently as possible.

A frying pan should be made of heavy-gauge metal, because the more bulk it has, the more heat it can hold. When you add room-temperature ingredients to a hot, thin pan they can rob enough heat from the metal that it falls below the optimum cooking temperature. Moreover, any hot spots on the range burners will go straight through the bottom of a thin pan to the food without being dispersed sideways, resulting in burned or scorched spots on the food. A thick pan, on the other hand, has enough heat reserves or "heat inertia" to maintain a steady cooking temperature in spite of these vicissitudes.

The most crucial property of a frying pan's metal is how well it conducts heat; it must have what scientists call a high thermal conductivity. That's true for three reasons.

First, you want the pan to transmit the burner's heat quickly and efficiently to the food. You wouldn't get much frying done in a pan made of glass or porcelain, which are terribly slow conductors of heat.

Second, you want all sections of the pan's surface to be at the same temperature, so that all the food gets the same treatment despite unevenness in the burner's temperature. Gas burners have separate tongues of flame lapping at different parts of the pan's bottom, while electric burners are coils of hot metal with cooler spaces in between. A high-conductivity pan bottom will quickly even out these irregularities.

Third, you want the pan to respond rapidly to changes in burner settings, both up and down. Frying and sautéing are constant battles to keep the food at a high temperature without burning it, so you must frequently adjust the burner. A pan made of high-conductivity metal will respond quickly to these changes.

Okay, so which metal is best?

And the winner is . . . silver! The best frying pan in the world would have a heavy bottom made of the one metal which conducts heat better than all others: silver.

You say you can't afford a sterling silver frying pan? Well, there is a very close second: copper, which conducts heat 91 percent as well as silver. Too much copper in the diet can be unhealthful, however, so the insides of copper pans must be lined with a less toxic metal. Tin was the standby for many years, but it is soft and melts at only 450°F. Modern metallurgical technology can bond thin nickel or stainless-steel layers to the insides of copper pans.

In my opinion, then, you can find nothing better than a heavy copper frying pan lined with stainless steel or nickel. Unfortunately, you may have to hock your wok to buy one. It's the most expensive cookware because copper is more expensive than aluminum or stainless steel, it's a difficult metal to work, and bonding steel or nickel linings onto it isn't easy to do on a mass-market scale.

Then what's the next-best metal? Aluminum. It's very cheap, yet it conducts heat 55 percent as well as silver does—still no slouch in the heat transmission derby. A thick aluminum pan can do a fine job of frying and sautéing, and it has the advantage of being only 30 percent as heavy (dense) as copper.

BUT (there's always a but): Aluminum is susceptible to attack by food acids, so it, too, is often lined with a nonreactive coating such as 18/10 stainless steel: an alloy that contains 18 percent chromium and 10 percent nickel. A hard stainless steel layer also conquers the main problem with aluminum: its relative softness. It scratches easily, and food will stick to a scratched frying pan surface.

There is another way to protect aluminum, however. Its surface can be electrochemically converted into a layer of dense, hard, nonreactive aluminum oxide by a process known as anodizing—passing an electric current between the aluminum and another electrode in a sulfuric acid bath. Calphalon is one popular brand of anodized aluminum cookware. The oxide layer, normally white or colorless but blackened by a dye in the acid bath, serves both to protect the aluminum's surface—it's 30 percent harder than stainless steel—and to protect it from acids, although the oxide is susceptible to alkaline chemicals such as dishwashing detergent. The anodized surface is also stick-resistant, but not actually nonstick. A really heavy anodized aluminum pan is certainly worth considering. It should be at least 4 millimeters thick.

At the bottom of the frying pan quality heap is solid stainless steel, which is the worst conductor of all among the common skillet materials: only 4 percent as good as silver. It can be shiny and pretty when new, but I call it "shameless steel" because it claims not to corrode or stain, yet it really does; salt can pit it and it discolors at high temperatures.

The individual virtues of copper, aluminum, and stainless steel can be combined by layering the metals, as we've seen with stainless-steel-lined copper and aluminum. All-Clad's Master-Chef pans, for example, have a core of aluminum sandwiched between two layers of stainless steel. Their Cop-R-Chef pans are a sandwich of aluminum between a stainless inside and a copper outside, but the copper is largely cosmetic; it isn't thick enough to compete with the arm-and-a-leg French solid copper pans. And speaking of layers, you can opt for a nonstick coating on the interior surfaces of many of these pans

Finally, most inexpensive of all and in a class by itself is that old, black cast-iron skillet that comic-strip wives used to hit their husbands over the head with. It is thick and heavy (iron is 80 percent as dense as copper), but a poor heat conductor: only 18 percent as good as silver. Thus, a cast-iron skillet will be slow to heat, but once heated—and it can be taken up to a couple of thousand degrees without warping or melting—it will hold onto its heat tenaciously. That makes it an excellent pan for certain specialized uses in which a high, uniform temperature must be held for a long time. No true southerner would make fried chicken in anything else.

You should certainly keep one handy for dealing with domestic fowls and domestic fouls, but it's not the general-purpose tool you inquired about.

MAGNETIC MAGIC

What's the best way to store my kitchen knives?
I've read that keeping them on a magnetic rack
somehow damages their blades. Is that true?

. . . .

No. Believe it or not, a magnetic rack might actually keep your knives sharp longer. In fact, in one of those slick catalogs of expensive gadgets that no one needs, I even saw a magnetic housing for storing your razor, allegedly to keep the blade sharp between shaves. (How it would otherwise get dull between shaves was not explained.)

You may have noticed that knives kept on a magnetic rack do become magnetized. (Try picking up paper clips with them.) And according to Professor Bob O. Handley of MIT's Materials Science and Engineering Department, a magnetized piece of steel will be somewhat stiffer than when it is not magnetized. It can probably then be sharpened to a keener edge and may stay sharp longer in use.

But don't count on it. Knife blades are made of several different steel alloys, and some of them may not retain their magnetism very long. The stiffening effect isn't likely to be very large in any case.

On the other hand, the careless use of a magnetic rack can indeed damage your knives if you whack or drag the cutting edges against the magnet bar when removing them or putting them back. That may be how the story got started that magnetic racks can dull the edges.

If you are worried about nicking your knife blades through hasty grabbing from a magnetic rack, you might prefer to keep them in a countertop wooden rack. Some people think that's really the best way. But who, besides Martha Stewart and the recipients of wedding gifts, owns a set of perfectly graduated knives, all tucked away in their custom-fitted, wooden slots? The downsides are that the slots are hard to clean and it's not easy to tell from the protruding handles which knife you're grabbing. With a magnetic rack on the wall, you can always select the right one for the job.

As every culinary textbook warns, a sharp knife is a safe knife; it won't slip off the food onto a finger. There are many good electric and manual knife sharpeners on the market, so the time-honored and time-consuming method of honing them on a stone is no longer necessary.

But a word of warning: Those brute-force sharpeners containing two interleaved sets of disks through which you draw the knife blade scrape off wholesale slivers of metal that will stick to the blade if it's magnetized. (These sharpeners are not recommended unless you like knives that get progressively skinnier.) Metal slivers are not nice to eat, however, so after you use such a sharpener wipe the knife carefully with a wet paper towel. That's a good idea if you keep your knives on a magnetic rack no matter what kind of sharpener you use, because abraded metal particles can be invisibly small.

GIVING A BRUSH THE BRUSH-OFF

I can't seem to keep my pastry brushes clean or
undamaged. I must have bought ten new ones in
the past year. Any suggestions?

. . . .

Yes. Wash them properly and don't use them for unintended purposes.

After being used to brush on an egg wash or melted butter, a pastry brush becomes gummy and rancid unless you wash it thoroughly before putting it away. Wet it with hot water and work up a lather by

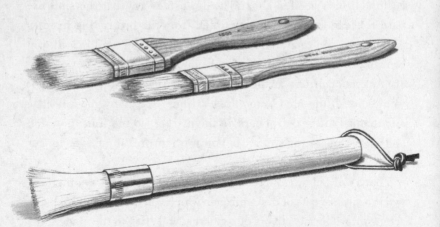

Two pastry brushes (top) and a basting brush (bottom).

swishing it around on a cake of soap, as if lathering up a shaving brush. Then work the lather well into the bristles against the palm of your hand. Or else plunge it up and down in a container of hot water and dishwashing liquid. In either case, rinse it well with hot water and air-dry it thoroughly before putting it away in the drawer.

Regarding the damage: Don't confuse a pastry brush with a basting brush, as several articles in popular food magazines have done. They're two separate tools, designed to do different jobs.

Pastry brushes aren't made to withstand heat; their soft, natural boar bristles can melt if used to apply oil or sauce to hot foods in the oven or on the grill. The longer-handled basting brushes, on the other hand, with their stiffer, synthetic bristles, can take the heat without melting.

Just as a pastry brush shouldn't be used for basting, a basting brush is too stiff for use on delicate pastry.

> The cheap paintbrushes with unfinished wooden handles and natural white bristles that are sold in hardware stores are virtually identical to the expensive pastry brushes sold in kitchen supply stores.

JIFFY LUBE

To cut down on my use of fat, I put some oil in a spray bottle, but all it did was shoot out a heavy, calorie-laden stream. Is there a better way to make my own "cooking spray"?

. . . .

Yes, there is a better way.

Ordinary plastic spray bottles are made to spray watery liquids, not oily ones. Water is thinner (less viscous) than oil and breaks up easily into a mist, but the paltry pressure from a trigger pump isn't enough to break oil down into microscopic droplets, the way a pressurized aerosol can can.

Cookware stores and catalogs sell olive oil sprayers that are great for oiling frying pans and grill pans, "greasing" baking pans, making garlic bread, spraying salad greens, and many other uses. You put the oil in them and pressurize them by pumping the cap. The oil then sprays out in a fine mist at the touch of a button, just as if from an aerosol can.

I keep a small, trigger-operated plastic bottle of plain water in the kitchen for a variety of moisturizing chores. The best way I've found to freshen up a loaf of French bread is to dampen it slightly with a spritz of water and put it in a 350°F toaster oven for two minutes. Many dishes will look brighter and fresher if misted just before being taken from the kitchen to the table. Almost any hot dish that has had to stand in the kitchen for a while before being served will benefit from this beauty treatment. Food stylists use this trick to make dishes look fresh for the camera.

A JUICY STORY

I often make lemon curd as a filling for small tarts, and of course I always use freshly squeezed lemon juice. But it seems that I waste a lot of juice by not getting it all out. Is there some way to get the maximum amount of juice out of a lemon or lime?

. . . .

You'll read in some food books and magazines that you should roll it firmly on the counter. Others recommend microwaving it for a minute or so. These actions sound perfectly reasonable, but I have always wondered whether they really work.

I had a chance to find out when my friend Jack, who loves to find bargains, discovered that a local supermarket was overstocked with limes and selling them at twenty for a dollar. With visions of endless margaritas dancing in his head, he bought forty for himself and called me to spread the news.

What an opportunity! Here was my chance to do the experiment I'd always wanted to do. But from my long experience as an academic scientist I knew that a proposal to the National Science Foundation would be unlikely to earn the necessary funding. So I dipped into my own reserves, procured four dollars' worth of limes without any competitive bidding or even so much as a purchase order, and delivered them personally via Toyota to my lab—uh, kitchen. They were large, green, good-looking Persian limes, the most common type in American supermarkets.

I wanted to find out whether heating a lime (or lemon; the principles should be the same) in a microwave oven or rolling it on the counter before squeezing will really produce more juice. I had always been suspicious of these recommendations which, like many tenets of kitchen lore, have never (to my knowledge) been scientifically investigated. I wanted to test them with all the rigor of a controlled scientific experiment. I did that, and the results may surprise you.

Here, in the lab-notebook style that they taught me to use in high school science, is what I did.

EXPERIMENT NO. 1

Procedure:

I divided 40 limes into four groups. (The math was easy.) One group, I microwaved for 30 seconds in an 800-watt oven; the second, I rolled firmly on the counter beneath the palm of my hand; the third, I both rolled and microwaved; to the fourth I did nothing, as a control. I weighed each lime, gave it its treatment, if any, cut it in half, extracted the juice with an electric juicer, and measured the amount of juice obtained. I then compared the yields in milliliters of juice per gram of fruit. I'll spare you the details of the weight, volume, and temperature measurements and the statistical analysis of the data.

Results and Discussion:

There was no detectable difference among the four groups of limes. Neither microwaving, nor rolling, nor rolling and microwaving produced any increase in the yield of juice.

Why should it, really? A fruit contains a certain amount of juice, depending on its variety, its growth conditions, and its post-harvest handling. Why on earth should anyone expect warming it or man-handling it to change that amount of juice? That's the part of citrus folklore that never made sense to me, and I have now proved it wrong.

But of course an electric juicer extracts virtually all of the juice that the lime contains. Maybe microwaving and rolling make it easier to get the juice out. When squeezing by hand, you may therefore get more juice for the same amount of squeezing pressure.

EXPERIMENT NO. 2

Procedure:

I divided another two dollars' worth of limes into four groups as before, but this time I squeezed them as hard as I could by hand. Naturally, I got less juice: on average, less than two-thirds of the machine yield. A much stronger man could undoubtedly get more. But I flatter myself that my right-hand strength probably exceeds that of the typical female cook.

Results and Discussion:

Hand-squeezing the limes as they came from the store yielded an average of 61 percent of their total juice. Microwaving yielded 65 percent, while rolling yielded 66 percent. All three of these results are the same, within experimental error. My skepticism was again justified; neither rolling nor microwaving prior to hand-squeezing significantly increases the amount of juice obtained.

But here's the big surprise: Rolling followed by microwaving made the limes so easy to squeeze that they yielded 77 percent of their total juice, some 26 percent more than untreated limes. They practically gushed juice, and I had to cut them over the juice collector to avoid losing any.

Here's what I concluded must be going on: Rolling breaks open some of the vacuoles—those little pillowcases full of juice in the fruit's cells. But the juice still can't flow out very easily because its surface tension (the "surface glue" that makes drops of liquid want to remain spherical) and its viscosity (its non-flowability) are both pretty high. But when the liquid is subsequently heated, its surface tension and viscosity drop substantially and the juice can flow out more easily, much more easily than I would have expected without looking up the actual viscosities. At the average before- and after-microwaving temperatures, it turns out that water (close enough to lime juice) flows four times as easily when it's hot. So the rolling breaks open the floodgates and the heating allows the flood to flow more easily.

Summary

If you are using an electric or mechanical juicer, rolling and/or microwaving will accomplish nothing. The same goes for those ribbed wooden or plastic reamers and the old-fashioned ribbed-glass juicers, because they also release virtually all of the juice that the fruit contains.

But if you are hand-squeezing limes and have a microwave oven, roll them on the counter and then microwave them. Rolling alone makes them softer and they appear to be juicier, but it hardly affects the yield. Microwaving alone accomplishes little more than to make the juice uncomfortably hot: 170 to 190°F in my experiments.

Although I didn't test them, I would expect that the same techniques to produce similar results with lemons. I've told Jack to keep an eye out.

Finally, what is the maximum amount of juice you can expect to get out of a lime? Limes are particularly fickle fruits, and recipes should therefore specify a number of ounces, rather than "juice of half a lime." The average electric-juicer yield of all my Persian limes was exactly two ounces, whereas rolling, zapping, and hand-squeezing yielded an average of 1.5 ounces. The champion in my sample contained 2.5 ounces, while two very healthy-looking specimens yielded only three-tenths of an ounce each.

As a result of my experiments, I now have enough lime juice for 130 margaritas. Just give me a little time. (If you'd like to join me, see the recipe on page 247.)

A Use for Juice

Lemon Curd

We can only assume that our lime-juicing technique works just as well on lemons, since we haven't received any word from Jack on lemon bargains. It's well worth the modest effort of squeezing them to make this delicious spread for toast or biscuits. It also makes a great tart or cake filling and is wonderful in a jelly roll. It will keep for months in the refrigerator.

---

5 **large egg yolks**
⅓ **cup sugar**
⅓ **cup lemon juice**
   Zest of two lemons
   Pinch of salt
¼ **cup (½ stick) unsalted butter**

---

1. In a heavy saucepan or the top of a double boiler, combine the egg yolks with the sugar and stir over low heat. Add the lemon juice, zest, and salt.
2. Stir, adding pieces of butter little by little. Cook until thick, 3 to 4 minutes, stirring constantly.
3. Pour into a clean jar, and place a round of waxed paper on the surface to prevent a skin from forming. Store in the refrigerator.

MAKES ABOUT 1 CUP

YOU CAN'T WASH YOUR CAR
WITH A WET MUSHROOM

All the cookbooks say that one should never wash
mushrooms because they soak up water like a
sponge and that we should give them only a quick
rinse or simply wipe them off. But aren't they
grown in manure?

. . . .

Soak up water? Not true. Those books are wrong.

Grown in manure? I'm afraid so.

First, let's deal with the manure.

The common white or brown button mushrooms in the super-markets (*Agaricus bisporus*) are cultivated in beds, or so-called substrate mixtures, that can include anything from hay and crushed corncobs to chicken manure and used straw bedding from horses' stables.

That knowledge bothered me for many years. Repeatedly warned against waterlogging my mushrooms by giving them a bath, however, I resorted to a soft-bristled mushroom brush that presumably whisked away the nasties from dry mushrooms without bruising them. It didn't do much. I sometimes even peeled my mushrooms, a time-consuming pain in the neck.

But as the hymn "Amazing Grace" would have it, *"I once was lost but now am found; was blind, but now I see."* I know now that the mushroom growers compost their substrate material for fifteen to twenty days, which raises its temperature to a sterilizing level. The compost, regardless of its origin, is germ-free before it is "planted" with the mushroom spores.

Nevertheless, I can't help thinking that there is more to manure than germs. So I still clean my mushrooms. And yes, I wash them in water, because they don't absorb more than a tiny bit, as I'll show below. Moreover, I seriously doubt that a water wash removes flavor, as some books claim. That would be true only if their flavor resided mostly on the surface and was predominantly water soluble.

I was always suspicious of the sponge model of mushroom flesh because it never appeared to me to be the least bit porous, even under a microscope. (Yes, I did that.) When I read Harold McGee's book *The Curious Cook* (North Point Press, 1990), I felt vindicated. An equally suspicious type, McGee weighed a batch of mushrooms, soaked them in water for five minutes—about ten times longer than any washing would take—wiped them off and weighed them again. He found that their weight had increased very little.

I have repeated McGee's experiment with two 12-ounce packages of white *Agaricus* mushrooms (a total of 40 mushrooms) and a 10-ounce package of brown ones (16 mushrooms). I weighed each batch carefully on a laboratory scale, soaked them in cold water with occasional stirring for McGee's five minutes, threw off most of the water in a salad spinner, rolled them around in a towel, and weighed them again.

The white mushrooms, all tightly closed buttons, had absorbed only 2.7 percent of their weight in water. That's less than three teaspoons of water per pound of mushrooms, in agreement with McGee's result. The brown mushrooms retained more water: 4.9 percent of their weight or five teaspoons per pound. That's probably because their caps were slightly separated from the stems and water was trapped in the gill spaces, not because their flesh is any more absorbent. Many other irregularly shaped vegetables would mechanically trap small amounts of water. And the timid "quick rinse" recommended for mushrooms by many cookbooks might trap just as much as my five-minute soak did.

So go ahead and wash your mushrooms to your heart's content—at least the common button kind; I haven't tested any of the more exotic varieties. But bear in mind that any brown dirt you see isn't manure; it's probably sterilized peat moss, with which the growers cover the composted substrate and through which the mushrooms actually poke their little heads.

And by the way, if you find your mushrooms releasing so much water in the sauté pan that they are steaming instead of browning, it's not because you've washed them. It's because the mushrooms themselves are almost entirely water and you've crowded them so much in the pan that the expelled steam can't escape. Sauté them in smaller batches or use a bigger pan.

Squeaky-Clean Mushrooms

Autumn Mushroom Pie

Brush 'em, rinse 'em, or wash 'em. Who cares? This woodsy mushroom pie will wow all comers.

Use a combination of richly flavored mushrooms such as cremini, porcini, chanterelle, and portobello. To keep the cost down, you can use half white button mushrooms, although the flavor won't be as 'shroomy. Make the filling up to a day ahead.

Pastry for a 9-inch double-crust pie

2½ cups finely chopped onions (3 to 4 medium onions)

4 tablespoons unsalted butter

8 cups coarsely chopped mushrooms, assorted, cleaned
(about 3 pounds)

1 teaspoon dried thyme leaves

¼ cup dry Marsala wine

Salt

Freshly ground black pepper

1 tablespoon all-purpose flour

1 egg yolk mixed with 1½ teaspoons water

Sprigs of fresh thyme for garnish, optional

---

1. To make the filling, sauté the onions in butter in a 12-inch skillet over medium heat. Cook the onions until soft and golden, but not brown, about 10 minutes. Add the mushrooms and dried thyme. The mushrooms will reduce in volume and release their juices.

2. Add the Marsala and continue cooking until the liquid reduces by half. Season generously with salt and pepper to taste. Sprinkle the flour over the mixture and stir for a minute or so until the juices thicken slightly. Remove from the heat. Cool this filling before making the pie.

3. Preheat the oven to 400°F. Fit the dough for the bottom crust into a 9-inch pie pan. Add the mushrooms, smoothing them evenly. Dampen the edge of the dough with water. Top with the remaining dough, pressing the edges to seal. Trim and flute the edges.

4. Place the egg yolk and water in a small dish and whisk together with a fork. Gently brush this egg wash over the top crust with your fingertips or a soft pastry brush. Bake the pie for 35 minutes, or until the crust is golden. Serve warm or at room temperature. Garnish the servings with sprigs of thyme if desired.

SERVES 6 AS LUNCHEON OR SIDE DISH

GRAMPA'S FOLLY

According to my dad, my grandfather used to go into the woods and collect wild mushrooms, which my grandmother would cook. My dad once asked her how she could tell if the mushrooms were safe to eat. She said she always put a silver dollar in the pan with the mushrooms, and if it didn't turn dark with tarnish the mushrooms were okay. My dad and I are wondering what the scientific basis is behind this method.

. . . .

Stop! I hope I caught you before you put Grandma's reputed wisdom to the test. There is no scientific basis whatsoever to the silver dollar trick. It's nonsense. I'd call it an old wives' tale, except that women who lived to be old wives never believed it.

There is no simple way of distinguishing poisonous mushrooms from safe ones, except by knowing and identifying the species. There are tens of thousands of known species of mushrooms, and many of the poisonous ones look very much like the edible ones. I personally don't have a good visual memory for shapes, so I permit myself to pick only two or three species that have no evil twins. I let the experts (or my favorite restaurants) supply me with the cèpes, morels, chanterelles, porcini, shiitake, enoki, and oyster mushrooms that have so enlivened American cuisine in recent years.

Incidentally, those ubiquitous portobellos that are on every menu these days are not a separate species; they're common brown *Agaricus* mushrooms that have been allowed to grow big before harvesting.

Your grandfather did your father a disservice, if I may say so, by letting him believe the silver coin test. He simply knew his mushrooms.

KEEPING COPPER PROPER

*I recently purchased a set of copper cookware and
it looks great. How can I keep it looking new?*

. . . .

Shiny copper is beautiful, and there are some wonderfully effective polishes on the market. But are you a cook or a decorator? The great virtue of copper or copper-clad cookware is that it conducts heat superbly and evenly. For that it deserves to be cherished, not polished. If you try to keep your copper cookware in its virginal state you will have taken on a full-time job.

But to avoid having them look too blotchy, there are a few simple things you can do. Don't ever put them in the dishwasher; the highly alkaline detergent can discolor the copper. Dry them completely after washing with dishwashing liquid. Make sure to get all the grease off with a mildly abrasive cleaner, because when heated it will burn into a black stain. Finally, don't heat the pans too hot, either with oil in them or especially when empty. Dark copper oxide forms most readily on the hottest spots, and you may wind up with the pattern of the burner imprinted on the pan's bottom.

MEASURE FOR MEASURE

WHEN AN OUNCE IS NOT AN OUNCE

Why do we have different measuring cups for wet and dry ingredients? A cup of sugar is the same volume as a cup of milk, isn't it?

. . . .

That depends on what your definition of "is" is.

A cup is indeed a cup throughout the land: eight U.S. fluid ounces, whether wet or dry. But you may be wondering: If a fluid ounce is a measure of fluids, how come we use it also to measure flour and other dry solids? And what's the difference between an ounce of volume and an ounce of weight?

The confusion stems from our antiquated American system of measurements. Here's what we were supposed to have learned in school (pay attention now, and follow the bouncing ounce): A U.S. fluid ounce is an amount of volume or bulk and is to be distinguished from a British fluid ounce, which is a different amount of volume, both of which are to be distinguished from an avoirdupois ounce, which is not an amount of volume at all but an amount of weight and is to be distinguished from a troy ounce, which is a different amount of weight and is *not* to be distinguished from an apothecary's ounce, which is exactly the same as a troy ounce except in February, which has 28. Is that perfectly clear?

Now if that isn't an argument for the International System of Measurement, known throughout the world as the SI, for *Système International* in French and to us as the Metric System, I don't know what is. In the SI, weight is always in kilograms and volume is always in liters. In the entire world, the United States is the only nation still using what used to be called the British system of measurement until even the British abandoned it and went metric.

Let's rephrase your question. Aren't eight good old American fluid ounces of milk the same amount of volume as eight good old American fluid ounces of sugar?

They certainly are. We'd really be in trouble if that weren't the case. But we still need a set of glass measurers for liquids and a separate set of metal measurers for solids.

Try to measure out a cup of sugar in a two-cup glass measurer and you'll have a tough time judging exactly when the sugar reaches the one-cup mark, because the sugar's surface isn't completely level. But even after you tap it on the counter to flatten it out and adjust it exactly to the mark, you won't have the amount of sugar that the recipe intended. That's because the recipe tester used a metal, one-cup "dry" measurer, filled flat to the brim. And believe it or not, that gives you a different amount of sugar than if you measured it out in a glass measurer.

Try it. Measure out exactly one cup of sugar by slightly overfilling a one-cup metal measurer and scraping off the excess with a straight edge, such as the back of a large chef's knife. Now pour the sugar into a two-cup glass measurer and jiggle it until the sugar's surface is flat. Betcha it doesn't come fully up to the one-cup line.

Could that be due to inaccuracies in the measuring cups themselves? Not unless you're using a flea-market special, with lines that look as if they were hand-painted in kindergarten; reputable kitchenware manufacturers are pretty careful about the accuracy of their products. No, the answer lies in a fundamental difference between liquids and granulated solids such as sugar, salt, and flour.

When you pour a liquid into a container it flows down into every crevice, leaving no spaces, not even microscopic ones. But a granulated solid can settle unpredictably, depending on the shape and size of the grains and of the container. Generally, when poured into a wide container, the grains get a chance to spread out more and fill in the spaces beneath them, so they settle down more compactly than if they were stacked up in a narrow container. And because they are settled more densely, they occupy less volume. The same weight of sugar will therefore actually occupy less volume in a wide container than in a narrow one.

Back to the kitchen and to your measuring cups. Dollars to doughnuts you'll find that at the same capacity level, the diameter of your glass measuring cup is substantially wider than the mouth of your metal one. Therefore, sugar and especially flour, which is notorious for its erratic settling, will occupy less volume in the glass measurer. If you use a glass measurer for your dry ingredients, you'll be adding more than the recipe intended.

To nail this down, I tested the opposite effect: I poured a leveled metal measuring cup of sugar into a tall, narrow measuring vessel—a chemist's graduated cylinder. As I expected, it filled the cylinder quite a bit higher than the eight-ounce (237-milliliter) mark.

Modern glass measuring utensils are, unfortunately, even wider than their predecessors, probably because people today want to heat milk or other liquids in them in their microwave ovens, and those liquids won't froth or boil over as easily in a wide container. So today's liquid measurers are particularly poor for measuring dry ingredients. But there's a problem even when measuring liquids in them. In a wide container, a small error in the filling height can make a relatively large error in the volume. Those big, widemouthed glass measurers are therefore not as precise in use as the older, narrower ones. If you still have one of the oldies, cherish it.

And then there's the problem of measuring out teaspoons and tablespoons of liquids. Have you noticed how surface tension makes the liquid bulge up above the rim of the measuring spoon? How accurate can that possibly be? Those spoons were made for solids, not liquids.

The perfect solution to all these problems, I've found, is the aptly named Perfect Beaker, made by EMSA Design of Frieling USA. It's calibrated in every kind of liquid measurement you could want:

**The Perfect Beaker. Its conical shape provides maximum
accuracy for small amounts of liquids.**

ounces, milliliters, teaspoons, tablespoons, cups, and pints, including fractions thereof. This single measuring device is all you need,
from one ounce to one pint. Its ice-cream-cone shape ensures that
smaller amounts of material are automatically measured in a narrower container, producing the highest accuracy in reading. You can
also use it to convert from one unit to another, which will come in
handy at the beginning of the next millennium when, judging by
progress thus far, the U.S. will finally be coming around to using the
Metric System. Just find your American amount on the scale and read
its metric equivalent at the same level.

(Or am I being too pessimistic? After all, it's been only twenty-
seven years since Congress passed a law requiring metric conversion, and already Coke and Pepsi come in two-liter bottles.)

The ultimate answer to accuracy and reproducibility in the
kitchen is quite simple, but except for professional bakers and other

chefs, we Americans just won't do it: Instead of measuring solid ingredients by volume, such as by tablespoons and cups, weigh them; that's what most cooks in the rest of the world do. In metric units, for example, one hundred grams of sugar is always the same amount of sugar, no matter whether it's granulated or powdered or what kind of container you put it in. For liquids, there's only one metric unit: the milliliter or its multiple, the liter (one thousand milliliters). No cups, pints, quarts, or gallons to fuss with.

Quick: How many cups in half a gallon?

See what I mean?

Coffee Cake Goes Metric

Black Raspberry Coffee Cake

Here's a recipe in SI or metric units, just to show you what it will be like in the year 3000. The American equivalents are in parentheses, so if you wish you can ignore the metrics.

You will find tables of metric equivalents in various cookbooks, but they are often inconsistent. For one thing, the numbers are all rounded off, and everyone seems to round them off differently, depending on how finicky they choose to be. The equivalents given in this recipe are from actual weighings, rounded off only to the nearest whole number of grams or milliliters. But if you round them off a bit more (for example, 300 instead of 296), the cake won't explode. We haven't converted amounts of less than half a teaspoon because the numbers of grams would be inconveniently small. Guess. Or use your fractional teaspoon measures when the metric police aren't looking.

This rich dessert lies somewhere between a confection and a pastry. Cut into wedges to serve warm with coffee. Or measure out all the ingredients the night before and bake in the morning for a special brunch. Black or red raspberries, blueberries, or blackberries can take turns in the starring role. It freezes well, but don't plan on leftovers.

FOR THE CRUMB TOPPING

- 108 grams (½ cup) firmly packed light brown sugar
- 18 grams (2 tablespoons) all-purpose flour
- 14 grams (1 tablespoon) unsalted butter, chilled
- 14 grams (½ ounce) semisweet chocolate, finely chopped

FOR THE CAKE

- 135 grams (1 cup) all-purpose flour)
- 160 grams (¾ cup) sugar
- 2 grams (½ teaspoon) baking powder
- ¼ teaspoon (¼ teaspoon) baking soda

   ¼   **teaspoon (¼ teaspoon) salt**

   1   **large egg**

  79   **milliliters (⅓ cup) buttermilk**

   5   **milliliters (½ teaspoon) vanilla extract**

  76   **grams (⅓ cup) unsalted butter, melted and cooled**

 175   **grams (1¼ cups) fresh black (or red) raspberries**

1. In a small bowl, mix the brown sugar with the flour and add the butter, cutting it in with a pastry blender or two knives until the mixture is mealy. Add the chocolate and mix well. Set aside until ready to use.

2. Preheat the oven to 190° Celsius (375°F) and spray a 20-centimeter (8-inch) springform pan with nonstick baking spray. In a medium bowl, sift together the flour, sugar, baking powder, baking soda, and salt. In another bowl, whisk together the egg, buttermilk, vanilla, and melted butter.

3. Pour the liquid mixture into the flour mixture all at once. Stir until just smooth. Spread the batter evenly in the prepared pan. Scatter the berries evenly over the top. Distribute the crumb topping evenly over the berries.

4. Bake until richly browned, 40 to 45 minutes. Serve warm.

MAKES 8 TO 10 SERVINGS

A LONG INSTANT

Why is my "instant-read" thermometer so slow to
tell me the food's temperature?

. . . .

There are two types of so-called instant-read thermometers: the dial-type and the digital readout type. But do they really give you the temperature reading in an instant? Don't you wish! These reputed speed demons can take anywhere from 10 to 30 seconds to climb up to their highest readings, which are, of course, the numbers you need to see. Withdraw one from the food before it has reached that maximum reading and you'll be underestimating the temperature.

Certainly, you're in a hurry to get the reading. You don't want to stand there with your hand in the oven until a dawdling thermometer decides to reveal your roast's actual internal temperature. But the sad truth is that no thermometer can register the temperature of a food until it itself—the thermometer, or at least its probe—has reached the temperature of the food into which it has been thrust. In fact, you might say that the only thing a thermometer can do is tell you its *own* temperature. There is little you can do about the time it takes for the thermometer to heat up to the temperature of the food, except to choose a digital, rather than a dial, thermometer because, as I'll explain below, digitals generally read faster than dials.

What you *can* do something about is knowing exactly where in the food you are measuring the temperature. The two types of "instant reading" thermometers differ substantially in this respect.

Dial types sense the temperature by means of a bimetallic coil in the stem: a coil made of two different metals bonded together. Because the two metals expand at different rates when heated, heat makes the coil twist, which in turn twists a pointer on a dial. Unfortunately, the temperature-sensing coil is usually more than an inch long, so you're actually measuring the temperature averaged over a substantial region of the food. But you often need to be able to measure a highly localized temperature. Inside a roasting turkey, for example, the temperature varies quite a bit from place to place, but to test for doneness you need to know the specific temperature in the thickest part of the thigh.

A digital thermometer, on the other hand, measures the temperature at a more precise spot in the food. It contains a tiny, battery-operated semiconductor whose electrical resistance varies with temperature. (Techspeak: a thermistor.) A computer chip converts the resistance into electrical signals that operate the numerical display. Because the tiny thermistor is down in the tip of the probe, a digital thermometer is especially good for monitoring a grilled steak

A digital thermometer manufactured by Component Design.

or chop, for example, where you need to know the temperature in dead center.

The other advantage of the digitals is that because their thermistors are so small, they acquire the food's temperature quickly. That's why they usually give you a faster reading than the dial types.

NOW WE'RE COOKING

COOKING UNDER PRESSURE

---

*My mother's diabolical pressure cooker from the
1950s seems to be coming back in modern dress.
Exactly what do they do?*

. . . .

They speed up cooking by making water boil at a higher-than-normal temperature.

In the process, they may hiss, rattle, and sizzle like an infernal machine, threatening to redecorate your kitchen in shades of goulash. But your mother's pressure cooker has been re-engineered to be more mannerly and nearly foolproof. As with all cooking appliances, though, safety is a matter of understanding. Unfortunately, the instructions that come with the pressure cookers are full of scary dos and don'ts that make no sense unless you understand how the things work. That's what I'm here for.

Pressure cookers burst—pardon me, appeared—upon the scene after World War II as the "modern" way to cook for homemakers whose time was overprogrammed with cooking, cleaning and kids. Today, those baby-boom kids have grown up and are themselves overprogrammed with jobs, gyms, and Jeeps. Any gadget that promises a gold medal for speed in the Kitchen Olympics is a sure sell.

No matter how many shortcuts you take, though, there are two unavoidable, time-consuming steps in all cooking. One is heat transmission—getting the heat into the interior of the food. That can be the bottleneck in many a "quick" recipe, because most foods are poor conductors of heat. The other slow step is the cooking reactions themselves. The chemical reactions that change our foods from raw to cooked can be quite slow.

Microwave ovens circumvent the slowness of heat conduction by generating the heat right inside the food itself. But many dishes such as soups and stews benefit from the slow marrying of flavors that takes place in water-based cooking methods such as braising: the searing and simmering of meats and vegetables in a small amount of liquid in a covered vessel. You can't do that in a microwave oven because the microwaves, not the simmering liquid, will do the cooking.

To speed up braising, we would like to use a higher temperature, because all chemical reactions, including those in cooking, go faster at higher temperatures. But there is a big obstacle: Water has a built-in temperature limit of 212°F, its boiling point at sea level. Turn up the heat to flame-thrower intensities and the water or sauce will certainly boil faster, but it won't get one bit hotter.

Enter the pressure cooker. It boosts the boiling point of water up to 250°F. How? I'm glad you asked, because the cookbooks rarely tell you, nor do the instructions that come with the cookers.

For water to boil, its molecules must gain enough energy to

escape from the liquid and go flying off freely into the air as a vapor or gas. To do that, they have to push against the blanket of atmosphere that covers our entire planet. Air is light, but it goes up more than 100 miles and the blanket is therefore quite heavy; every square inch of it weighs about 15 pounds at sea level. Under ordinary conditions, water molecules must achieve energies equivalent to a 212°F temperature before they are able to push through that 15-pound-per-square-inch (psi) blanket and boil away.

Now let's heat a small amount of water in a pressure cooker, a tightly sealed container with a small, controllable vent for releasing air and steam. As the water begins to boil, it generates steam and, with the vent closed, the pressure inside the container builds up. Only after it has reached a total pressure of 30 psi—15 from the atmosphere plus an extra 15 from the steam—does the vent controller allow the excess steam to discharge into the kitchen. Thereafter, it maintains the pressure at that 30 psi level.

To push through this higher "blanket" pressure and keep on boiling, the water molecules must now achieve a higher energy than before. To overcome 30 psi of pressure, they require an energy equivalent to 250°F, and that becomes the new boiling temperature. The high-temperature, high-pressure steam speeds cooking by permeating all parts of the food.

As you start to heat the sealed pressure cooker, the vent releases air until the water begins to boil and steam forms. The steam pressure is held at the desired 30-psi level by some kind of pressure-limiting device. In many cases it's a little weight on top of the vent tube. During cooking, the weight wobbles aside to release all higher-than-30-psi steam, which hisses as it escapes and scares people into thinking the thing is about to explode. It's not. Newer pressure cooker designs use a spring valve instead of a weight to maintain the pressure at the desired level.

During cooking, you adjust the burner so that the contents boil fast enough to maintain the steam pressure, but not so fast that an excessive amount of steam is lost through the vent. In any event, the pressure regulator won't let you turn it into a bomb. After the allotted cooking time, you cool the pot down, so that the steam inside condenses—returns to liquid—and relieves the pressure. A safety device assures you that the pressure is gone (some models won't even let you open them until then), whereupon you may open and serve.

KITCHEN MAGNETISM

My neighbors just remodeled their kitchen and installed an induction-heating cooktop. How does it work?

. . . .

Microwave ovens were the first new way of making heat for cooking in more than a million years. Well, now there's a second one: magnetic induction heating.

Magnetic induction has been used for the past decade or so in some European and Japanese foodservice kitchens, and more recently in commercial American kitchens. They are now beginning to appear in the home.

Induction ranges differ from electric ranges in that electric cooktops generate heat by the *electrical* resistance of metal (the burner coils), while induction cooktops generate heat by the *magnetic* resistance of metal: the metal in the cooking vessel itself.

Here's how it works.

Beneath that beautiful, smooth ceramic surface on your neighbor's cooktop are several coils of wire like the coils of wire in a transformer. When one of the heating units is turned on, the house's 60-cycle alternating (AC) electric current begins to flow through it. For reasons that we won't go into (and that even Einstein couldn't really explain to his complete satisfaction), whenever electricity flows through a coil of wire it makes that coil behave like a magnet, complete with North and South poles. In this case, because the AC current is reversing its direction 120 times per second, the magnet is reversing its polarity back and forth 120 times per second.

So far, there's no evidence in the kitchen that anything at all is happening; we can't see, feel, or hear magnetic fields. The cooktop is still cool.

Now place an iron frying pan on top of the coil. The alternating magnetic field magnetizes the iron, first in one direction and then the other, switching its polarity back and forth 120 times per second. But magnetized iron isn't quite so easily persuaded to reverse its polarity, and it resists the vacillations to a significant degree. That causes much of the magnetic power to be wasted, and the wasted power shows up as heat in the iron. As a result, only the pan gets hot. There's no flame or red-hot electric coil, and the kitchen stays cool.

Any magnetizable (Techspeak: ferromagnetic) metal will be heated by this magnetic induction process. Iron will, of course, whether enameled or not. Many, but not all, stainless steels will. But aluminum, copper, glass, and pottery won't. To see whether a given utensil can be used on a magnetic induction cooktop, take one of those silly magnets off your refrigerator and see if it sticks to the bottom of the pan. If it does, the pan will work for induction cooking.

So in addition to the substantial cost of a magnetic induction cooktop, you can't use those treasured and expensive copper pans. Did your neighbors think of that before springing for their impressive, high-tech cooker?

LET THERE BE . . . HEAT!

*There's a new kind of oven that supposedly cooks
with light instead of heat. How does it work?*

. . . .

Is this a fourth new way of making heat for cooking, after fire, microwaves, and induction ranges? No. The so-called light oven

makes heat in pretty much the same way your electric range does:
through the electrical resistance-heating of metal.

Light ovens have been in specialized commercial use since about
1993 but are now being produced for home use. A countertop or
wall-mounted FlashBake oven manufactured by Quadlux Inc. has
been available since December 1998, while General Electric Appliances' built-in Advantium ovens have been available since October
1999 to builders and contractors for installation in new kitchens.

When I first heard about the light oven, my skeptic button was
pushed hard. Some of the promotional statements sounded like
pseudoscientific hype: They "harness the power of light." They cook
"with the speed of light" and "from the inside out."

Light does indeed travel, appropriately enough, at the speed of
light, but it doesn't penetrate most solids very far. Try reading this
page through a steak. How, then, can light deposit enough energy
inside the food to cook it, unless it is incredibly intense? I thought of
lasers, those ultrapowerful beams of light that we use for everything
from eye surgery to annoying the neighbors with little red dots, but
their light is so compact and concentrated that at most they could zap
one grain of rice at a time.

Ah, but there is "light," and then again there is "light." The secret
of the light oven lies not only in the intensity of its radiations but in
the blend of wavelengths that it generates. Here's how it works, based
on information I gathered from some of GE's techies. (They wouldn't
divulge *all* their secrets.)

"AND GOD SAID, 'Let there be visible light, but also ultraviolet,
infrared and an entire electromagnetic spectrum of longer and
shorter wavelengths'" (not an exact quote). What we humans call *light*
is the mere, thin slice of the solar energy spectrum that our eyes are
capable of detecting. But in a broader sense, the word "light" really
requires a more exact specification.

The light ovens contain banks of specially designed, long-life,

1500-watt halogen lamps that are not vastly different from the halogen lamps in many modern light fixtures. But only about 10 percent of a household halogen lamp's energy output is visible light; 70 percent is infrared radiation and the remaining 20 percent is heat. The light ovens' halogen lamps produce a secret mixture of visible light, various infrared wavelengths, and heat. It's the combination of all three that does the cooking.

(Regardless of what many science books may tell you, infrared radiation is not heat; it's a form of radiant energy that is converted to heat only when absorbed by an object. I call it "heat in transit." The sun's infrared radiation isn't heat until it is absorbed by the roof of your car. The "heat lamp" that some restaurants use to hold your plated food until the server comes back from vacation is sending out infrared radiation, and the food is warmed by absorbing that radiation.)

The light ovens' visible and near-visible light do indeed penetrate meat to some extent—you can shine a flashlight through your thumb in a dark room. And they aren't absorbed by water molecules as microwaves are, so they can deposit all their energy directly into the solid portions of the food, rather than wasting their energy by making hot water first. Some of the wavelengths put out by the halogen lamps can penetrate foods up to three- or four-tenths of an inch. That may not sound like a lot, but the deposited heat then gets conducted deeper into the food from there. And the ovens cheat by supplementing the halogen lamps with microwaves, which penetrate more deeply. (You can use the light ovens also as independent microwave ovens.)

Meanwhile, the longer-wavelength infrared radiations and the heat are being absorbed in the food's surface, browning and crisping it—something that microwave ovens can't do. Ordinary ovens take a long time to brown food because only some of their heat gets to the food by infrared radiation; the rest has to get there through the air, which is a poor conductor of heat. The light oven's infrared radiation heats the food's surface directly to a higher temperature than an ordinary oven can, so the browning is faster.

Speed, in fact, is the main selling point of light ovens. When GE's market research teams asked what consumers wanted most in their cooking appliances, the top 3 answers they got were speed, speed, and speed. People said they would love to be able to roast a whole chicken in 20 minutes and broil a steak in nine.

What's really remarkable about the light ovens is their computer technology. A microprocessor driven by proprietary software programs the on-off cycling of the lamps and the microwave generator in a carefully worked out sequence for the optimal cooking of each dish. GE's market research discovered that 90 percent of all American consumers' cooking entailed only 80 recipes (no comment), so these 80 recipes are programmed into the oven's data bank for push button cooking. Just punch in what kind of steak you have, its thickness and weight and how you want it done, and it's on your plate before you can say grace.

Now if we only had a computer that would dispense with all of that time-wasting soft music, candlelight, conversation, and wine.

HIGH-TECH, LOW-TECH, NO-TECH

WHY CRACKERS ARE HOLEY

. . . .

Why do crackers and matzos have all those little holes in them?

Saltines, Wheat Thins, Triscuits, Ritz Crackers, grahams, you name it—there's hardly a cracker anywhere that doesn't have a pattern of little holes in it.

The makers of matzos, the unleavened flatbread of the Jewish Passover, seem to have gone hog wild (you should excuse the expression) on perforations. Matzos are much hole-ier than secular crack ers. But it's not just a tradition; it's for a very practical purpose. And no, the 18 holes in a Keebler Club cracker are not a golf course for the elves.

According to a spokesperson at Keebler, there's a sort of mystique about cracker holes that occupies the minds of people who seem to have very little to do. They're prone to calling Keebler's customer relations line to ask questions such as, "Why are there 13 holes in saltines, while graham crackers have various numbers and a Cheez-It has a sole hole?" The answer: "It just turns out that way."

Here's a primer on the science of crackerpuncture.

When you're whipping up a 1,000-pound batch of dough by putting flour and water into an enormous mixer, as they do down at the cracker factory, there's just no way to avoid getting some air beaten into the mix. Then, when you roll the dough out real thin and put it into a hot oven (saltines are baked at 650 to 700°F), the trapped air bubbles will expand into bulges and can even explode. Air expands when heated because the molecules are moving faster and pushing harder against their confines.

Besides being unsightly, thin-skinned bulges can bake too fast, scorching before the rest of the dough is done. And if they burst, they leave pockmarks and craters in the surface. A cracker that looks like a scorched, foxhole-riddled battlefield makes a very poor impression on the tea table.

So just before a thin sheet of dough goes into the oven, a "docker"—a big cylinder with spikes or pins sticking out—rolls over its surface. The pins puncture the air bubbles, leaving those telltale pinholes in the dough. The pins are spaced differently for different kinds of crackers, depending on their ingredients, the baking temperature, and the desired final appearance. On saltines, for example, consumers seem to prefer a gentle, rolling-hills terrain, so some bubbles are allowed to billow between the dimples. And those square little Cheez-Its, with their one central hole, have the look of a punched pillow.

If that isn't already more than you want to know about cracker

holes, consider this: In crackers that contain leavening agents such
as baking soda, the rising, expanding dough will partially obliterate
the holes while resting or baking. But they'll usually still be there, at
least as slight depressions. You think there are no docker holes in
Wheat Thins? Hold one up to the light and you'll see the "fossilized"
remains. Even a rugged-surfaced Triscuit has 42 holes in it.

Puncturing bubbles is especially important in matzos, because
they're baked quickly at a very high temperature: 800 to 900°F. At
these temperatures the surface of the dough dries out quickly, and any
expanding bubbles would tend to blast through the hardened crust,
producing an oven full of kosher shrapnel. So some heavy-duty bubble perforating is in order. It's done by rolling over the dough sheet
with a "stippler," which is much like a docker, but with close-together
lines of teeth. That's what leaves those parallel furrows.

Because the dietary laws of Passover preclude the use of any leavening agents, matzos are made of flour and water only. One reason
for the thoroughness of the stippling, in fact, is to avoid the mere
appearance of leavening, even if it is produced innocently by expanding air bubbles. Because it is unleavened, matzo dough doesn't swell
in the oven to cover up the stippler tracks, and they remain quite
prominent in the finished product. You'll still see some blisters
between the tracks on a matzo, however. They come from very small
air bubbles that evaded the stippler but didn't get the chance to grow
to a destructive, explosive size. These unburst blisters contribute to
an interesting appearance in the finished product because their thin
skins brown faster than the rest of the dough.

Now you know why you have to prick the dough of a pie shell
before baking it or, for extra insurance, hold the dough down with
beans or pie weights. In addition to air pockets in the dough itself,
there may be some air hiding between the dough and the bottom of
the pan. Nothing will explode, but you're likely to end up with an
arched pie bottom if you don't take precautions.

Here's an easy way to remove an olive or gherkin from a densely packed jar. (How do they get them in there, anyway?) Hardware and kitchenware stores sell a little pickup tool for grasping small objects. It looks like a hypodermic. You press on the plunger and three or four spring-wire fingers emerge from the bottom. Lower them onto your prey, release the plunger, and the wire fingers try to spring back into the barrel, holding firmly onto their quarry. Press again to release the captive.

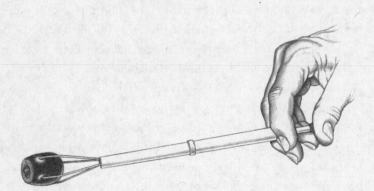

An olive and pickle picker.

SOME ILLUMINATION ON IRRADIATION

There is a lot of controversy about food irradiation. Exactly what is irradiation? And is it safe?

. . . .

Food irradiation is the practice of producers' subjecting their food products to intense fields of gamma rays, X rays, or high-energy electrons before shipping them to market.

Why would they want to do this?

- Irradiation kills harmful bacteria, including E. coli, Salmonella, Staphylococcus, and Listeria, among others, thereby reducing the danger of food-borne illness.
- Irradiation kills insects and parasites without the use of chemical pesticides. (Many of the spices, herbs, and seasonings used in the United States today have for some time been irradiated for this purpose.)
- Irradiation inhibits the spoilage of foods, and can stretch the world's available food supply. In more than thirty countries around the world, some forty different kinds of food, including fruits and vegetables, spices, grains, fish, meats, and poultry, are routinely being irradiated.

There are two classes of opposition to the widespread use of food irradiation. One centers on socioeconomic issues, and the other on safety.

The main socioeconomic objection is that food irradiation might be taken advantage of by the food industry for its own, self-serving purposes. Instead of cleaning up its less-than-satisfactory sanitation act, the food and agriculture industry might come to depend upon irradiation as an end-of-the-line cop-out to "neutralize" contaminated, sloppily produced meats and other foods.

I am no apologist for agribusiness, or for that matter for any enterprise whose sole purpose is to make money—even, when expedient, at the expense of public safety. There exists an undeniable history of illegal dumping of toxic wastes, for example, not to mention the collusion within a certain industry to conceal its knowledge of the lethal effects of burning and inhaling the smoke from its product. In this light it is difficult not to believe that food irradiation is tempting to food producers for what many would consider to be the wrong reasons.

But I hereby sidestep the political, social, and economic arguments for and against food irradiation, on which I have opinions in my role as a citizen, and focus purely on the scientific issues, which I deem myself more qualified to address. Only after the scientific facts are clear can the other issues be fought out with some semblance of objectivity.

Is food irradiation safe? Are airplanes safe? Are flu shots safe? Is margarine safe? Is living safe? (Of course not; it invariably ends in death.) I don't mean to belittle the question, but "safe" is probably the most useless word in the English language. It is so loaded with contexts, connotations, interpretations, and implications that it loses all meaning. And, of course, a meaningless word belies the very purpose of language.

Any scientist will tell you that proving a negative is virtually impossible. That is, trying to prove that something (for example, an untoward event) *won't* happen is futile. It is relatively easy to prove that something *does* happen; just try it several times and note that it happens. But if it doesn't happen there is always the next time, and predicting the next time is prophesy, not science. When you come right down to it, science can deal only in probabilities.

Allow me, then, to rephrase the question. What are the chances—the probabilities—that consuming irradiated food will in some way produce unhealthful effects? The scientific consensus is "very slim."

Here are some quick answers from a nuclear chemist (me), who in his time has both generated and been exposed to his share of radiation:

Do irradiated foods cause cancer or genetic damage? It has never happened.

Does irradiation make food radioactive? No. The energies of the radiations are too low to cause nuclear reactions.

Does irradiation change the chemical composition of whatever it irradiates? Of course it does. That's why it works. More about this later.

ONE BIG PROBLEM is that many people first came upon the word *radiation* in the context of the "deadly radiation" (the media love to use that phrase) that spews from atomic bombs and broken nuclear reactors. But radiation is a much broader—and more benign—concept than that.

Radiation is any energetic wave or particle that is traveling from one place to another at approximately the speed of light. The lamp on your desk sends out visible radiation called light. The broiler element in your oven sends invisible infrared radiation to your steak. Your microwave oven sends microwave radiation into your frozen peas. Cell phones, radio, and TV stations send out radiations bearing inane chatter, trash music, and moronic sitcoms.

And yes, inside a nuclear reactor there are intense nuclear radiations emanating from radioactive materials, including the very same gamma rays that are used in food irradiation. These, along with the X rays and high-energy electron beams also used in food irradiation, are called "ionizing radiations," because they have enough energy to break atoms apart into "ions"—charged fragments. They are indeed very dangerous for living things, from microbes to humans.

But the heat that we cook with is the very same heat that rages in the fires of Hell. You wouldn't want to be in the oven alongside your roast any more than you'd want to be inside a nuclear reactor or alongside the food while it's being irradiated. That doesn't make either cooking or irradiation dangerous. It's all a matter of who or what is being exposed.

X rays and gamma rays penetrate deeply into plant and animal tissue, doing damage to atoms and molecules in living cells along the way. These two kinds of radiations, along with beams of electrons, are used to irradiate foods precisely because they *do* damage the cells of insects and microorganisms, altering their DNA and preventing them from reproducing or even from staying alive. Heat, of course, does the same thing. That's why milk, fruit juices, and other foods are pasteurized by heating. But many germs are harder to kill than the bacteria that pasteurization is designed to deactivate. More drastic measures are necessary, but higher temperatures would change the taste and texture of the foods too much. That's where irradiation comes in.

Ionizing radiations can break the chemical bonds holding molecules together, whereupon the fragments may recombine in new and unusual configurations, forming molecules of new compounds called radiolytic products. Thus, irradiation does indeed cause disruptive chemical changes. That's how it kills bacteria. But while the changes in the bacteria's DNA are lethal to them, the amount of chemical change in the food itself is minuscule at the radiation intensities used. Ninety percent of the new chemicals formed are naturally present in foods anyway, especially in cooked foods. (Cooking causes chemical changes too, of course.) The other 10 percent? In more than four hundred studies reviewed by the FDA before approving food irradiation, no unfavorable effects were found from eating irradiated foods, either by humans or throughout several generations of animals.

While nothing, not even chocolate pudding, can definitively be shown to be absolutely "safe," I believe in the well-known scientific principle that the proof of the pudding is in the eating. Apparently, so do the FDA, the USDA, the Centers for Disease Control and Prevention, the Institute of Food Technologists, the American Medical Association, and the World Health Organization, all of whom have approved the safety of various forms of irradiated foods.

A frequently expressed concern is that the widespread use of food irradiators would pose a serious problem of radioactive waste disposal. Mindful of the huge amounts of intensely radioactive waste generated during the reprocessing of nuclear reactor fuels, people may naturally wonder about the disposal of used food irradiators. But food irradiators, dangerous as they are, are as different from a nuclear reactor as a flashlight battery is from an electric generating plant. Radioactive materials are indeed being used, but there is no waste buildup from their use.

Let's look at the hazards of the three types of food irradiators, one at a time.

X rays and electron beams used in food irradiation disappear like lamp light as soon as the switch is turned off. There is no lingering hazard and no radioactivity involved at all.

Cobalt-60 irradiators have been used safely in cancer therapy for decades all over the world. The radioactive cobalt, which must be

shielded from people by massive concrete walls, is in the form of little "pencils" of solid metal that can't leak. No one is going to throw
one into the nearest creek. Opponents of food irradiation point out
that in 1984 a cobalt radiotherapy unit somehow found its way to a
scrap yard in Mexico, its radioactivity eventually winding up in recy-
cled steel consumer products such as table legs. But that was not a
matter of radioactive waste. It was a deplorable instance of either stu-
pidity or cupidity, two traits that no amount of precaution or regula-
tion can erase from the human psyche.

Cesium-137, the other radioactive gamma ray source used in some
irradiators, is in the form of a powder encapsulated in stainless steel.
A byproduct of reactor fuel reprocessing, its half-life is thirty years,
so after its long useful lifetime is over it can be returned to reactor
waste as one more grain on the sand pile. A cesium-137 source being
used for the sterilization of medical supplies did leak disastrously in
1989, but the problem is understood and has been fixed.

Here are some of the commonly voiced "technical" objections to
food irradiation:

*"Food irradiation uses the equivalent of 1 billion chest X rays, which is
enough radiation to kill a person 6,000 times over."*

How is that relevant, I ask? Food irradiation is used on foods, not
on people. In a steel mill, the temperature of the molten steel is
3,000°F, which is hot enough to vaporize a human body. Workers in
steel mills and food irradiation facilities are therefore well advised
not to bathe in vats of molten steel or take naps on the food irradiation conveyor belts.

*"With each bite of irradiated food we receive indirect exposure to ioniz-
ing radiation."*

There is absolutely no radiation in the food, either direct or indirect, whatever that means. With each piece of steel we touch, do we
receive "indirect exposure" to that 3,000° temperature?

*"Ionizing radiation can kill beneficial microorganisms as well as
dangerous ones."*

That's true. So do canning and virtually all other food preservation methods. But so what? A serving of food without beneficial microorganisms is not harmful.

"Ionizing radiation cannot discriminate between, for instance, E. coli bacteria and Vitamin E. Everything in its path can be changed, including nutrients."

That's also true to some extent, depending on the food and the radiation dose. But I don't see the loss of some vitamins as a reason to ban the sterilization of foods by irradiation. All food preservation methods change the nutrient profile of foods to some extent. And I doubt if anyone's diet is going to be limited exclusively to irradiated foods.

SO, IS FOOD IRRADIATION safe? Can anything be proven to be absolutely safe? Just read the finely printed "possible side effects" notice in every package of health-giving and lifesaving prescription drugs. We would have no marketable drugs if "absolute safety" were the criterion for approving new medicines. As pointed out by James B. Kaper, Professor of Microbiology and Immunology at the University of Maryland School of Medicine, who has seen the devastating effects of E. coli poisoning in children, "Perhaps some minor adverse effects might eventually be linked to ingestion of irradiated food. But by that time, many people, mostly children, will have died from E. coli when they would have been protected by ingesting irradiated food."

Life is a continual risk-benefit analysis; some degree of risk is the inevitable dark shadow of any technological advance. Until the last decade of the nineteenth century, for example, we had no electricity in our houses. In the last decade of the twentieth, an average of more than two hundred people were electrocuted in the United States each year from household electrical devices such as lamps, switches, TVs, radios, washers, dryers, and so on, with another three hundred killed in some forty thousand electrical fires. We deplore and yet accept these consequences of having electricity in our homes because the benefits so vastly outweigh the risks.

We must compare the benefits of preserving foods and destroying harmful bacteria, insects and parasites—of stretching the world's food supply and saving lives—against the vastly less likely, and certainly not life-threatening, risks.

TALKING IN A WINTER WONDERLAND

I'm confused by all the separate compartments in my refrigerator. What am I supposed to keep in each? What, for example, does the "crisper" do?

. . . .

Every time I open the refrigerator door, Alex, my Siamese cat, eyes the contents like Willie Sutton peeking into Fort Knox. He knows that that big, white impregnable strongbox contains all the pleasures life has to offer. (He's neutered.)

We humans aren't much different. Our refrigerators are our treasure houses. Their contents reflect our individual lifestyles even more than the clothes we wear or the cars we drive.

The main purpose of a refrigerator, of course, is to exhibit every silly object that can conceivably be glued to a magnet, not to mention the scribbled "art" of children or grandchildren. But in addition, refrigerators produce low temperatures, and low temperatures slow down every process that spoils food, from chemical enzyme reactions to the ravages of living spoilers such as bacteria, yeasts and molds.

There are two kinds of bacteria that we want to inhibit: pathogenic (illness-causing) bacteria and spoilage bacteria. Spoilage bacteria make food repulsive and inedible, but they generally won't make us sick. Pathogenic bacteria, on the other hand, may be completely undetectable by taste or appearance, but are still dangerous. Low temperatures inhibit them both.

AND NOW, ALICE, would you like to take a tour of Refrigerator Wonderland? Just drink this bottle labeled "Drink Me" to make you small, and follow the white rabbit into the fridge.

Alice: Brrr. It's freezing in here!

White Rabbit: Exactly. We've landed in the freezing compartment, which is often at the top because any cold air leakage will fall down and help cool the lower parts.

A: Just how cold is it in here?

WR: A freezing compartment should always be at 0°F or colder. That's 32 degrees below water's freezing temperature.

A: How can I tell if my freezer at home is cold enough?

WR: Buy a refrigerator-freezer thermometer, which is specially designed to be accurate at low temperatures. Nestle it among the frozen food packages in your freezer, close the door, and wait six to eight hours. If the thermometer doesn't read within a couple of degrees of zero, adjust the freezer's temperature control knob and check again six to eight hours later.

Now let's climb down into the main part of the fridge, where it's quite a bit warmer.

A: You call this warm?

WR: Everything's relative. Outside in the kitchen it's at least 30 degrees warmer. The refrigerator mechanism is removing heat from the box we're in, but heat is energy, and you can't just destroy energy; remove it from one place and it has to go someplace else. So the refrigerator throws it out into the kitchen. The Mad Hatter claims that a refrigerator is really a kitchen heater, and he's right. In fact, a refrigerator puts out more heat than it removes from its interior, because the removal mechanism creates heat. That's why you can't cool off the kitchen by leaving the refrigerator door open; you'd just be moving heat around from one place to another and even adding some, but not getting rid of any.

A: How does the refrigerator remove heat?

WR: It contains an easily vaporizable liquid called Freon, or at least it did before scientists discovered that Freon destroys Earth's ozone layer; new refrigerators contain a friendlier chemical with the jabberwocky name of HFC134a. Anyway, when a liquid vaporizes (boils), it absorbs heat from its surroundings, which consequently get colder. (No room in here to explain why). When the vapor is compressed back into a liquid, it releases that heat back out again. A refrigerator lets the liquid vaporize here inside the box, cooling those metal coils you see on the wall. Then it compresses the vapor to a liquid again (that humming you hear is the compressor motor), and dissipates the resulting heat outside the box, through a maze of coils tucked away behind or beneath it. A thermostat turns the compressor on and off as needed to maintain the proper temperature.

A: What is considered proper for a temperature?

WR: The main compartment of a refrigerator should always be below 40°F. Above that temperature, bacteria can multiply fast enough to be dangerous.

A: Can I use my new thermometer to measure that?

WR: Absolutely. Put it in a glass of water in the middle of your fridge and wait six to eight hours. If it doesn't read 40°F or below, adjust the refrigerator's main control knob and check the temperature again six to eight hours later.

A: I'm certain that any refrigerator of mine will prove to be at precisely the proper temperature, thank you. But whatever shall I keep in it?

WR: You know, the usual stuff. Live crabs—it sedates them so they don't throw off their claws when you steam them; tablecloths with candle wax on them—you can scrape it off after it gets hard; damp laundry in a plastic bag whenever you can't iron it right away; old corsages . . .

A: All right, smarty. Is there anything that should *not* be kept in the refrigerator?

WR: Yes. Tomatoes lose flavor when chilled below about 50°F because an important flavor chemical dissipates. Potatoes get unpleasantly sweet because some of their starch turns to sugar. Bread dries out and gets stale if not tightly wrapped, yet mold spores might grow inside a plastic bag. Best to freeze it. And a large amount of left-over food that is still warm can raise the fridge's temperature to a dangerous, bacteria-friendly level. Divide it up into small, easily cooled containers and chill them in cold water before putting them in. Don't let them cool on the counter, because they'll be at a dangerous temperature too long.

Alice, watch out! You're too close to the edge of the shelf!

A: Help! I've fallen down into this drawer. Where am I?

WR: You're in the crisper.

A: I don't think I want to be crisp.

WR: It's only for fruits and vegetables, and it controls humidity, rather than temperature. Vegetables will dry out and get flabby unless the humidity is kept relatively high. The crisper is a closed box that keeps water vapor in. But fruits require a lower humidity than vegetables, so some crispers have adjustable openings that you're supposed to readjust every time you change the contents.

A: Yeah, sure. Now what's that other compartment below us?

WR: That's the meat keeper. It's the coldest part of the fridge, except for the freezer. It's at the bottom of the fridge because cold air sinks. Meats and fish have to be kept as cold as possible, but fresh fish shouldn't be kept more than a day anyway.

And speaking of meats, I'm late for a very important "meating." Here. Drink this other bottle of "Drink Me" to make you big again and we'll get out of here.

Don't forget to turn out the light.

The world of food is limitless. The world of science is limitless. No single work can do more than etch a tiny scratch into the surface of either one or, for that matter, into the interface between them.

In this book I have selected a number of practical issues that I hope will be useful to the curious home cook, and I have discussed them in language that is as nontechnical as possible. The most I can hope for is that these apéritifs have whetted the appetites of my readers for further understanding of kitchen science. For those whose appetites have been whetted, I list here some works that delve more deeply into the science of foods.

TECHNICAL SCIENCE BOOKS
(WITHOUT RECIPES)

Belitz, Hans-Dieter, and Grosch, Werner. *Food Chemistry*. Second Edition. Berlin, Heidelberg: Springer-Verlag, 1999. The detailed, advanced chemistry of foods and cooking, with a comprehensive index.

Bennion, Marion, and Scheule, Barbara. *Introductory Foods*. Eleventh Edition. Upper Saddle River, N.J.: Prentice-Hall, 2000. A college textbook for food science courses.

Fennema, Owen R., Editor. *Food Chemistry*. Third Edition. New York: Marcel Dekker, 1996. Twenty-two academic food scientists contributed chapters on their specialties to this reference book.

McGee, Harold. *On Foods and Cooking: The Science and Lore of the Kitchen*. New York: Macmillan, 1984. A comprehensive, ground-breaking classic, covering the detailed history, traditions, and chemistry of foods and cooking.

McWilliams, Margaret. *Foods, Experimental Perspectives*. Fourth Edition. Upper Saddle River, N.J.: Prentice-Hall, 2000. Compositions, structures, testing, and evaluation of foods.

Penfield, Marjorie, and Campbell, Ada Marie. *Experimental Food Science*. Third Edition. San Diego, Calif.: Academic Press, 1990. Laboratory testing and evaluation of foods.

Potter, Norman N., and Hotchkiss, Joseph H. *Food Science*. Fifth Edition. New York: Chapman & Hall, 1995. A college textbook on food science and technology.

LESS-TECHNICAL BOOKS
(WITH RECIPES)

Barham, Peter. *The Science of Cooking*. Berlin: Springer-Verlag, 2000. Introductory chemistry followed by chapters on meats, breads, sauces, etc. With 41 recipes.

Corriher, Shirley O. *Cookwise: The Hows and Whys of Successful Cooking*. New York: Morrow, 1997. What various recipe ingredients do, how they do it, and how to use them to best advantage, with particular emphasis on baking. With 224 recipes.

Grosser, Arthur E. *The Cookbook Decoder, or Culinary Alchemy Explained*. New York: Beaufort Books, 1981. A whimsical but practical collection of kitchen science information by a Canadian chemistry professor. With 121 recipes.

Hillman, Howard. *Kitchen Science*. Boston: Houghton Mifflin, 1989. Questions and answers. With 5 recipes.

McGee, Harold. *The Curious Cook: More Kitchen Science and Lore*. San Francisco: North Point Press, 1990. A collection of special topics, discussed in detail. With 20 recipes.

Parsons, Russ. *How to Read a French Fry and Other Stories of Intriguing Kitchen Science.* Boston: Houghton Mifflin, 2001. Down-to-earth, practical discussions of frying, vegetables, eggs, starch, meats, fats, etc. With 120 recipes.

(Words defined separately are in italics.)

ACID – Any chemical compound that produces hydrogen *ions* (H⁺) in water. (Chemists sometimes use broader definitions.) Acids are inherently of differing strengths, but they all taste sour.

ALKALI – In everyday usage, any chemical compound that produces hydroxide *ions* (OH⁻) in water, such as lye (sodium hydroxide) and baking soda (sodium bicarbonate). Chemists call such compounds bases. More strictly speaking, an alkali is a particularly strong kind of base: the hydroxides of sodium, potassium, or one of the other so-called alkali metals. Acids and bases (including alkalis) neutralize each other to form *salts*.

ALKALOID – Any of a family of bitter-tasting, physiologically potent chemical compounds found in plants. Alkaloid family members include atropine, caffeine, cocaine, codeine, nicotine, quinine, and strychnine.

AMINO ACID – An organic compound that contains both an amino group ($-NH_2$) and an acid group ($-COOH$). In these formulas, N=nitrogen, H=hydrogen, C=carbon, and O=oxygen. About twenty different amino acids constitute the natural building blocks of proteins.

ANTIOXIDANT— A chemical compound that prevents undesirable *oxidation* reactions in foods or in the body. In foods, the most common oxidation reaction to be prevented is the production of rancidity in fats. Antioxidants commonly used in foods include butylated hydroxytoluene (BHT), butylated hydroxyanisole (BHA), and *sulfites*.

ATOM— The smallest unit of a chemical element. Each of the more than one hundred known chemical elements consists of atoms that are unique to that element.

BTU— British thermal unit, a unit of energy. Four Btu's are approximately equal to one nutritional *calorie*. Range burners, whether gas or electric, are rated in the number of Btu's of heat they generate per hour.

CALORIE— A unit of energy, most often used in the context of how much energy a food provides when metabolized in the human body.

CARBOHYDRATE— One of a class of chemical compounds found in living things, including sugars, starches, and cellulose. Carbohydrates serve as sources of energy in animals and as structural components in plants.

DIPOLE— A *molecule* whose two ends bear relative positive and negative charges with respect to each other.

DISACCHARIDE— A sugar whose *molecules* can be broken down (hydrolyzed) into two molecules of simple sugars, or *monosaccharides*. A common disaccharide is sucrose, the main sugar in sugar cane, sugar beets, and maple sugar.

ELECTRON — One of the very light, negatively charged elementary particles that occupy the regions of space outside the very heavy nuclei of *atoms*.

ENZYMES — Proteins produced by living organisms that serve the function of speeding up (catalyzing) specific biochemical reactions. Because biochemical reactions are inherently very slow, most won't occur without the proper enzyme. Being proteins, many enzymes can be destroyed by extreme conditions such as high temperatures.

FATTY ACIDS — Organic *acids* that are bound to glycerol to form glycerides in natural fats and oils. Most natural fats are *triglycerides*, containing three molecules of fatty acids per fat *molecule*.

FREE RADICAL — An *atom* or *molecule* that has one or more unpaired *electrons* and is therefore highly reactive, because atomic electrons are most stable when present in pairs.

GLUCOSE — A simple sugar, or *monosaccharide*. It circulates in the bloodstream and is the major energy-producing unit of *carbohydrates*.

HEMOGLOBIN — The red, iron-containing protein that transports oxygen through the bloodstream.

ION — An electrically charged *atom* or group of atoms. A negatively charged ion has an excess of *electrons*, while a positively charged ion lacks one or more of its normal complement of electrons.

LIPID — Any fatty, waxy, or oily substance in living things that will dissolve in organic solvents such as chloroform or ether. Lipids include actual fats and oils, together with other related compounds.

MICROWAVE — A unit of electromagnetic energy whose wavelength is longer than infrared radiation and shorter than radio waves. It penetrates solids to a depth of several centimenters.

MOLECULE — The smallest unit of a chemical compound, consisting of two or more *atoms* bound together.

MONOSACCHARIDE — A simple sugar that cannot be broken down (hydrolyzed) into other sugars. The most common monosaccharide is *glucose*, or blood sugar.

MYOGLOBIN — A red, iron-containing protein similar to *hemoglobin*. It is found in the muscles of animals, serving as an oxygen-storage compound.

NUCLEATION SITE — A spot, speck, scratch, or tiny bubble in a container of liquid that serves as a location at which *molecules* of a dissolved gas can congregate to form bubbles.

OSMOSIS — The process in which water *molecules* move through a membrane, such as a cell wall, from a more dilute solution of a dissolved substance to a more concentrated solution of the substance, thus tending to equalize the concentrations.

OXIDATION — The reaction of a substance with oxygen, usually with the oxygen in the air. More broadly, a chemical reaction in which an *atom*, *ion*, or *molecule* loses *electrons*.

POLYMER — A huge *molecule* consisting of many, often hundreds, of identical molecular units, all bound together.

POLYSACCHARIDE — A sugar whose molecules can be broken down (hydrolyzed) into several *monosaccharides*. Examples are cellulose and starches.

SALT — The product of a reaction between an *acid* and a base, or *alkali*. Sodium chloride, table salt, is by far the most common.

SULFITE — A salt of sulfurous *acid*. Sulfites react with acids to form sulfur dioxide gas, used as a bleach and bactericide.

TRIGLYCERIDE — A *molecule* consisting of three *fatty acid molecules* bound to a glycerol molecule. Natural fats and oils are mostly mixtures of triglycerides.

ROBERT L. WOLKE is professor emeritus of chemistry at the University of Pittsburgh and a syndicated columnist for *The Washington Post*.

He received his Ph.D. in nuclear chemistry from Cornell University, following which he did research at the Enrico Fermi Institute of the University of Chicago, the General Atomic Division of General Dynamics, the University of Florida, and the Oak Ridge National Laboratory.

In 1960 he joined the faculty of the University of Pittsburgh, where he has served as associate and full professor, director of the Wherrett Laboratory of Nuclear Chemistry, and director of the University's Office of Faculty Development.

In 1990 he left academe to devote full time to writing. In 1998 he was asked to write a food science column, "Food 101" for *The Washington Post*, which he continues to do today. The column is nationally syndicated by the United Feature Syndicate.

He is the winner of a Golden Quill Award for Distinguished Achievement in Journalism, a James Beard Foundation Journalism Award for newspaper food columns, the International Association of Culinary Professionals' Bert Greene Award for newspaper food writing, and awards from the Association of Food Journalists and the National Society of Newspaper Columnists.

INDEX